# THE LANGUAGE OF INCLUSIVE EDUCATION

*The Language of Inclusive Education* is an insightful text which considers the writing, speaking, reading and hearing of inclusive education. Based on the premise that humans use language to construct their worlds and their realities, this book is concerned with how language works to determine what we know and understand about issues related to in/exclusion in education. Using a variety of analytical tools, the author exposes language-at-work in academic and popular literature and in policy documents. Areas of focus include:

- what inclusive education means and how it is defined;
- how metaphor works to position inclusive education;
- how textbooks construct inclusive education;
- how we use language to build what we understand to be difference and disability, with particular reference to AD(H)D and Asperger's syndrome;
- listening to children and young people as a means to promote inclusion in schools.

Woven through this volume is the argument for a more critical awareness of how we use language in the field that we call 'inclusive education'. This book is a must-read for any individual studying, practising or having an interest in inclusion and exploring the associations with language.

**Elizabeth Walton** is a Senior Lecturer in Inclusive Education at the School of Education, University of the Witwatersrand, Johannesburg, South Africa.

# THE LANGUAGE OF INCLUSIVE EDUCATION

Exploring speaking, listening, reading and writing

Elizabeth Walton

LONDON AND NEW YORK

First published 2016
by Routledge
2 Park Square, Milton Park, Abingdon, Oxon OX14 4RN

and by Routledge
711 Third Avenue, New York, NY 10017

*Routledge is an imprint of the Taylor & Francis Group, an informa business*

© 2016 E. Walton

The right of E. Walton to be identified as author of this work has been asserted by her in accordance with sections 77 and 78 of the Copyright, Designs and Patents Act 1988.

All rights reserved. No part of this book may be reprinted or reproduced or utilised in any form or by any electronic, mechanical, or other means, now known or hereafter invented, including photocopying and recording, or in any information storage or retrieval system, without permission in writing from the publishers.

*Trademark notice*: Product or corporate names may be trademarks or registered trademarks, and are used only for identification and explanation without intent to infringe.

*British Library Cataloguing in Publication Data*
A catalogue record for this book is available from the British Library

*Library of Congress Cataloging in Publication Data*
Names: Walton, Elizabeth.
Title: The language of inclusive education : exploring speaking, listening, reading, and writing / Elizabeth Walton.
Description: New York, NY : Routledge, [2016]
Identifiers: LCCN 2015024902
Subjects: LCSH: Inclusive education. | Discourse analysis.
Classification: LCC LC1200 .W35 2016 | DDC 371.9/046—dc23
LC record available at http://lccn.loc.gov/2015024902

ISBN: 978-1-138-79434-4 (hbk)
ISBN: 978-1-138-79435-1 (pbk)
ISBN: 978-1-315-75927-2 (ebk)

Typeset in Bembo
by Cenveo Publisher Services

# CONTENTS

*List of illustrations*   *vi*
*Foreword*   *vii*
*Acknowledgements*   *ix*
*Acronyms*   *xi*

Book beginnings   1

1   Inclusive education as a discourse   9

2   Inclusive education as an ideology or field   29

3   The meaning of inclusive education   47

4   Metaphors that matter in inclusive education   66

5   Inclusive education on the (university) library shelf   85

6   Languaging ADHD   103

7   Reading and writing in/exclusion   119

8   Speaking and hearing in/exclusion   136

Book ends   155

*Index*   *162*

# ILLUSTRATIONS

## Figures

| | | |
|---|---|---|
| 3.1 | Definition two | 52 |
| 3.2 | Change in school and schooling | 54 |
| 3.3 | Shifts in what inclusive education entails | 57 |

## Tables

| | | |
|---|---|---|
| 4.1 | Conceptual metaphors, metaphorical items and their sources | 78 |
| 5.1 | 'Gateway issues' in inclusive education textbooks | 94 |
| 8.1 | Five voice research projects | 139 |

# FOREWORD

Are there conventions to which foreword writers are bound? I'm not sure. If such conventions exist I would guess that commencing this foreword for Elizabeth Walton's splendid book *The Language of Inclusive Education* with a discussion point arising from the second chapter presents a breach. In that chapter entitled 'Inclusive education as an ideology or field', the author summons Terry Eagleton who declares: 'Marxists want nothing more than to stop being Marxists.' In fact, I will actually start in 1971, the release date of Graham Nash's first album called *Songs for Beginners*. The first track on that album is an angry and visceral protest directed against the Vietnam War fittingly called 'Military Madness'. I recently went to a Crosby, Stills and Nash concert and some 44 years later the song is tragically just as relevant, just as angry. As the theatres of conflict change they are condemned to its eternal performance. After all, in their amusing book of *Advanced Banter* John Lloyd and John Mitchinson (2008: 352) point out that Ambrose Bierce told us that: 'War is God's way of teaching Americans geography.'

As I read this I thought of the antiquity and ubiquity of exclusion and that, as Elizabeth Walton suggests, many of us are destined to advocate for inclusion for the foreseeable future and thereafter. Ours is a life of what Walton calls alertness. We are forever listening out for the canary. A teaching assistant responsible for working with children with disabilities in a rural elementary school in Victoria, Australia once said to me: 'Roger, my job is to make myself as redundant as possible as quickly as possible.' Her hopeful confidence was endearing and it stays with me. The truth is that exclusion and disclusion, as Lerato declares, are a part of the human condition, at least as we have come to live and know it.

It is good to be reminded that inclusive education is a political imperative, a deeply ideological task. For self-proclaimed scientists ideology is a pejorative reference and there is no place for it in their laboratory. This book refreshes the work of Ellen Brantlinger who reminds us of Žižek's (2012: 4) instruction that a particular ideology's 'inversion is no less political'. Interviewing Dave Gillborn and Deborah Youdell with Julie Allan, Dave put it in all its gritty reality. 'Ideology is like sweat,' he ventured; 'You smell everyone else's but never your own.' *The Language of Inclusive Education* is a timely reminder that we must continue to advance our partisan science. At the heart of this political struggle is the analysis of language and its deployment in non-random intent.

Returning to Lerato, who in the opening pages instructs us in the spatial properties of discourse, I am much taken by the notion of disclusion. Inclusion has become, as Walton demonstrates, a vehicle of proximal exclusion. In many respects the inclusion unit is the modern metaphor of segregated schooling. Education policy has been a project of the progressive co-option of insurrection into the neo-liberal agenda. The depiction of the mobilisation of ADHD across South Africa is illustrative: 'the languaging of the child as a burden' and excusing schooling and teaching from the diagnostic lens. Like Naomi, the army of ADHD sufferers endure a daily reminder of what they can't presently do.

Let me not delay you further from your read or disclose more to you, for Elizabeth Walton better expresses it and you should enjoy the pages ahead as I did – with no sense of expectation. This is an important book and will quickly find its way onto the shelves of our colleagues who share the project of resisting exclusion.

Roger Slee
Melbourne, 2015

## References

Lloyd, J. and Mitchinson, J. (2008) *Advanced Banter. The QI Book of Quotations*. London: Faber & Faber.
Žižek, S. (2012) *Mapping Ideology*. London: Verso.

# ACKNOWLEDGEMENTS

I have discovered that it takes a village to write and produce a book. I would like to express my gratitude to people in my 'village' and acknowledge the role they have played in enabling me to complete this project.

First, thanks go to Sarah Tuckwell and the team at Routledge for their editorial assistance and support. Then I am most grateful to Professor Roger Slee for being willing to write the foreword of this book. I also thank the editors of *Perspectives in Education* and *Acta Academia* for their permission to use material which originally appeared in articles published in these journals.

Then I acknowledge with gratitude the many critical friends who willingly gave of their time and expertise to read different chapters of this book, and to offer suggestions for change and improvement. They are: Dr Marian Baker, Professor Nazir Carrim, Dr Ana Ferreira, Professor Linda Graham, Professor Sumaya Laher, Professor Kiki Messiou, Professor Norma Nel and Dr Reville Nussey. Karen McCarthy, once in my high-school English class and now friend and expert language practitioner in her own right, provided a thoughtful, 'bird's eye' view of the whole manuscript. I owe a debt of gratitude to Dr Lee Rusznyak, my friend, colleague and part of my 'package'. Lee gave critical feedback on first drafts of all the chapters and was kind enough to be honest and tell me when I needed to rephrase, reduce and delete. She has been unfailingly encouraging during this book writing process, celebrating small triumphs and commiserating when the writing fairy (which we share) was nowhere to be found.

I am grateful to the Faculty of Humanities at the University of the Witwatersrand for a Research Promotion Grant that enabled me to complete the manuscript. I would also like to express my thanks to the many supportive colleagues I have in the Wits School of Education. These include Professor Ruksana Osman (Dean of the Faculty of Humanities), Professor Jean Baxen (Head of the Wits School of Education) and Professor Karin Brodie (Deputy Head of the Wits School of Education and my mentor in the academy). I am privileged to work in a vibrant and generative intellectual environment where my thinking has been challenged and enriched by colleagues such as Lynne Slonimsky, Professor Hilary Janks, Professor Yael Shalem and Professor Brahm Fleisch. In addition to those mentioned, I would like to thank the staff community of the Wits School of Education for their friendship and support, and also make mention of the helpful library staff at the Wits School of Education.

I would also like to thank the many high-school learners, undergraduate and postgraduate students whom I have had the privilege of teaching over the years and who have shaped my thinking in so many ways. In particular, I wish to express gratitude to the five students whose 'voice' research formed the focus of Chapter 8 – their engagement with those whom the system seems to have forgotten is highly commendable. I am grateful for the support I have had from my family: my parents, my sister, my uncle and my children. I have dedicated this book to my husband Grant. This book would not have been written if it were not for Grant's encouragement and belief in me; his forbearance when I was distracted by writing; his regular supply and delivery of tea, coffee and wine; his planning and cooking of meals; and his technological expertise and forward planning that secured working computer hardware, software and Internet access, even through electricity blackouts.

Thank you all.

# ACRONYMS

*Note*: Education has a proclivity for acronyms and inclusive education is no different. The use of acronyms serves purposes beyond a preference for shorter terms. Acronyms signal insider knowledge in a discourse by presuming familiarity with their meanings. The effect of their use is to mark insiders and outsiders, those in the know and those who are cast as ignorant.

| | |
|---|---|
| ADHASA | Attention Deficit and Hyperactivity Support Group of Southern Africa |
| ADHD | Attention Deficit Hyperactivity Disorder |
| APA | American Psychiatric Association |
| CD | Conduct Disorder |
| DBD | Disruptive Behaviour Disorder |
| DBE | (South African) Department of Basic Education (the Department of Basic Education was renamed when the Department of Education split into two departments in 2009: basic education is concerned with schools and adult literacy, and higher and further education and training is concerned with universities and technical/vocational colleges) |
| DoE | (South African) Department of Education |
| DSM | Diagnostic and Statistical Manual |
| GDE | Gauteng Department of Education (Gauteng is one of South Africa's nine provinces) |
| ICD | World Health Organisation, *International Classification of Diseases* |
| ICT | Information and Communications Technology |
| IEP | Individual(ised) Education Programme/Plan |
| LCT | Legitimation Code Theory |
| NGO | Non-Governmental Organisation |
| ODD | Oppositional Defiance Disorder |
| ORF | Official Recontextualising Field |

| | |
|---|---|
| PLC | Professional Learning Community |
| PRF | Pedagogic Recontextualising Field |
| RSA | Republic of South Africa |
| SAALED | South African Association for Learning and Educational Differences |
| SEN | Special Educational Needs |
| SIAS | South African National Strategy for Screening, Identification, Assessment and Support |
| TRC | Truth and Reconciliation Commission |
| UNESCO | The United Nations Educational, Scientific and Cultural Organisation |
| WHO | World Health Organisation |

# BOOK BEGINNINGS

'They discluded me'[1] was 11-year-old Lerato's explanation for why she was alone and tearful in the playground of a Johannesburg school. As an English teacher at the time, ever alert for opportunities to help learners[2] improve their language use, I suggested that perhaps she meant that she had been *excluded*. But she assured me that she did not mean *ex*cluded, because she still regarded herself as part of her friendship group; rather, in some configuration of pre-teen girls' social politics, she wasn't welcome to sit with her friends during that particular break-time (Walton 2011). While a growing concern about bullying in schools would make the behaviour of these girls interesting, what captured my attention was her confident use of the neologism 'discluded'. It suggests that the words *inclusion* or *exclusion* are not sufficient to express the complexities and nuances of people's experiences of access, participation and belonging. It seems, at least from Lerato's perspective, that it is possible to be neither included nor excluded, but something in between. People can be included and excluded simultaneously, depending on time and place, and exclusion may even be the experience of people who have been included. The prefix *dis* in *dis*cluded is telling. It conveys the negation or absence of inclusion rather than the eviction implied in *ex*clusion, and suggests that it is possible that at a later stage she will be *re*(in)cluded. *Dis* carries the additional meaning (used informally either as a noun or verb) of insult or put-down. 'Dissing' takes place between members of a community, and its informality ironically signifies the commonality of members of that community. It is also indicative of the ruptures that can occur within a community into which people have ostensibly been 'included'.

The words *include* and *exclude* stem from the Latin *cludere*, which means to close or to shut. So, embedded in inclusion and exclusion is the idea of closing or shutting in, or indeed closing and shutting out. Words mean more than their definitions, however; the various forms of include, for example, inclusion, inclusive, inclusivity and inclusively have acquired particular meanings in the context of education.

Inclusive education (or 'inclusion', which is often used synonymously) has, since the 1980s, become the term broadly applied to the international move towards educating all children (particularly those deemed disabled or as having special needs) in the 'regular' classroom. Given impetus by *The Salamanca Statement* (UNESCO 1994), inclusive education has found its way into education systems across the world. It appears in education policies, academic journals, conferences, books, teacher education courses, textbooks, websites, non-governmental organisations (NGOs) and the media. Much has been said and written about inclusive education in different contexts, but not much attention has been given to *how* it is said and written. This lacuna has not gone unnoticed by scholars in the field.

In 2008, Graham and Slee wrote that they hoped their paper, 'An illusory interiority: interrogating the discourse/s of inclusion', would renew debate about 'what is meant by talk of inclusion' (278), commenting that 'inclusive education scholars need to explicate the discourses of inclusion' (279). In *The Irregular School*, Slee (2011) makes four propositions for approaching inclusive education in the future. His second proposition is 're-righting language' (156). Such an endeavour, according to Slee, involves recognising that language does not merely describe the world, but shapes it, and can be made to work for change. He notes that the use of the term 'inclusive education' can be 'imprecise and misleading' (156) as it often invokes dichotomised notions of 'special' and 'ordinary' schools. He motivates for deconstructing such language and hearing the voices of marginalised people. This book, *The Language of Inclusive Education*, responds to these statements and represents a contribution to the conversation about how inclusive education is languaged.

## The language of inclusive education

The words 'language' and 'inclusive education' typed together into a search engine will yield hits in three areas important to the overall concerns of inclusive education. These are the recognition of home or mother language (including sign language) as a means to more inclusive teaching and learning; language and communication learning in inclusive classrooms, with a particular focus on augmentative or alternative communication; and the drive for inclusive language that is not prejudiced, discriminatory or exclusionary. None of these, however, is the focus of this book. Instead, I am concerned with the ways in which language has been used in the development of what we know as 'inclusive education'. Language works in various ways and has different effects. This was highlighted by South Africa's Truth and Reconciliation Commission (TRC), which, in its report on apartheid-era violence and discrimination, said:

> Language, discourse and rhetoric *does* things: it constructs social categories, it gives orders, it persuades us, it justifies, explains, gives reasons, excuses. It constructs reality.
>
> *(TRC 1998: 294, emphasis in the original)*

This book is premised on the need to consider what the language of inclusive education does and what realities it constructs. Over the decades spanning the inception, growth and spread of inclusive education, people (including myself) who identify their work as the pursuit of inclusive education have been languaging[3] inclusive education. We have used language to convey what we mean by the concept, but we have also used language to make that very meaning.

Inclusive education is (and has been) languaged by those who write and speak it. These 'languagers' are often people with power, either because of their status or because of their influence. Like other languages, inclusive education is spoken with many 'accents' and written in many styles. People are also languaged *by* inclusive education. These people include actors in the education sphere, but especially teachers and learners, particularly those who are devalued by society and marginalised in education. Chapters in this book will show how the language of inclusive education constructs them in various ways. Textbook writers, for example, language teachers as unskilled, needing short-term solutions and quick-fixes to enable them to 'manage' the problem of learner diversity in their classrooms. Learners who cannot concentrate for what is deemed an appropriate amount of time are languaged as diseased and as a burden on teachers. Popular fiction languages young people with diagnoses of autism as being utterly aberrant, potentially dangerous, but ultimately entertaining.

The four language strands of writing, reading, speaking and listening are woven through this book. Written language predominates, because text-based sources offer an enduring record of how inclusive education is languaged. Various types of texts are scrutinised in this book, and the reader will find an analysis of policy documents, newspaper reports, textbooks for teachers, academic publications and popular fiction. Writing presupposes reading, and the language strand of reading is given attention through a critical literacy approach to the texts, with a particular focus on understanding 'the relationship between texts, meaning-making and power' (Janks and Vasquez 2011:1). A critical reading of inclusive education texts engages with questions about the assumptions that the text producers make about the reader and the subject. I also question what they present as 'natural', which when interrogated reveals problematically constructed views of 'the way things are'. The analytic tools used in this critical reading are eclectic and draw on critical discourse analysis (Gee 2011; Janks 2010), functional linguistics (Halliday and Matthiessen, 2004), Thompson's analysis of the workings of ideology (Thompson 1990) and metaphor analysis (Cameron and Deignan 2006; Schmitt 2005). The language strands of speaking and listening are the focus of Chapter 8, where the challenges and possibilities of 'hearing the voices of marginalized people' (Slee 2011: 156) are explored. Speaking and listening are also foregrounded in many of the anecdotes that introduce each chapter.

## Anecdotes, critical incidents and noticing

Each chapter of this book begins with an anecdote, most of which are recollections of an incident that piqued my interest or challenged my thinking. These can loosely be described as 'critical incidents', although they are not used in the context of teacher reflection towards improved practice that Tripp (1993) initially described. What makes an incident critical, says Tripp (1993: 25), is not necessarily that it is dramatic or unusual, but rather that it is deemed significant because it indicates 'underlying trends, motives and structures'. Thus an incident is '... made into a critical incident by what was subsequently seen in and written about it'. I am not using critical incidents systematically as either a research technique or a professional learning device, but rather as a route into my reflections. The anecdotes also reflect something of Mason's (2002: 33) discipline of 'noticing', which he says is 'to make a distinction, to create foreground and background'. In these recollections, I am in effect 'marking' certain incidents and recognising them as salient (Mason 2002).

The use of anecdotes in this book echoes that of Tzur (2001: 259) who interwove reflections on 'experience fragments' from his development as a mathematics teacher educator 'as a tool to abstract notions of general implication'. My accounts of interactions with teachers and learners point to some of the conceptual issues in the language of inclusive education, and they serve as a useful springboard for the discussion that follows. Anecdotes, too, are a way of inserting the human experience into academic writing and responding to a natural interest in narratives (Sword 2012). They offer scholarship 'not as a list of abstractions or logical proofs but as a vibrant presence' (Pelias 2005: 421). In this book I have used personal reflection to show something of myself as a writer and the context in which this book is written.

## Writing 'I' with a South African voice

Over two decades ago, Barton and Clough (1995: 3) asked important questions about research in inclusive education, disability and special education needs. The first of these questions was: 'What assumptions about SEN [special education needs]/disability do I have which are inevitably present in the way I conceive of the study?' This question was echoed more recently by Allan and Slee's (2008: 98) discussion of 'smelling your own sweat' by recognising the ideological biases that inevitably inform research and writing about inclusive education. One of the ways to respond to this challenge is to insert the author into writing about inclusive education. An authorial presence is not always preferred in scholarly writing, and the convention of many journals in the field is to expunge the 'I' in preference for a more 'scientific' style. This book, however, heeds Jean McNiff's (2008) injunction to put the 'I' back into educational research in order to contribute to an ongoing conversation.

The 'I-ness' of this book is inextricably linked to its 'South African-ness'. South Africa is one of the countries associated with a second generation of efforts towards inclusive education (Kozleski et al. 2011) and the country's efforts in this regard are bound up with the challenges of the post-colonial and post-apartheid state. I write as a South African, and while some of the chapters of this book are primarily rooted in the South African experience, the principles are nevertheless applicable wherever inclusion is talked and written about. Other chapters make scant reference to South Africa and should be of immediate relevance to international readers.

The South African context offers more to inclusive education than a mere cross-national comparative study. On a national scale, the country continues to struggle to realise an inclusive society, after the pernicious and systematic exclusion of people who were constructed as inferior. There are profound similarities between the South African quest for transformation and the various international endeavours to realise more inclusive education. The South African experience in this book is thus not only a contextual referent, it also offers the potential for reflection on what it might mean to transform education to make it inclusive.

## The chapters in *The Language of Inclusive Education*

Bookends have various functions. Not only do they transform a surface into a bookshelf, they hold books together and demarcate the beginning and end of a particular collection. It is in the latter sense that I denote the first and last chapters of this book as bookends. This short introductory chapter is a bookend, but because I do not want to end before I have begun, I have called it 'book beginnings'. In it, I have shown the impetus for the book, and how it contributes to a conversation on the language used in and for inclusive education. The chapters in this book are a collection of essays, designed to stand alone if need be, but linked by common themes and references to each other. The topics selected for inclusion in this volume are by no means exhaustive and the language of inclusive education encompasses far more than the content of these chapters. Furthermore, I acknowledge my own interests and biases in the topics chosen, and recognise that others could well argue for the exclusion of some of these topics and the inclusion of others in a discussion of the language of inclusive education.

Because language is inextricably bound up with making and communicating meaning, the first three chapters of this book concern themselves with the meaning of inclusive education as mediated through language. Chapters 1 and 2 are founded on the notion that before working with what inclusive education does, can or should mean, attention should be given to what inclusive education *is*. In other words, these chapters consider what inclusive education is as a unit of analysis. Three identities for inclusive education are explored, each offering different analytical possibilities. The first chapter considers inclusive education as a discourse found in professional, policy and public domains. The language of inclusive education is different in each of these domains, and this chapter identifies and discusses various distinctive discourses. The second chapter considers inclusive education first as an ideology and then as a knowledge field. Drawing on Thompson's (1990) modes of the operation of ideology, I explore some of the characteristics of inclusive education that distinguish it as an ideology. The chapter then moves to a close examination of the claims that inclusive education is a field. Here, I draw on the sociology of education and the work of Basil Bernstein (2000) and Karl Maton (2000) and others to examine whether inclusive education can be regarded as a knowledge field, and if so, what kind of knowledge the field represents. The third chapter considers definitions. A tired mantra of inclusive education is that definitions vary across contexts and that it is impossible to offer a precise definition. I interrogate the effect of this permissive approach to defining inclusive education, arguing that it *does* matter how it is defined, because what we say matters. But instead of critically analysing how other writers have defined inclusive education, I look back over the years of my own study and writing in the field, and critically engage with the definitions that I have used. In this way, I explicate some of the ways in which language reveals (and conceals) how inclusive education is understood and constructed.

Metaphors are integral to the way inclusive education is languaged. Chapter 4 presents a systematic analysis of the metaphors used for inclusive education in South Africa. The prevailing metaphors for inclusive education are those of goals, buildings, journeys and hospitality. The combined effect of these metaphors is to locate inclusive education in some distant future, and casts the amorphous 'department of education' as responsible for the realisation of inclusion in South African schools. Hospitality metaphors are shown to be particularly insidious as they conceal othering in the guise of welcoming learners into the system and accommodating their needs. An example of this can be found in various textbooks about inclusive education, which advise teachers on how to 'accommodate' the educational needs of learners 'with disabilities/difficulties/challenges/barriers'. Three such textbooks are scrutinised in Chapter 5, with a focus on ways in which different textual and visual devices construct a particular pedagogic discourse of inclusive education for pre- and in-service teachers.

Chapters 6 and 7 turn their attention to the ways in which ADHD and Asperger's syndrome have been languaged. There is little contestation in South Africa of the psycho-medical approach to learners whose attention span and ability to concentrate are deemed to be developmentally inappropriate. In Chapter 6, I show how ADHD is languaged in various South African texts to pigeonhole learners who display ADHD-type characteristics as diseased, requiring medication, and disordered, requiring management. While Asperger's syndrome is not recognised by name in the latest *Diagnostic and Statistical Manual of Mental Disorders* (American Psychiatric Association 2013), it has entered the popular imagination through television, film and fiction. Chapter 7 looks at two novels, both written after Asperger's syndrome was recognised as a discrete condition. Both books, *The Curious Incident of the Dog in the Night-time* by Mark Haddon (2003) and *House Rules* by Jodi Picoult (2010), portray young men with characteristics of Asperger's syndrome. Using a critical literacy approach, I explore what it is that people come to 'know' about Asperger's syndrome as a result of reading popular fiction, and what linguistic and textual features of these books build this knowledge.

Chapter 8 moves from reading and writing to listening and hearing. The marginalisation of many children and young people includes the silencing of their voices. There have been many calls to listen to the voices of children when implementing inclusive education and in this chapter I focus on listening in the context of research. The schooling experiences of young South Africans show that exclusion is very much their experience of education, even under the providence of 'inclusive education'. The final chapter, the second 'bookend', concludes (literally 'closing together') with a reflection on what is built (Gee 2011) by our speaking, listening, writing and reading 'inclusive education'. The book ends with an unapologetic call to vigilance, and a critical consciousness (Rice 2006) of the workings of the language of inclusive education.

## Notes

1  The permission of *Perspectives in Education* is acknowledged and readers are referred to the original article where this anecdote was first published (Walton 2011).
2  South Africa uses the term 'learners' to denote children and young people who are in the schooling (as opposed to the higher and further education) system. While I am aware that this term is not necessarily internationally preferred, I have chosen to keep this terminology in this book. It serves as a reminder that because of the lingering deleterious effects of apartheid, many people in the South African schooling system are adults, and calling them 'pupils' is disparaging. I note, however, Soudien's (2006: 11) reservations about the imagination of the 'learner' as 'defined in terms of middle-class singularity' when in fact learners represent a highly diverse group of young people in South Africa.
3  Much of the work on languaging comes from the literature on second or additional language acquisition and proficiency (Swain 2006). The idea of languaging offers the important link between language and cognitive activity. Swain (2006: 96) contends that language is not only 'a conveyer of meaning' but it is also 'an agent in the making of meaning'. I appropriate the term 'languaging' to indicate the human actors who do the languaging, and also to emphasise the role that language plays in the development of the idea of inclusive education. I revisit the term with reference to ADHD in Chapter 6.

## References

Allan, J. and Slee, R. (2008) *Doing Inclusive Education Research*. Rotterdam: Sense Publishers.
American Psychiatric Association (2013) *Diagnostic and Statistical Manual of Mental Disorders*, 5th edn. Washington, DC: APA.
Barton, L. and Clough, P. (1995) 'Conclusion: many urgent voices', in P. Clough and L. Barton (eds), *Making Difficulties: Research and the Construction of Special Educational Needs*. London: Paul Chapman, pp. 143–7.
Bernstein, B. (2000) *Pedagogy, Symbolic Control and Identity: Theory, Research and Critique*, revised edn. Lanham, MD: Rowman & Littlefield.
Cameron, L. and Deignan, A. (2006) 'The emergence of metaphor in discourse', *Applied Linguistics*, 27 (4): 671–90.
Gee, J. P. (2011) *An Introduction to Discourse Analysis*, 3rd edn. New York: Routledge.
Graham, L. J. and Slee, R. (2008) 'An illusory interiority: interrogating the discourse/s of inclusion', *Educational Philosophy and Theory*, 40 (2): 277–93.
Haddon, M. (2003) *The Curious Incident of the Dog in the Night-time*. London: David Fickling Books.
Halliday, M. and Matthiessen, M. (2004) *An Introduction to Functional Grammar*, 3rd edn. London: Arnold.
Janks, H. (2010) *Literacy and Power*. New York: Routledge.
Janks, H. and Vasquez, V. (2011) 'Editorial: Critical literacy revisited: writing as critique', *English Teaching: Practice and Critique*, 10 (1): 1–6.
Kozleski, E. B., Artiles, A. J. and Waitoller, F. R. (2011) 'Introduction. Equity in inclusive education', in A. J. Artiles, E. B. Kozleski and F. R. Waitoller (eds), *Inclusive Education: Examining Equity on Five Continents*. Cambridge, MA: Harvard Education Press, pp. 1–14.

McNiff, J. (2008) 'The significance of "I" in educational research and the responsibility of intellectuals', *South African Journal of Education*, 28: 351–64.

Mason, J. (2002) *Researching Your Own Practice: The Discipline of Noticing*. London: Routledge.

Maton, K. (2000) 'Languages of legitimation: the structuring significance for intellectual fields of strategic knowledge claims', *British Journal of Sociology of Education*, 21 (2): 147–67.

Pelias, R. J. (2005) 'Performative writing as scholarship: an apology, an argument, an anecdote', *Cultural Studies ↔ Critical Methodologies*, 5 (4): 415–24.

Picoult, J. (2010) *House Rules*. London: Hodder & Stoughton.

Rice, N. (2006) 'Teacher education as a site of resistance', in S. Danforth and S. Gabel (eds), *Vital Questions Facing Disability Studies in Education*. New York: Peter Lang, pp. 17–31.

Schmitt, R. (2005) 'Systematic metaphor analysis as a method of qualitative research', *Qualitative Report*, 10 (2): 358–94.

Slee, R. (2011) *The Irregular School*. London: Routledge.

Soudien, C. (2006) 'Disaffected or displaced?', *International Journal of School Disaffection*, 4 (1): 6–12.

Swain, M. (2006) 'Languaging, agency and collaboration in advanced second language proficiency', in H. Byrnes (ed.), *Advanced Language Learning: The Contribution of Halliday and Vygotsky*. London: Continuum, pp. 95–108.

Sword, H. (2012) *Stylish Academic Writing*. Cambridge, MA: Harvard University Press.

Thompson, J. (1990) *Ideology and Modern Culture*. Cambridge: Polity Press.

Tripp, D. (1993) *Critical Incidents in Teaching: Developing Professional Judgement*. London: Routledge.

Truth and Reconciliation Commission (TRC) (1998) Truth and Reconciliation Commission Report, Volume Five. Accessed from: www.justice.gov.za/trc/report/finalreport/Volume%205.pdf.

Tzur, R. (2001) 'Becoming a mathematics teacher-educator: conceptualizing the terrain through self-reflective analysis', *Journal of Mathematics Teacher Education*, 4 (4): 259–83.

UNESCO (1994) *The Salamanca Statement and Framework for Action*. Paris: UNESCO.

Walton, E. (2011) '"They discluded me": the possibilities and limitations of children's participation in inclusion research in South Africa', *Perspectives in Education*, 29 (1): 83–92.

# 1
# INCLUSIVE EDUCATION AS A DISCOURSE

## What is inclusive education?

Picture a situation of social introduction, which typically proceeds as follows:

*Other Person*: So I hear you are a lecturer. What is your subject?
*Me*: I lecture in the field of inclusive education.
*Other Person*: Inclusive education? What is that?
*Me*: Well … it's an education reform initiative that's concerned with reducing exclusion, so it's about every child's right to education and valuing diversity. It's policy in South Africa and my field of research. I work with teachers and student teachers to enable them to teach diverse learners effectively.
*Other Person* (politely attempting not to look bored): Huh? What do you mean by 'diverse learners'?
*Me*: Unlike when we were at school, South African classrooms now include learners who come from a variety of language, racial and socio-economic backgrounds, and there may be learners with disabilities too. We aim to …
*Other Person* (interrupts): Oh, you mean special education – why didn't you say so? You know, my husband/wife/sister once worked with someone whose kid was special needs. Shame,[1] hey? It's nice to know that there are people like you who can help them, I know I would never have the patience. Nice to meet you.

And Other Person goes off to mingle and I am left contemplating the impossibility of distilling 'inclusive education' for cocktail party use. Situations like these are a reminder that inclusive education is not easily pigeon-holed. Not only is its *meaning* contested, what it actually *is* is not often interrogated. I suggest that while debates about definitions have value, they should come second in the quest to clarify the nature of inclusive education. This is because its meaning could well be different, depending on what we are assuming inclusive education is. Inclusive education can be identified in different ways. In this and the next chapter, three possibilities will be explored: inclusive education as a discourse, as an ideology and as a field. Each of these positions inclusive education differently, and offers different analytical possibilities. To begin, I will explore inclusive education as a discourse, and then discuss inclusive education discourses operating in the professional, policy and public domains.

## Inclusive education as discourse

I am not alone in suggesting that inclusive education is a discourse. Rose (2010a: 5) writes of 'discourses of inclusion' and Kalijanpur (2011: 98) reviews a book, saying that it would contribute to the 'critical discourse on international inclusive education'. But before examining inclusive education as a discourse, discourse itself needs to be understood. There are various useful definitions of discourse. Fairclough offers discourse as 'language use conceived of as socially determined' (2001: 18), and Blommaert (2005) says variously that it is 'language-in-action' (2) and 'all forms of meaningful semiotic human activity seen in connection with social, cultural, and historical patterns and developments' (3). Gee (2008: 154) suggests that discourse is 'language in use'. So 'discourse' is more than a pretentious word for language, it encompasses the multiple contexts in which language and other semiotic activity takes place. Gee maintains that discourse is a part of Discourse (big 'D' deliberate) which is 'saying (writing)-doing-believing-valuing combinations' (2008: 154). Big D Discourse is associated in Gee's schema with the capacity to couple ways of speaking and writing with ways of behaving and believing to realise various socially recognisable identities.

The Discourse of inclusive education enables a variety of identities to be enacted in different domains. Participation in the Discourse takes different forms and is legitimated in different ways.[2] But what is particularly useful in calling inclusive education a discourse is the idea, emphasised by Gee's hyphens, of the interconnectedness of speaking, writing, doing, believing and valuing. Inclusive education can readily be seen as a combination of speaking and writing (evidenced in policies and legislation, conference presentations, workshops, journal articles and books), particular beliefs and values about equity and participation in schools and various systemic, school and classroom practices. These elements cannot be separated – what is said/written and done cannot be considered apart from the belief systems that inform and sustain the saying, writing and doing.

A seminal piece on inclusive education discourses was Dyson's 1999 contribution to the *World Yearbook of Education*. In this article, Dyson maintained that inclusion was 'located within a limited number of discourses' (39). From those offering a rationale for inclusion he identified a rights and ethics discourse and an efficacy discourse and, from those promoting the realisation of inclusive education, a political discourse and a practical discourse. Importantly, Dyson recognised that these different discourses constructed different notions of inclusion, and made different questions possible. He concluded that we should talk of 'inclusions' (46) to acknowledge its many versions. Fifteen or more years have passed since Dyson categorised inclusion discourse, and while much of what he said is still valid, things have changed. I agree that we still have discourses (emphasising the plural) of inclusive education, but it is my sense that Dyson's rationalisation discourse has diminished over the years. Its place has been taken by a multi-disciplinary, critical and theoretical discourse of inclusion that interrogates the concept and the ways it has been encoded and enacted. The practical discourse that seeks to realise inclusion is flourishing.

I argue that it is fruitful to consider inclusive education as operating as a discourse in three overlapping domains, which I have categorised as the professional domain, the policy domain and the public domain. The saying-doing-believing of inclusive education in each of these domains is different, but their boundaries are blurred, and the discourses seep into one another. I am reminded by Gee (2011: 36) that 'Discourses are not "units" with clear boundaries' and that I am engaged in 'recognition work' (37). Recognising discourses and labelling them is thus a tentative exercise, because discourses change over time and not everyone will agree on the distinctions I make. Despite this, it is productive to look at the different domains to examine how inclusive education is languaged in each and to what effect.

## Inclusive education as a discourse in the professional domain

By the professional domain,[3] I refer to places and spaces where inclusive education knowledge is produced, recontextualised and reproduced[4] (Maton 2014). I am deliberately collapsing finer distinctions that could be made between the field of practice and the field of knowledge production, or between academics and practitioners, and am considering a broad domain that encompasses universities, schools and publishing houses. There could be various ways to classify the discourse of inclusive education in this domain. Slee (2011: 62–3), for example, has identified clusters of influence on inclusive education[5] and an argument could be made that each of these clusters could be identified and analysed as a discourse of inclusive education. My categorisation of the discourse of inclusive education in this domain is broader, as I draw on Aristotelian terms and read two main discourses which are contrasted and connected – *epistēmē* and *technē*.[6] These two terms have a complex history and have been used differently by different ancient philosophers, some of whom used the terms interchangeably (Parry 2008). However, using Kemmis and Smith's (2008: 23) definitions, *epistēmē* can be said to represent the disposition of seeking truth, with the associated actions of contemplation and theoretical reasoning, and *technē* can refer to the disposition to act in a reasoned way, according to the rules of a craft, with a means-ends orientation. My use of these Greek terms deliberately resists calling one discourse 'theory' and the other 'practice', given the many meanings and contestations embedded in those terms. *Epistēmē* and *technē* serve my purpose well, not only for their relative unfamiliarity which dislodges the conventional ascriptions of meaning, but also because they are both contrasted and connected. So thinking of these two inclusive education discourses as dichotomies is less helpful than thinking of them as bifurcations. Bifurcation is both branching and linked, and is generative, suggestive of new possibilities. It is also a reminder of partiality (Davis 2004), both my own as I recognise my bias in drawing distinctions, but also the incompleteness of the distinctions drawn.

The *epistēmē* discourse in inclusive education represents multiple disciplinary and theoretical gazes. These include Allan (2005, 2007), who puts philosophers' ideas to work on inclusive education; Slee's (2010) sociological lens on inclusive education; various (critical) disability theories (Barton 2010; Gable 2014; Oliver 2013; Oliver and Barnes 2012; Terzi 2008); comparative education, particularly with reference to globalisation (Rizvi and Lingard 2010); and policy studies (Liasidou 2012). The discourse is conceptual and analytical, not empirical, and is often critical as it reflects on the epistemology/epistemologies of inclusive education and interrogates policy and practice. Alan Dyson recognises this *epistēmē* discourse as he is quoted in Allan and Slee (2008: 35):

> … [Y]ou get a kind of wing of the inclusion movement which is very much about conceptualization, critical thinking. If it has a home in academic disciplines it's probably within philosophy of education, sociology of education, where people do not feel it is necessary to do empirical work out there in the field because it doesn't actually tell you very much.

This *epistēmē* discourse offers theoretical understandings of the problem(s) of exclusion and marginalisation in schools. In some iterations (for example, Brantlinger (2006) and Slee (2011)), it is critical of the ways in which prevailing special education norms and practices have been thinly overlaid with a veneer of inclusive-sounding language.

Various grammatical and semiotic devices indicate the abstract nature of the written *epistēmē* discourse of inclusive education. Consider the first sentence of Allan's (2007: 281) chapter titled 'Inclusion as an ethical project' as an example:

> The inclusion of disabled students within mainstream schools continues to be debated amid criticisms of conceptual confusion among those holding opposing views (Gallagher 2001), and accusations that inclusion has become an ideological battlefield.

This sentence has a complex grammatical structure, and employs a number of features that signal this as abstract, specialised language. These include nominalised verbs, such as 'inclusion', 'confusion' and 'accusations'. Nominalisation removes actors, tense and modality from verbs, and changes them from being processes into abstract things. Allan's sentence also uses noun phrases, like 'conceptual confusion' and 'opposing views'. Noun phrases work to condense 'a whole sentence's worth of information' (Gee 2011: 8) into a couple of words, thereby complexifying the content of the sentence. The verb processes in these sentences are not material, i.e. about 'actions and events' (Halliday and Matthiessen, 2004). The processes are verbal ('continues to be debated'), mental ('holding opposing views') and relational ('inclusion has become an ideological battlefield') which dislodges them from specific contexts.[7] Neither the writer nor the audience are explicitly present in this sentence, reinforcing its abstraction. Other features, like in-text citations and predominant verbal text (i.e. minimal diagrams, pictures, tables, etc.) would characterise this kind of discourse.

The *epistēmē* discourse of inclusive education is, in my experience, not always highly valued by those working directly in schools. When invited to conduct workshops on inclusive education, I am usually reminded that teachers want 'practical' ideas, not theory, and that I should provide information that teachers can go away with and put into practice the next day. The teachers in Du Toit and Forlin's (2009) study confirm this, saying, 'we want it [training] in layman's terms: ten easy steps to pinpoint a problem' (656). In other words, they are clamouring for the *technē* discourse of inclusive education.

The *technē* discourse could be said to focus on presenting the solution to the problem(s) of exclusion and marginalisation in schools by providing the 'how to' of inclusive education. The attributes of the Aristotelian term *technē* are very evident in this discourse, as it has a strong focus on practical knowledge and it suggests a 'rational ability to intervene and change the surrounding world' (Saugstad 2002: 380). The idea of the rules of a craft is inherent in *technē*, and learning the rules requires apprenticeship with an accomplished craftsperson. So the *technē* discourse in inclusive education presents, *The Teachers' Guide to Inclusive Education: 750 Strategies for Success!* (Hammeken 2007) and *What Successful Teachers Do in Inclusive Classrooms: 60 Research-Based Teaching Strategies That Help Special Learners Succeed* (McNary et al. 2005). Titles like these position teachers as un(der) - skilled apprentices who can learn how to apply the rules (described as guides, programmes or strategies) in order to achieve inclusion. Various verbal and visual features distinguish the *technē* discourse from the *epistēmē* discourse. For example, the cover of *The Teachers' Guide to Inclusive Education: 750 Strategies for Success!* (Hammeken 2007) presents a colourful line drawing of young people of different races holding hands across the globe. The optimism of the visual is complemented by the word 'Success!' in the title, and the exclamation mark signals this as an informal and accessible text. Indications that the reader is expected to interact with the text are the provision of lined pages for notes and questions for discussion. The book contains a number of 'tips' for teachers and also offers forms and checklists for them. Books in this vein are characteristic of what Brantlinger (2006: 54) calls '*technical* knowledge' (emphasis mine) which must be 'learned or mastered by pre- or in-service teachers'.

The *technē* discourse in the professional domain extends to research. McNary et al.'s (2006) volume links research with classroom practice in a form accessible to teachers. In research, the *technē* discourse in inclusive education usually involves an empirical orientation that seeks to understand 'what works' at individual, classroom, school and systemic levels. Dyson (quoted in Allan and Slee 2008: 35) comments on this orientation, saying that it is a view that

> ... there is a set of practices, relationships, conditions, whatever, which are more or less inclusive and *you can study them*, you can intervene in them[,] you can change them ...
>
> *(emphasis mine)*

This discourse reflects a belief that evidence-based strategies employed by teachers can make a difference to the educational outcomes of children and young people. The premise of evidence-based practice is that interventions that have been shown through large-scale, experimental research to be effective should be used when teaching learners who are deemed to have 'special needs'. There is, by virtue of this premise, a need to identify and describe the deficits of 'the excluded' in order to facilitate 'their' inclusion.

Rose (2010a: 5) implicitly recognises the *epistēmē* and *technē* discourses of inclusive education as he introduces his volume entitled *Confronting Obstacles to Inclusion*. He maintains that some of the writers in the book aim to deepen 'philosophical understanding' about inclusion, with others being more concerned to explore 'responses from schools'. The fact that there are differing approaches, he suggests, is a strength rather than a weakness in terms of understanding inclusion. Such an inclusive approach to these potentially contradictory discourses may be commendable, but glosses the critique that the *epistēmē* discourse makes of the *technē* discourse. Allan (2007: 48), for example, is scathing about texts that purport to guide users on how to 'do' inclusion as she raises questions about the purposes of inclusion, asking 'inclusion into what?' Slee (2011: 39) does not dismiss the importance of policies, strategies and resources in the pursuit of inclusive education, but argues that these constitute a 'second-order discussion' which should be preceded by a 'recognition of the unequal social relations that produce exclusion'.

## The policy domain

Educational policy-making is a topic too vast and unwieldy to be neatly or comprehensively inserted into a few paragraphs within a broader topic of inclusive education discourse. Like many of the words used in this chapter, 'policy' is contested, with multiple definitions (Liasidou 2012). There are, however, some observations that can be made about discourses of inclusive education within policies at various levels. The international call for inclusive education to be made policy (if not law) by all governments was made by the Salamanca Statement (UNESCO 1994) and there is evidence that a number of countries have given effect to this. Policies do not appear from nowhere; they are conceived and written by people in and with power, who have vested interests themselves, or have an eye to vested interests, and are intended to serve particular purposes. Slee (2010: 119) confirms this by saying:

> In the sphere of public policy, words are instruments tactically employed in the service of power. They are made to talk in particular ways for specific ends.

There are at least three types of inclusive education discourse in the policy domain: inspiration, aspiration and implementation. Inspiration consists of statements of the values and beliefs on which the inclusive education policies are founded. The language of inspiration is one of abstract nouns, a call to collective responsibility and a reminder of basic rights that must be realised. Aspiration refers to descriptions of the ideal schooling system envisaged by the policy. The language is of vision, and what could be or should be. Finally, implementation is about *how* inclusive education should be realised. In this discourse, the content is detailed and strongly directive. These three discourses can be exemplified with reference to South Africa's policy on inclusive education.

In this chapter, and in this book as a whole, I refer to the South African policy on inclusive education. My intention is not to comment on the policy provisions *per se*, but to show language at work in the published policy documents. *White Paper Six: Special Needs Education* (Department of Education (DoE), 2001) is the seminal policy intended to describe the building of an inclusive education system. Subsequent to *White Paper Six*, the country has seen the publication of various guideline documents that develop the ideas of *White Paper Six* and offer some direction for the implementation of inclusive education. Exemplifying the inspirational discourse, the introduction to *White Paper Six* begins with the words:

> Our Constitution (Act 108 of 1996) founded our democratic state and common citizenship on the values of human dignity, the achievement of equality and the advancement of human rights and freedoms (Section 1a). These values summon all of us to take up the responsibility and challenge of building a humane and caring society, not for the few, but for all South Africans. In establishing an education and training system for the 21$^{st}$ century, we carry a special responsibility to implement these values and to ensure that all learners, with and without disabilities, pursue their learning potential to the fullest.
>
> *(DoE 2001: 11)*

The first sentence of this extract foregrounds the Constitution of South Africa by making it the theme of the sentence (i.e. the first part of the sentence, or the 'launch pad for the clause' (Janks 2010: 76)). This invokes the legal and moral authority of the Constitution at the outset. The Constitution is not preceded by an article ('a/n' or 'the') but by the possessive plural pronoun 'our'. This indicates shared ownership and presumes a unity of understanding of its purposes and provisions. The use of first person plural pronouns is striking in this extract. The policy writers imagine 'we' and 'our' and 'us' to include the policy reader, and use the pronouns to create a sense of collective identity. There is thus an 'imagined community' (Anderson 1983) that this policy addresses. Other noteworthy grammatical choices include the use of the present tense in these sentences which makes for a strong sense of certainty. Unlike other sections of *White Paper Six* where the passive voice prevails, this introduction is characterised by verbs in the active voice and the indicative mood. This represents a focus on actors and action. These sentences are laden with abstract nouns ('citizenship', 'dignity', 'equality', etc.) which are identified as 'values'. These values have the power to 'summon', but also can be implemented, making them both the subject and object of action. These sentences typify the inspirational discourse of inclusive education in policy, and are written to evoke a sense of shared purpose with an appeal to what are imagined as common values. This discourse operates at the level of generality, and rehearses ideas and ideals that are assumed to be generally understood and cherished.

The aspiration discourse of inclusive education in the policy domain includes descriptions of the roles and functions of different types of schools (ordinary schools, full-service schools and special schools), and the different responsibilities of people at various levels of the system (province, district, school, etc.). This aspirational discourse is typified by the following extract from *White Paper Six*:

> This strengthened education support service will have, at its centre, new district-based support teams that will comprise staff from provincial district, regional and head offices and from special schools. The primary function of these district support teams will be to evaluate programmes, diagnose their effectiveness and suggest modifications. Through supporting teaching, learning and management, they will build the capacity of schools, early childhood and adult basic education and training centres, colleges and higher education institutions to recognise and address severe learning difficulties and to accommodate a range of learning needs.
>
> *(DoE 2001: 29)*

In contrast to the previous extract, this one uses the future tense to describe the ideal functioning of the inclusive education system in terms of education support services. There are no modals which would suggest uncertainty or tentativeness, with the verbs indicating confidence that the events described will take place. This is not a discourse that describes how the support teams might achieve their envisaged functions, but one that pronounces on what the system will comprise and entail. There is no call to shared values or use of personal pronouns, it is a statement of what will be. This particular extract is characterised by lists. There is a list of the composition of staff, a list of the functions, a list of all the institutions where they will build capacity and a list of what capacities will be built. The cumulative effect of these lists is to inundate the reader with requirements such that the task becomes overwhelming. The aspirational discourse is not one of *why* or *how*, but *what*.

*White Paper Six* is characterised by inspirational and aspirational discourses of inclusive education. Its intention is both to persuade and communicate that inclusive education is both a moral imperative and a vision that can be realised in the South African context. There is little about implementation in *White Paper Six*. This discourse is found in subsequent guideline and strategy documents like *The National Strategy on Screening, Identification, Assessment and Support* (SIAS) (DoE 2008; Department of Basic Education (DBE) 2014). The latter document typifies the implementation discourse and is explicitly identified as supporting 'the *implementation* of the main principles of Education White Paper 6' (DBE 2014: front matter, emphasis mine). The following extracts come from the first two chapters of the 2014 version of this policy:

> The policy directs the system on how to plan, budget and programme support at all levels.
>
> *(DBE 2014: 1)*

> Through a set of forms, this policy outlines the protocol that has to be followed in identifying and addressing barriers to learning that affect individual learners throughout their school career.
>
> *(DBE 2014: 6)*

Here the vocabulary of action is privileged, and the language is used to inform and instruct. The verbs are in the indicative mood (providing information), and frequently in the imperative mood (giving instruction). The SIAS process is not optional, it is a protocol 'that has to be followed'. The word 'must' appears throughout the SIAS document, with directives for things that various people are required to do in the process of identifying and addressing 'support needs'. The language of this policy is authoritative and personal pronouns do not feature in the 2014 version. Unlike the inspirational discourse, this is not the generalised rhetoric of why inclusive education is pursued, nor the aspirational description of what is envisaged. Instead, a detailed and complicated procedure is outlined, replete with 'forms' and 'protocols'. It is also worth noting how the 'policy' is the subject of the verbs used in these extracts. This means that the policy assumes the power of agency, and is decoupled from the human actors who formulated it, enforce it or enact its directives.

The implementation discourse has textual features which are similar to the *technē* discourse in the professional domain. The SIAS policy contains, in addition to visual texts like tables, forms and checklists, a one-page flow-chart as a visual representation of the 'SIAS Process for Individual Learners' (DBE 2014: 38). This flow-chart has 17 textboxes variously linked to each other with bold arrows. This signals a process that is clearly boundaried and with finite possibilities. Visual texts that accompany the verbal text are a feature of the implementation discourse, and they suggest that although inclusive education might seem complex, it is in fact a logical process, with identifiable steps and procedures with a logical end point.

The implementation discourse of inclusive education is clearly intended to provide explicit guidance as to how the aspirational discourse might be realised. The extent to which this occurs has been a matter for research (Donohue and Bornman 2014; Wildeman and Nomdo 2007). One needs to look no further than newspaper reports to know that the ideals and aspirations of policy are *not* the experience of many children and their families.

## Inclusive education as a discourse in the public domain

Issues of educational inclusion and exclusion have seeped into the public domain, and we cannot ignore the in/exclusion discourse found in the media, popular fiction, film and web and blog sites. These have the potential to influence ways of viewing the world, how things are and should be, and who or what constitute society's problems. The discourse of in/exclusion in this domain is not constrained by academic peer review but is influenced by the need to produce what sells. It reflects and constructs a range of popular ideas about difference, schools and schooling. So television documentaries reminiscent of the freak shows of yesteryear are made of people with severe or unusual disabilities for a voyeuristic audience. These emphasise the otherness of these individuals, and ensure that viewers see disability as individual tragedy and triumph. Fictional films and books build life-worlds for characters with an array of 'disabilities'. Only some of this fiction successfully portrays these characters as developed, nuanced characters, without essentialising their identities as disabled.

While not discounting the role of television, film, fiction and other media, I am particularly interested in the role of newspapers in developing the public discourse of inclusive education. Newspapers are not averse to commenting on educational policy, and sometimes their take on the issue reflects and reinforces the opinion of newspaper owners and their niche market. An example is a report in *The Independent*, a conservative daily newspaper in the UK. The headline and subheading read (Wilce, 2006):

> **Special-needs education: does mainstream inclusion work?**
>
> Labour wants children with learning difficulties to attend mainstream schools. But critics say that the policy of inclusion isn't working. Hilary Wilce investigates a very political issue.

In this instance, the 'policy of inclusion' is packaged not as an educational, but a 'very political issue', associated with a particular political party. Across the Atlantic, Ferri and Connor (2006) engaged in a comprehensive analysis of US newspaper editorials and compared the language used for racial desegregation with that of inclusion in education. In that country, issues of inclusive education seem to have occupied a significant amount of editorial space and reader response. The same cannot be said for South Africa, where inclusive education finds itself the subject of various newspaper reports and not a matter for editorial attention. There is also little evidence of reader comment on the reports, and it seems that inclusive education does not engage the public[8] in the same way as it does in other countries. Despite this, it is possible to identify a number of common themes that emerge when considering the news coverage of inclusive education in South Africa.[9] My purpose here is to isolate the use of language in the themes of disability neglect, information about inclusive education and efforts to be inclusive.

## *Disability neglect*

Many newspaper articles are concerned with disability 'neglect' (Macleod 2005; Taylor 2013) and report the ways in which learners with disabilities are excluded by schools or the schooling system. In some cases, these accounts of neglect or exclusion are disability specific while others are more general. The trend in these accounts is to make the point either at the level of the individual story and provide details of names, places and specific difficulties, or to offer numbers and statistics to show the magnitude of the problem, or to do both. So, for example, there is the story of Linda who has cerebral palsy and whose mother had to quit her job and educate at home 'after she approached four mainstream schools in her area that would not accept her' (Chipangura 2013). In the same article, Bongani has been rejected by various pre-schools because he is 'disruptive, hyperactive, does not listen, doesn't like to be helped or needs individual attention that they cannot afford as they have many other children to take care of'. In another article, Mandre, a 'wheelchair-bound [sic] Roodepoort teenager', skipped breakfast and ate nothing during the day because he 'could not use his school's toilets as they lacked railings and he was too shy to ask for help'. He left that school because he was 'lonely and not reaching his full potential' (Grobbelaar 2011). Stories that evoke this theme seem to offer a human face to the scandal of exclusion by using learners' first names and a few personal details. But these details are superficial, as their identities are framed by their problems. The description of the litany of difficulties that these learners encounter achieves two things. It contributes to a public discourse of disability as a problem and people with disabilities as victims and in need of charitable help (Stadler 2006). It also deepens alterity, by casting these young people as being so very different.

The story of the named individuals is set against the numbers story, which, taken across all the sources, seems quite imprecise. The numbers of children with disabilities reported as being out of school[10] ranges between 165,000 and 467,000 children. Officially, there are about 200,000 South African learners out of school in total, with 'special needs' given as one of the reasons for this (DBE 2011). Mentioning these numbers in newspaper reports is clearly meant to have shock value and to indicate the enormity of the problem of the exclusion of learners with disabilities. I would argue, however, that employing the numbers inadvertently feeds the idea that the problem is overwhelming and ultimately unsolvable. The solution that is offered is inclusive education, with descriptions of what inclusive education is, what the benefits are and who is responsible for its implementation.

## *Information about inclusive education*

A second concern of newspaper articles that contribute to a public discourse of inclusive education is the provision of information. The newspaper-reading public could be forgiven for having a very reductionist understanding of inclusive education, given that it is usually explained simply as the move towards educating learners with disabilities or 'special needs' in mainstream schools (Anthony 2013; Dale-Jones 2014; Erasmus 2005; Nkosi 2011). In most cases, this is coupled with reference to various policy documents, an association which might work to assure the public that inclusive education is not a whimsical idea but has the authority of policy. It might just as well make inclusive education sound like one more policy 'fad', which may or may not survive successive educational administrations.

The information given in newspapers about inclusive education extends to the rationale for inclusive education and its benefits. Details of who is responsible for the implementation of inclusive education are provided, together with determinants of its success. In these sections of the articles, the report writers foreground expert comment. These experts include high-level South African education officials, spokespersons for NGOs and South African and international academics. The contribution of these experts reflects some of the inspirational and aspirational discourse that I identified in the policy domain. This is set against stories from the ground. There are some optimistic accounts of individuals who, against the odds, have been 'included', and I will return to these stories shortly. There are also the bleak accounts of exclusion experienced by learners like Linda, Bongani and Mandre. In effect, we have two stories of inclusive education in the public domain. One story is from experts in positions of power and authority who can imagine and pronounce on what an inclusive education system could or should entail. The other story is from experts by experience of the education system who 'carry and shed real tears over stories of the devaluing and rejection of their children' (Slee 2011: 53). Pervading both stories, though, is the refrain that inclusive education represents a massive challenge.

Often accompanying the information about inclusive education are reports of the 'challenges' and 'barriers' to its implementation. The word 'challenge' appears repeatedly where inclusive education is described in the newspaper reports. The 'challenges of implementing inclusive education' is a familiar theme in the inclusive education discourse in the professional domain, yielding numerous research projects and academic texts.[11] As the theme permeates the public domain through newspaper reports, these challenges are compressed and compounded to meet the space constraints of an article, and so become overwhelming to a reader. In some instances, the challenges are deemed 'barriers' to implementation (IOL news 2006; Keating 2006; Pretorious 2006) and, as such, they seem insurmountable. These challenges or barriers are the well-known list of poor teacher education, systemic constraints (inadequate resources, overcrowded classrooms, distance and transport) and negative attitudes towards children with disabilities and their inclusion in 'mainstream' classrooms. In this discourse, it is significant to note that the problem of systemic and endemic exclusion quickly shifts to being a problem of inclusion, which is seen as 'difficult to achieve' (Dale-Jones 2014). One article is entirely given to a report on a school's decision no longer to include d/Deaf learners because of the financial costs which the school is unable to bear (Mohlala 2005).

This particular article is written in such a way that it secures a good impression of the school's efforts, while demonstrating the unaffordability of inclusion. The use of language in the report is revealing and I comment on just three excerpts:

> The school enrolled five deaf learners in 2001, but has been forced to decline any further applications from disabled learners because the cost of teaching them is prohibitive.

The construction of this sentence is worth examining. The main clause and theme of the sentence is the school which enrolled five deaf learners. This secures the reader's focus on what the school did, with its subsequent decision to decline further applications coming second to the school's effort. 'Force' is a strong word, and it suggests that the school had no option; the decision to decline further applications was taken against its will. Who is doing the forcing is obscured because the passive voice is used. In fact, what emerges is that there is no outside force; the school itself has taken the decision. There is a telling conflation of 'deaf learners' and 'disabled learners', who come together in the pronoun 'them'. 'Them' are clearly not us, who are not too costly to educate. The cost of teaching 'them' is not merely expensive, it is 'prohibitive', which suggests that the school has no choice. Providing access for these learners is seen as a drain on the school's resources:

> Two interpreters were hired and their salaries were paid from the school's coffers and this proved too expensive to sustain, she [the principal] says, adding that it was not an easy decision, because the school believed it was important not to isolate disabled learners.

In South Africa, some state schools (including this one) are allowed to charge school fees from parents who can afford to pay. The school's 'coffers' would thus represent the contribution of parents, and these funds are usually used to supplement the staff complement that the government supplies and to provide additional facilities and maintenance. To a South African parent reading this article, the mention that the interpreters were paid from the school's coffers would be highly significant, because it signals money collected from the whole parent body and used for only five learners. That learners with disabilities use up more than their fair share of resources is a complaint that Ferri and Connor (2006: 162) identify in the US press as they note a rhetoric that focuses 'on the unfairness of "wasting resources" … on so few students'. The school in this article is presented as making a rational yet difficult decision, with their belief in not isolating disabled learners having to be sacrificed because of cost. The absent voice in this account is the Department of Education who might have been expected to employ the interpreters. The learners, though, are grateful for their opportunity:

> They are full of praise for [the school] for accommodating them. 'We are very thankful indeed to [the school] for being a home away from home to the

five of us. At the beginning we felt out of place, but now we feel welcome.'
... The girls consider themselves lucky to have been at [the school] and
wish it were possible for other deaf learners to follow in their footsteps.

The school (a 'School for the Deaf') that these learners previously attended did not offer a matriculation certificate that enabled access to university, hence their enrolment at this mainstream school. The learners have appropriated the language of hospitality and see themselves as guests in the school, thankful that they have been accommodated and made to feel welcome. They know that their place in the school has been a concession which they were 'lucky' to have been granted, but which will not be extended to other d/Deaf learners. This article sets up inclusion of disabled learners (a positive and worthwhile idea) and financial prudence (a necessary responsibility) as being irreconcilable opposites, that is we can have one or the other, but not both. In the end, financial prudence wins the day and there'll be no more 'disabled' learners at this particular school. The 'battle' between the two ideals in this school is implicit in this report. But fighting language is quite explicit in other reports.

Two battles are evident in the discourse of inclusive education in the public domain. The first is the 'battle' or 'struggle' for parents of children with disabilities to find schools which will enrol their children (Anthony 2013; Chipangura 2013). The learners themselves also 'struggle' to gain access and acceptance (Grobbelaar 2011). The second battle is over inclusive education itself. The media, schools and parents 'battle' to accept inclusive education, says Mitchell in the report by Pretorious (2006). Dale-Jones (2014) reported on a teachers' seminar where she saw evidence of the 'contestations that dog inclusive education' and learned that 'schools should fight for inclusion'. Resistance to inclusive education comes from teachers (Dale-Jones 2014; Macleod 2005; Pretorious 2006) and parents (Pretorious 2006). In the US newspaper debates on desegregation and inclusion, Ferri and Connor (2006: 156) also found 'analogies to war or battle' and account for this both in terms of the seriousness of the reforms under consideration and the 'preponderance of binaries' in the discussion. One of the binaries in South African news reports about inclusive education is that either inclusion is a good idea but is impossible, or that inclusion is possible – look at the evidence.

## *Efforts to be inclusive*

There are a number of newspaper articles which are solely, or in part, given to reporting on various efforts towards greater inclusivity. These articles trumpet the strides made by the Department of Education (provincial or national), NGOs or individual schools or institutions to promote or implement inclusive education. Departmental initiatives include the upgrading of infrastructure (Dunlap 2011; Nkosi 2011), the allocation of funds (Taylor 2013) and policy development (Dale-Jones 2014; Pretorious 2006). NGOs have a role to play in promoting and supporting 'positive models' of inclusive education (Taylor 2013) and recognising the efforts of teachers and principals who are 'taking the initiative' to promote inclusion (Nkosi, 2011).

The stories of individual school efforts are of particular interest in the development of the public discourse of inclusive education, exemplified in the following extracts:

> ... a partially-sighted girl currently attends ... a mainstream school in Cape Town. She uses a desk lamp to aid her note-taking during class and is assisted by a facilitator, who is paid for by her parents and who ensures that all her learning materials are accessible.
>
> *(Dunlap 2011)*

> At [a preparatory school] every effort has been made to accommodate [a learner], who uses a wheelchair. Ramps have been constructed for him, and his classroom, which would have been on the first floor, has been brought down to the ground floor.
>
> *(Dunlap 2011)*

> ... [B]ecause [a girls' high school in Cape Town] building is over 100 years old, it's difficult to ensure that it is entirely disabled-friendly, but they have made it work in individual situations. Currently, they have a learner who is hearing impaired. Teachers make use of a device that is linked to her hearing device so she can pick up what is being said in class.
>
> *(Dunlap 2011)*

> [A learner] was born with spina bifida and is confined to a wheelchair ... [S]he was determined to attend a mainstream high school and was eventually accepted at [a high school] where staff have made several changes to accommodate her. [The] acting ... deputy principal said: 'When we accepted [her] it was a new challenge, but we are trying continuously.' [The acting deputy principal] said [the learner with spina bifida] was the only pupil with a disability at the school but there were others who faced learning barriers. By providing extra support every day, she said, the staff had accommodated these pupils.
>
> *(Keating 2006)*

These stories have a celebratory tone, and yet they rehearse a discourse of inclusive education as being a series of compensatory measures introduced in response to individual deficits. Three of these extracts mention specific 'accommodations' made for these particular individuals. Thus inclusive education is not presented as systemic reform, but as support strategies offered to individuals in a system which remains largely unchanged. This orientation to inclusive education is revealed in these extracts in various ways. In the first, the facilitator is 'paid for by the parents'. This signals inclusion as the preserve of the privileged, and warns the reader not to expect that this kind of support would be generally available to learners in all schools. The second and third extracts show schools making an 'effort' to 'work' to ensure accessibility in response to individual needs. Access is not the right of these learners, it represents an extra effort that the school must make. A similar sentiment is expressed in the fourth extract, where the learner's acceptance constitutes a 'challenge', requiring continuous 'trying' for the school. In these extracts, the school is lauded as making a valiant effort, but there is no doubt that 'the child seeking inclusion is an outsider and a potential burden' (Slee 2011: 157). These comments are not intended to criticise these schools' endeavours – it is indeed difficult to be inclusive in a system that mitigates against inclusivity in various ways. Rather, they show how inclusive education is languaged in and by these reports, and how they contribute to a public discourse of inclusive education.

## Conclusion: the appearances and dispersion of inclusive education

If inclusive education is a discourse, or a constellation of related discourses, then its discursive formations can be analysed. This chapter has been an exercise in exploring the interplay of the 'appearances and dispersion' (Foucault 2002: 39) of inclusive education, as it is said-done-believed in different domains. The domains are not sealed from each other and the echoes of the saying-doing-believing in one domain are heard in the others. It is clear that the discursive community of inclusive education is characterised by hybridity and variability (Artiles 2004) and its reach extends beyond the professional and policy domains into the public domain. A result of this discursive breadth is the diffusion of understandings of inclusive education, as it is invoked for various purposes and languaged with different effects. This variability ought to be expected if inclusive education is a discourse. There are, however, alternatives when considering the nature of inclusive education, and these are explored in the chapter that follows.

## Notes

1 'Shame' is a common South African colloquialism that does not mean shame at all. It is an expression of sympathy.
2 This is explored further in Chapter 2 where I discuss inclusive education as a knower code, in which personal dispositions and attributes are emphasised in legitimising participation and achievement in the field.
3 By contrast, Kozleski *et al.* (2011: 3) do not recognise a profession domain, but rather 'multiple professional discourses about inclusive education'.
4 Drawing on Maton (2014: 51), production fields are the 'sites where "new" knowledge is created'; recontextualisation fields are sites where the knowledges from the fields of production are 'selected, rearranged and transformed to become pedagogic discourse'; and reproduction fields are the 'sites of teaching and learning'.
5 These include special education, with its origins in medicine and psychology; critical theories, including disability theories; curriculum, pedagogy; and assessment and teacher education.
6 Phronesis, the third Aristotelian disposition, is 'the moral disposition to act wisely, truly and justly' (Kemmis and Smith 2008: 23). Allan (2008: 48) has strongly advocated for a focus on phronetic research, noting 'the failure to position research on inclusion phronetically'. She argues further that '… with its central interest in values and power, [it] appears to be the most appropriate kind of research to be undertaken in relation to inclusion' (148). There is some evidence of the use of the idea of phronesis in inclusive education research (Rayner 2009), but I do not recognise this as a distinctive discourse in the professional domain.

7   In other words, this is a discourse characterised by stronger semantic density (Maton 2014). Chapter 2 explores this in more detail.
8   I acknowledge the complexity of imagining a public in relation to texts, with Warner (2002: 16) speaking of the 'mutually defining interplay between texts and publics'. It does not seem worth speculating about the public who would be the assumed readers of the articles under discussion, beyond making some superficial comments about access to online media sources and interest in the topic. But it is worth noting that this public is both addressed and made by these texts.
9   My sources are the online platforms of four prominent South African newspapers, and one online news site, all of which offered search results to the words 'inclusive education'. I examined 16 news articles and one letter to the editor from 2005 to 2013 and the analysis was made using the QDA Miner (Lite) software package.
10  Grobbelaar (2011) reports that: 'Tens of thousands of disabled children struggle to access decent education' with '47% of disabled children aged 16 to 18 not in any form of education'". Moeketsi (2012) reports: 'At least 467,000 disabled children are not going to school', suggesting that '10 percent of children with disabilities were not attending school in South Africa'. Monama (2012) offers a figure of 'at least 400,000 disabled children of school-going age' who are not 'in the system', while a fellow reporter on the same newspaper suggests a more conservative '165,000 children with disabilities' who are out of school (Mashaba 2012). The discrepancy between the reported and official numbers is difficult to account for, since the Department of Basic Education is usually quoted as the source of the figures given in newspaper reports.
11  See, for example, Rose (2010b).

## References

Allan, J. (2005) 'Inclusion as an ethical project', in S. Tremain (ed.), *Foucault and the Government of Disability*. Ann Arbor, MI: University of Michigan Press, pp. 281–97.
Allan, J. (2007) *Rethinking Inclusive Education*. Dordrecht: Springer.
Allan, J. (2008) *Rethinking Inclusive Education. The Philosophers of Difference in Practice*. Dordrecht: Springer.
Allan, J. and Slee, R. (2008) *Doing Inclusive Education Research*. Rotterdam: Sense Publishers.
Anderson, B. (1983) *Imagined Communities: Reflections on the Origin and Spread of Nationalism*. London: Verso.
Anthony, L. (2013) 'KZN bid for autistic kids'. Accessed from: http://www.iol.co.za/dailynews/opinion/kzn-bid-for-autistic-kids-1.1533214#.U76sRfmSw6g.
Artiles, A. J. (2004) 'The end of innocence: historiography and representation in the discursive practice of LD', *Journal of Learning Disabilities*, 37 (6): 550–5.
Barton, L. (2010) 'Response', *British Journal of Sociology of Education*, 31 (5): 643–50.
Blommaert, J. (2005) *Discourse*. Cambridge: Cambridge University Press.
Brantlinger, E. (2006) 'The big glossies: how textbooks structure (special) education', in E. Brantlinger (ed.), *Who Benefits from Special Education? Remediating (Fixing) Other People's Children*. Mahwah, NJ: Lawrence Erlbaum Associates, pp. 45–76.
Chipangura, C. (2013) 'No room in school for disabled kids', *IOL News*. Accessed from http://www.iol.co.za/lifestyle/family/kids/no-room-in-schools-for-disabled-kids-1.1549502#.U76sEfmSw6g.
Dale-Jones, B. (2014) 'Teaching that embraces difference', *Mail and Guardian*. Accessed from: http://mg.co.za/article/2014-04-07-teaching-that-embraces-difference.
Department of Basic Education (DBE) (2010) *Guidelines for Inclusive Teaching and Learning*. Pretoria: Government Printers.

Department of Basic Education (DBE) (2011) *Action Plan to 2014: Towards the Realisation of Schooling 2025*. Pretoria: Government Printers.

Department of Basic Education (DBE) (2014) *The National Strategy on Screening, Identification, Assessment and Support*. Pretoria: Government Printers.

Department of Education (DoE) (2001) *Education White Paper Six: Special Needs Education. Building an Inclusive Education and Training System*. Pretoria: Department of Education.

Department of Education (DoE) (2008) *The National Strategy on Screening, Identification, Assessment and Support*. Pretoria: Government Printers.

Donohue, D. and Bornman, J. (2014) 'The challenges of realising inclusive education in South Africa', *South African Journal of Education*, 34 (2): 1–14.

Du Toit, P. and Forlin, C. (2009) 'Cultural transformation for inclusion, what is needed? A South African perspective', *School Psychology International*, 30 (6): 644–55.

Dunlap, J. (2011) 'Are our schools disabled friendly?' Accessed from: http://www.parent24.com/Back-to-School/Are-our-schools-disabled-friendly-20110504.

Dyson, A. (1999) Inclusion and inclusions: theories and discourses in inclusive education', in H. Daniels and P. Garner (eds), *World Yearbook of Education: Inclusive Education*. London: Kogan Page, pp. 36–53.

Erasmus, B. (2005) 'Opening windows for the visually impaired'. Accessed from: http://mg.co.za/article/2005-11-10-opening-windows-for-the-visually-impaired.

Fairclough, N. (2001) *Language and Power*, 2nd edn. Abingdon: Routledge.

Ferri, B. and Connor, D. (2006) *Reading Resistance*. New York: Peter Lang.

Foucault, M. (2002) *The Archaeology of Knowledge*, trans. M. Sheridan Smith. London and New York: Routledge.

Gable, A. (2014) 'Disability theorising and real-world educational practice: a framework for understanding', *Disability and Society*, 29 (1): 86–100.

Gee, J. P. (2008) *Social Linguistics and Literacies: Ideology in Discourses*, 3rd edn. Abingdon: Routledge.

Gee, J. P. (2011) *An Introduction to Discourse Analysis*, 3rd edn. New York: Routledge.

Grobbelaar, R. (2011) 'Disabled pupils miss out', *Times Live*. Accessed from: http://www.timeslive.co.za/local/2011/08/15/disabled-pupils-miss-out.

Halliday, M. and Matthiessen, M. (2004) *An Introduction to Functional Grammar*, 3rd edn. London: Arnold.

Hammeken, P. (2007) *The Teachers' Guide to Inclusive Education: 750 Strategies for Success!* Thousand Oaks, CA: Corwin Press.

IOL news (2006) 'Give special-needs pupils inclusive education'. Accessed from: http://www.iol.co.za/news/south-africa/give-special-needs-pupils-inclusive-education-1.285734#.U76r3fmSw6g.

Janks, H. (2010) *Literacy and Power*. London: Routledge.

Keating, C. (2006) 'Kamielah finds niche at mainstream school'. Accessed from: http://www.iol.co.za/news/south-africa/kamielah-finds-niche-at-mainstream-school-1.291982?ot=inmsa.ArticlePrintPageLayout.ot.

Kemmis, S. and Smith, T. (2008) 'Personal praxis', in S. Kemmis and T. Smith (eds), *Enabling Praxis*. Rotterdam: Sense Publishers, pp. 15–35.

Kozleski, E. B., Artiles, A. J. and Waitoller, F. R. (2011) 'Introduction. Equity in inclusive education', in A. J. Artiles, E. B. Kozleski and F. R. Waitoller (eds), *Inclusive Education: Examining Equity on Five Continents*. Cambridge, MA: Harvard Education Press, pp. 1–14.

Liasidou, A. (2012) *Inclusive Education, Politics and Policymaking*. London: Continuum.

Macleod, C. (2005) 'Why inclusive education must work'. Accessed from: http://mg.co.za/article/2005-05-07-why-inclusive-education-must-work.

McNary, S., Glasgow, N. and Hicks, C. (2005) *What Successful Teachers Do in Inclusive Classrooms: 60 Research-Based Teaching Strategies That Help Special Learners Succeed*. Thousand Oaks, CA: Corwin Press

Mashaba, S. (2012) 'Little hope for children with disabilities'. Accessed from: http://www.sowetanlive.co.za/news/2012/01/05/little-hope-for-children-with-disabilities.

Maton, K. (2014) *Knowledge and Knowers*. Abingdon: Routledge.

Moeketsi, S. (2012) 'Many disabled kids not in school'. Accessed from: http://www.iol.co.za/news/south-africa/many-disabled-kids-not-in-school-1.1428147#.U76sH_mSw6g.

Mohlala, T. (2005) 'The end of a learning curve'. Accessed from: http://mg.co.za/article/2005-11-22-the-end-of-a-learning-curve.

Mohlala, T. (2007) 'Education for all', *Mail and Guardian*. Accessed from http://mg.co.za/article/2007-01-03-education-for-all.

Monama, T. (2012) 'Many disabled not at school'. Accessed from: http://www.sowetanlive.co.za/news/2012/05/24/many-disabled-not-at-school.

Nkosi, B. (2011) 'Only 108 SA schools offer inclusive education'. Accessed from: http://mg.co.za/article/2011-12-06-only-108-sa-schools-offer-inclusive-education.

Oliver, M. (2013) 'The social model of disability: thirty years on', *Disability and Society*, 28 (7): 1024–6.

Oliver, M. and Barnes, C. (2012) *The New Politics of Disablement*. New York: Palgrave Macmillan.

Parry, R. (2008) '*Episteme* and *Techne*', in E. N. Zalta (ed.), *The Stanford Encyclopedia of Philosophy*, Fall 2008 Edition. Accessed from: http://plato.stanford.edu/archives/fall2008/entries/episteme-techne/.

Pretorious, C. (2006) 'A formula for success'. Accessed from: http://mg.co.za/article/2006-10-09-a-formula-for-success.

Rayner, S. (2009) 'Educational diversity and learning leadership: a proposition, some principles and a model of inclusive leadership?', *Educational Review*, 61 (4): 433–47.

Rizvi, F. and Lingard, B. (2010) *Globalizing education policy*. London: Routledge.

Rose, R. (2010a) 'Understanding inclusion', in R. Rose (ed.), *Confronting Obstacles to Inclusion*. Abingdon: Routledge, pp. 1–6.

Rose, R. (ed.) (2010b) *Confronting Obstacles to Inclusion*. Abingdon: Routledge.

Saugstad, T. (2002) 'Educational theory and practice in an Aristotelian perspective', *Scandinavian Journal of Educational Research*, 46 (4): 373–90.

Slee, R. (2010) 'A cheese-slicer by any other name? Shredding the sociology of inclusion', in M. Apple, S. J. Ball and L. A. Gandin (eds), *The Routledge International Handbook of the Sociology of Education*. Abingdon: Routledge, pp. 99–108.

Slee, R. (2011) *The Irregular School*. London: Routledge.

Stadler, J. (2006) 'Media and disability', in B. Watermeyer, L. Swartz, T. Lorenzo, M. Schneider and M. Priestley (eds), *Disability and Society*. Pretoria: HSRC Press, pp. 373–86.

Taylor, C. (2013) 'Wake up to pupil neglect', Letter to the editor, *Mail and Guardian*. Accessed from: http://mg.co.za/article/2013-09-27-00-letters-to-the-editor-september-27.

Terzi, L. (2008) 'Beyond the dilemma of difference', in L. Florian and M. J. McLaughlin (eds), *Disability Classification in Education: Issues and Perspectives*. Corwin: Thousand Oaks, pp. 244–62.

UNESCO (1994) *The Salamanca Statement and Framework for Action on Special Needs Education*. Paris: UNESCO.

Warner, M. (2002) *Publics and Counterpublics*. New York: Zone Books.

Wilce, H. (2006) 'Special-needs education: does mainstream inclusion work?' Accessed from: http://www.independent.co.uk/news/education/education-news/specialneeds-education-does-mainstream-inclusion-work-470960.html.

Wildeman, R. A. and Nomdo, C. (2007) *Implementation of Inclusive Education: How Far Are We?* IDASA Budget Information Service Occasional Paper. Available from: https://www.nelsonmandela.org/omalley/cis/omalley/OMalleyWeb/dat/provinccial%20education%20depts%20not%20up%20to%20the%20job.pdf.

# 2
# INCLUSIVE EDUCATION AS AN IDEOLOGY OR FIELD

## Inclusionists working themselves out of a job

'Marxists want nothing more than to stop being Marxists,' says Terry Eagleton (2011: 1). People whose work is in inclusive education might be similar. Inclusionists (as Brantlinger (1997) calls them) might want nothing more than to stop being inclusionists. That is, of course, if they see inclusive education as radical reform. They would want to work themselves out of a job, because then, like Eagleton's political radicals, inclusionists 'would no longer be necessary because their goals would have been accomplished' (1). Inclusive education is supposed to be an interim idea. In the future, when the goal has been achieved, the adjective 'inclusive' would be unnecessary to describe 'education' because education, by definition, would have become inclusive. I wish to continue from the previous chapter that began to consider what inclusive education may be as an object of study. Moving from the idea that inclusive education is a discourse, I will consider two other possibilities. The first is that inclusive education is an ideology, and the second is that it is a field. Each of these identities offers different analytical possibilities. They each also offer a different position from which inclusive education might be judged. If inclusive education is an ideology, its power as a social or political agenda should determine its credibility. But if it is a field, then its epistemological claims must withstand scrutiny.

## Inclusive education as ideology

Gramsci (1971/1999: 706) in his *Prison Notebooks* bemoaned the 'arbitrary elucubrations of particular individuals' as the widespread, 'bad sense' use of the name 'ideology'. More recently, others have noted that the word ideology is often used vaguely and has various and contradictory definitions and approaches (Bourdieu and Eagleton 2012; Eagleton 1994). Althusser's (1970/2012) work must be regarded as seminal in a discussion of ideology, and is valuable as inclusive education is considered as ideological.[1] Developing the Marxist theory of the State, Althusser proposed the concept of ideological state apparatuses (religion, education, family, communication, etc.) which contribute to the reproduction of the relations of production. In positing a theory of ideology in general, rather than a theory of specific ideologies, Althusser examined various hypotheses. The first is that ideology is an imaginary or illusory rather than a real representation of the material conditions and relations of existence. The second is that ideology has a material existence and 'exists in an apparatus, and its practice or practices' (Althusser 1970/2012: 126). From these, Althusser derived his central thesis, which is that ideology is made possible by the subject, and that the function of ideology is to constitute individuals as subjects. This occurs through interpellation, or as ideology hails individuals and transforms them into subjects. Drawing on Althusser's hypotheses, ideology can fruitfully be considered in relation to power, material processes and their functioning. These, in turn, can be related to inclusive education as an ideology.

It seems useful to begin by exploring what makes an idea an ideology, or when an idea becomes an ideology, because inclusive education has been described as both an idea (for example, Ainscow (2005: 109)) and an ideology. An idea functions as an ideology, says Young (1990), when believing it reproduces or justifies relations of domination and oppression and obscures more emancipatory relations. Thus ideas become ideologies through the workings of hegemonic power. For Althusser (1970/2012), ideological state apparatuses reflect and perpetuate the ideology of the ruling classes and although the ideological state apparatuses function predominantly through ideology, they also function by repression, even if this is concealed or symbolic. Ideologies may thus be regarded as the generalised and dominating ways of thinking and acting that are regarded as normative in a society and which are sustained by various social practices and oppressive power relations. Ideology is usually invisible to those with hegemonic power. To those who subscribe to (and benefit from) ideologies, they seem un-ideological – they simply represent the way things are and should be.

Hegemonic power may not be necessary for ideas to become ideologies. Eagleton (1994: 6) suggests that when ideas are 'granted an active political force' rather than being reflections on the world, we are dealing with ideologies. Relations of power are certainly not absent in these processes, but this understanding makes room for counter-hegemonic ideas, those that challenge dominant ideologies, also to be regarded as ideological. Althusser (1970/2012) shows that ideological state apparatuses may be the site of struggle as the resistance of exploited classes can find the 'means and occasions' (113) to express itself there. Gramsci differed from Althusser by saying that the site of the struggle against hegemonic power was not state apparatuses but civil society and, significant for the discussion of inclusive education that will follow, Gramsci (1971/1999: 707) espouses the idea of 'organic ideology'. For Gramsci, organic ideologies can be distinguished from arbitrary or 'willed' ideologies. Organic ideologies are historically necessary and valid in that they 'create the terrain' for people to acquire consciousness of their position and to struggle (Gramsci 1971/1999: 707). This means that there is the potential for ordinary people to resist dominant ideologies.

Ideas also become ideologies through their insertion into material processes and practices (Blommaert 2005). Althusser (1970/2012) makes it clear that the ideas that make up an ideology do not have an ideal or spiritual, but a *material* existence, and that the practices of ideological state apparatuses are a realisation of ideology. For Gramsci (1971/1999), ideas (or 'individual fancies' (707)) require material forces to make them ideological. The materiality of ideology makes analysis of its working possible, and Thompson (1990) maintains that an analysis of ideology concerns the ways in which symbolic forms (which he defines as 'a broad range of actions and utterances, images and texts' (59)) intersect with relations of power. The study of ideology, says Thompson (1990: 7) calls us to '… ask whether the meaning constructed and conveyed by symbolic forms serves, or does not serve, to maintain systematically asymmetrical relations of power'.

Exploring ideology with respect to inclusive education is not breaking new ground, and I acknowledge the pioneering work of Brantlinger (1997), Allan and Slee (2008), Liasidou (2012) and Allan (2013) as I develop this topic. Inclusive education (or inclusion) is widely regarded as an ideology, both by those who reject it and those who support it. Those who reject inclusive education and name it as 'ideological' are using the term as a pejorative descriptor. Used thus, 'ideology' is an insult (Bourdieu and Eagleton 2012), suggesting bias and partisanship (Blommaert 2005) and even fanaticism (Eagleton 1994). In their critique of full inclusion, Kavale and Forness (2000) and Kavale and Mostert (2003) say that inclusion is ideological, as opposed to being rational, scientific and evidence-based. The 'ideology of full inclusion', claim Kavale and Mostert (2003: 191), 'has influenced policy and practice disproportionately to its claims of efficacy'. These authors mockingly call themselves, and others who do not share the 'vision' of inclusion, 'the benighted' (193), and contrast themselves with 'the anointed' whose 'alternate vision is empowered by cultish certainty and presumptive rightness'[2] (192). They describe the workings and consequences of the 'ideology of the anointed' as it is 'promulgated' in order to 'propagandize the real world' (194). By calling inclusion an 'ideology', these authors are clearly not intending to be complimentary. Nor, perhaps, is Baroness Warnock, who twice in her report to the House of Commons Education and Skills Committee quotes a Member of Parliament's words about a local authority that represented 'the extreme end of the ideology of inclusion' (UK Parliament 2006). Sir Bob Balchin, chair of the Tory enquiry into special education, agrees, saying: 'The ideology of inclusion ought to be consigned to history. We need to look at the whole thing in a more pragmatic light' (Wilce 2006).

The advocates of inclusive education do not shy away from saying that it is an ideology or that it is ideological. Forlin (2006) writes in the context of the Australian experience about 'the ideology of inclusion' (269) and that 'inclusive education is an ideology that is being promoted' (273), and, more recently, Paliokosta and Blandford (2010: 179) note that 'inclusion has been a dominant ideology' in the

United Kingdom. In her rebuttal of the claim of 'traditionalists' that inclusion is an ideology, Brantlinger (1997: 448) concedes the presence of ideology in the stance of inclusionists, but says that separate special education as espoused by the 'traditionalists' is no less ideological. This echoes Žižek's (2012: 4) contention that when something is pronounced ideological, we can be sure that 'its inversion is no less ideological'. In recognising inclusive education as an ideology, Brantlinger (1997) positions it in terms of Gramsci's idea of an organic ideology, one which works for emancipation from oppressive social structures. This suggests that while inclusive education may be ideological, it is not a hegemonic ideology.

Many of the tenets of inclusive education make it counter-hegemonic, resisting dominating beliefs and practices in schools that are based on normalising principles and sustained by oppressive structures and unequal social relations. Inclusive education challenges the assumptions about 'the way things are', the sorting, categorising and labelling of children that results in the inequitable provision of educational goods, and the school and classroom practices that go unchallenged, but which marginalise and exclude. As such, inclusive education seeks to subvert hegemonic ideologies and promote emancipatory and socially just ways of being. But this position is not unassailable. Inclusive education has been seen as first-world knowledge which has penetrated developing countries, spreading 'evangelical belief in the inclusion of diversity' (Armstrong *et al.* 2011: 33). These authors say that first-world and donor countries exhort developing countries to adopt inclusive education as a 'policy prescription to address system failure' (33). Couched like this, inclusive education becomes another imposition on developing countries, in the tradition of colonising and missionary endeavours – hegemonic indeed. Inclusive education in this sense is not only an ideology, as donor aid functions to coerce countries into compliance, but also idealistic. If we cannot ensure epistemic access for the children already in our system, the argument goes, how can we possibly consider those on the margins, or outside the system? In other words, inclusive education exists as an 'ideal' (Kozleski *et al.* 2011: 5), practically unworkable in developing contexts.

Further complicating matters is the question of whether inclusive education is an ideology rather than a term under which multiple (inconsistent and conflicting) ideologies are subsumed. Concern has been raised about ways in which ideologies reproduced in special education processes and practices have been rebranded as inclusive education (Brantlinger 2006; Graham and Slee 2008; Slee 2011). Policies in many countries, my own included, attest to this, as do books and textbooks which name and position some children as Other and describe how to include 'them' in an unproblematised pre-existing mainstream or regular education. So, in many iterations, inclusive education is hardly an emancipatory ideology. It has been domesticated (Slee 2009) or mainstreamed to make it fit into prevailing, dominant discourses and practices in education, and made palatable to teachers, therapists, academics and others with a vested interest in preserving the status quo. Whether inclusive education is hegemonic ideology, co-opted by hegemonic ideology, radical and subversive ideology or some combination of these, there are good reasons to regard inclusive education as (an) ideology.

The interpellative role of inclusive education also signals it as an ideology. Using language, inclusive education hails individuals and produces them as subjects – learners become the included, the excluded, the about-to-be included and so forth; teachers are hailed as inclusive teachers, resistant teachers, negative teachers, etc. The ideology provides a script (Gonsalves 2007) which directs the thinking and saying of these subjects and thus ensures that the ideology of inclusive education is enacted and given material existence. Furthermore, as I explore in some detail in this chapter, the ideology of inclusive education interpellates the *individual* and makes individual subjects. These subjects are, as Goodley (2007: 322) says, fixed as 'eternally lacking' and always with needs to be met.[3]

Inclusive education can be regarded as ideological in the sense that it is reproduced in material processes and practices. These include research, publications and other texts, teaching and conferences. As such, the meanings created by its symbolic forms can be scrutinised in terms of the relations of domination that they create or maintain. To do this, Thompson's (1990) five modes of the operations of ideology (legitimation, dissimulation, unification, fragmentation and reification) can be used to frame an analysis. These modes, or processes, and the strategies associated with them can be identified in various texts. I will return to some of these as I examine various aspects of the language of inclusive education in the course of this book, but for now I would like briefly to suggest how inclusive education or inclusion works ideologically in terms of Thompson's modes of operation.

## *Legitimation*

Legitimation works to sustain relations of domination by representing them as legitimate. Referring to Max Weber, Thompson (1990) claims three grounds on which legitimacy is promoted – rational grounds, traditional grounds and charismatic grounds. If inclusive education is a counter-hegemonic ideology, it is difficult to argue that it legitimises relations of domination and oppression which could be identified in prevailing educational structures and practices. But it is possible to argue that inclusive education promotes its own legitimacy and 'persuades an audience that it is worthy of support' (Thompson 1990: 61).

Rational grounds, which Thompson (1990) says is an appeal to legality and rules, can be found in the 'rights and ethics discourse' of inclusive education that Dyson (1999: 39) expounds, in the appeals to various United Nations (UN) Conventions (in particular the Convention of the Rights of People with Disabilities (UN 2006)) and with reference to *The Salamanca Statement and Framework for Action* (UNESCO 1994). As various countries have incorporated inclusive education into their educational policies and legislation, it has been further legitimated. The legitimacy of inclusive education on traditional grounds is promoted as inclusionists link segregated special education with the rise of modern schooling. The argument is made that special education arose from the failure of modern schooling to teach all children, and became a repository for children who were deemed to have characteristics that fell outside the parameters of 'normal'. Nostalgic accounts of the inclusion of children with disabilities in one-room schools in the US prior to the First World War (Frost 2009) combine with idyllic pictures of the inclusion of children with disabilities in indigenous community education (Kisanji 1998) to create the impression that inclusive education is the true and natural way of schooling. The presentation of inclusive education as legitimate also occurs as charismatic leaders and people in authority endorse inclusive education. One of the textbooks on inclusive education that I discuss in Chapter 5, for example, has a foreword written by Archbishop Emeritus Desmond Tutu, the famed anti-apartheid activist (Bornman and Rose 2010).

Inclusive education thus legitimates itself in various ways. This is not to say that the same devices do not work to legitimate segregated special education and other forms of educational exclusion. But the effect of legitimation is that critique and question are forestalled, if not disallowed. A critique of inclusive education might come either from those convinced of the merits of segregated special education, or from those who deem inclusive education unworkable or unrealistic in a competitive, globalised world, or from those who question the legitimacy of inclusive education as a field of study and its place in the academy (see the discussion of inclusive education as a field later in this chapter). Critique may equally come from those who support the idea of inclusive education but are dissatisfied with the form that it has taken.

## *Dissimulation*

Dissimulation is the mode that Thompson (1990) maintains conceals, denies or obscures the workings of power. Euphemism is one way[4] in which dissimulation works, and it refers to 'naming slippage' (Janks 2010: 41) and the ways in which things are renamed for positive effect. Just like in South Africa where institutionalised racism was renamed a couple of times to make it appear less sinister (it was variously called segregation, apartheid and separate development), so renaming of children deemed 'different' continues as successive terms to identify 'diverse' children and young people are recruited. We have thus seen terms like 'handicapped' and 'retarded' replaced with 'special needs' and, in South Africa, 'barriers to learning'. Even the term 'diversity' conceals the power of some to name others as 'diverse', as diversity is usually identified from some norm from which others diverge (Zanoni *et al.* 2010). Inclusion, or inclusive practice, or inclusive policy are, in some places at least, little more than euphemisms for traditional, segregated special education thinking and doing.

## *Unification*

Also at work in the ideology of inclusive education is Thompson's third mode of unification, that process that 'embraces individuals in a collective identity, irrespective of the differences and divisions that may separate them' (Thompson 1990: 64). Inclusion is a term that Graham and Slee (2008: 277) argue assumes 'a benign commonality'.

The deep and important contestations about what inclusive education is or could or should be are glossed in a unified term that (incorrectly) suggests standardisation. 'Inclusion' has become a popular and easy term to use, meaning everything and anything to anyone. It suggests a shared understanding, where in fact there is little, and captures a wide spectrum of (sometimes contradictory) beliefs and practices under one label.

## *Fragmentation*

Fragmentation in the working of an ideology emphasises difference, particularly among groups who might unite. It also expunges the Other by constructing an enemy that must be repelled (Janks 2010). Fragmentation works in inclusive education by emphasising the claims on inclusive education by different groups and by stressing the individual learner. First is the fragmentation of people around professional or identity interest groups. Inclusive education apparently calls for different orientations by various therapists, allied professionals and teachers.[5] There are also separate identity groups which are preserved within inclusive education discourses. These identities relate to disability (Bender and Mathes 1995; Lynch and Irvine 2009) and other groups that may be vulnerable to marginalisation, like refugees or Travellers (Bhopal 2004; Taylor and Sidhu 2011). This increasing fragmentation of what Maton (2010a: 54) calls 'knower groups', which become smaller with increasing specification, emphasises difference rather than similarity and reduces the basis for collective social action. Their difference, rather than their common experience of oppression, is made to matter.

The emphasis on the individual in inclusive education is also a site of fragmentation. *The Salamanca Statement* (UNESCO 1994) makes frequent mention of inclusive education's responsibility to meet 'individual needs'. Other writers emphasise responsiveness to individual difference (Florian and Rouse 2009) and the need for Individualised Education Plans (Soodak 2003). This attention to the individual sounds noble, and might be read as an effort to ensure that the specific educational requirements, particularly of those with disabilities, will not be compromised in inclusive, general classrooms. The effect, however, is to depoliticise exclusion and exclusionary practices, and reduce the struggle for inclusion to dealing with isolated cases of individual 'need' or, as McCall and Skrtic (2009: 12) say:

> ... needs ... [are] stripped of their oppositional meanings and redefined in ways that recast the collective agents of a political movement as individual victims and passive recipients of predefined services.

Under the protective mantle of confidentiality and individual responsiveness, schools can keep parents from finding common cause among themselves to challenge the structures that result in the exclusion of their children. Dealing with a succession of individual 'cases' allows teachers and other therapeutic personnel to see each individual as the problem, rather than identifying the problem in the way we do schooling.

Fragmentation is also about naming the enemy. In the inclusion wars[6] there has been no shortage of vitriol as camps (Allan and Slee 2008) set up positions in opposition to each other. The most obvious enemy that inclusive education has made is with traditional special education, and various inclusive education scholars have positioned themselves either to sleep with this enemy, collaborate with it or engage in outright war with it. Inclusive education is also not averse to naming other enemies – usually those who are blamed for obstructing the realisation of inclusive education. Teachers come in for much of this opprobrium, as if it is easy to be an inclusive teacher in a schooling system that is built with the architecture of exclusion (Slee 2011). Negative attitudes are also named as the enemy of inclusion, as if attitudes exist apart from the structures that engender and maintain them (Slee 2011).

## *Reification*

When an action or a process which has actors and agents and occurs in time and space becomes a 'thing', it is reified (Janks 2010). This is Thompson's final mode of the operation of ideology. The reification of inclusion involves the process of nominalisation, as the verb 'to include' becomes the noun 'inclusion' and actors, agents and objects are deleted. There is no human agency in 'inclusion'. It is much easier, and more respectable, to say 'I don't agree with inclusion', or 'Inclusion won't work' than to say 'I won't include Xolani (or whoever) in my lesson.' By this I am not suggesting that the verb form 'to include' is not problematic. It is. As Graham and Slee (2008: 278) rightly point out, 'to include is not necessarily to *be* inclusive' (italics in the original) and formal access to education does not assure epistemic access. But at least the verb form does not allow the elision of people (as both subjects and objects) in the construction and execution of what we call inclusion. Identifying and resisting the reification of inclusion forces the confrontation of the processes involved and the social relations of power that position and legitimise some as the includers and some as the included, and, as a result, some as the excluded.

By making inclusion some*thing*, the process of nominalisation works to distinguish it from something else. Nouns are identifiers or classifiers, so in naming something, we make it distinct from anything else. I would suggest that another effect of the nominalisation of inclusion is to make it appear distinct from exclusion, as if these are two separate or separable things. If inclusion is regarded as something different from exclusion, it becomes easy to consider inclusion as the antidote to exclusion, instead of seeing inclusion and exclusion either as one concept (Popkewitz and Lindblad 2000), or as linked experiences in Benjamin *et al*.'s (2003) notion of multiple inclusions and exclusions. The distinction between inclusion and exclusion and the either–or binary that it suggests, obscures how inclusion can really mean assimilation, denying the possibility that for some, the experience that is called inclusion (by those with appellative power) is in fact an experience of exclusion, marginalisation, paternalism and authoritarianism (Young 1990). So if something is inclusion, nominalisation suggests, it can't be exclusion, and it can't be special education either. And yet much special education discourse has been repackaged as inclusive education, and the processes by which some children are identified as 'having barriers to learning' and then placed in separate special schools continue unquestioned.

Recognising inclusive education as ideological, or recognising ideology in inclusive education, is regarded as important for research (Allan and Slee 2008) and for practice (Brantlinger 1997). When research and practice are imagined together, then a field is assumed (see, for example, Norwich (2014), in the case of inclusive education). I now turn to the idea that inclusive education may be a field and explore the knowledge claims that it might make as a field.

## Inclusive education as a field

Education is widely regarded as a field (if not a discipline) (Furlong 2013). The case has also been made for specific sectors and particular interests within education to be regarded as a field. As examples, Maton (2005) makes the claim for higher education as a field in its own right, and Chen and Derewianka (2009) claim language education as a field. Inclusive education is regarded as a field by those who write under its banner (see, for example, Singal 2005; Slee 2011; Norwich 2014) and is acknowledged as a 'field of enquiry' (Allan and Slee 2008: 28). A field, however, is a term used with varying degrees of abstraction, either very broadly to indicate an ambit, or scope of interest, or quite specifically, to indicate a structured space. To conceptualise and interrogate inclusive education as a field in epistemological terms, I draw on some of the theoretical tools from the sociology of knowledge in education. This offers the possibility of examining inclusive education specifically as a knowledge field, with a focus on *what* the knowledge of inclusive education might be.

Legitimation Code Theory (LCT) emerged in the 1990s and has grown in the years since then, with applications in education and beyond. LCT proposes that fields are 'knowledge-knower structures' (Maton 2010b: 161). The knowledge structures and knower structures of a field, according to LCT, are analytically distinguishable (Maton 2010b) which is useful for the purposes of examining inclusive education. The particular affordances of LCT are that it 'enables knowledge practices to be seen, their organising principles to be conceptualised and their effects to be explored' (Maton 2014: 3). There are five 'strands' of LCT and I have chosen to focus on just two – specialisation and semantics, and one idea within each.

*Specialisation* in LCT includes a number of key concepts and here I want to examine inclusive education in terms of the legitimation of its knowledge. Maton (2010a) suggests that there are two rules for knowledge claims – *what* counts as legitimate knowledge and *who* can claim to produce legitimate knowledge. The legitimation of inclusive education knowledge comes to a large extent from *who* claims the knowledge, rather than *what* the knowledge is. In other words, it is a 'knower code'. Maton's (2010a: 46) description of a knower code is a good fit for inclusive education:

> The specialized knower may claim unique knowledge of more than a delimited object of study; the knower's focus for truth claims may be hypothetically

boundless, difficult to define, or encompass a host of disparate and seemingly unconnected objects of study.

We might focus on two types of 'specialist knower' in the intellectual field of inclusive education. The first is the endlessly proliferating and fragmenting 'client knowers' who are given 'voice' in inclusive education. The (inter)subjective experiential knowledge of these knowers becomes the 'truth' of inclusive education. The progressive 'hyphenation' (Maton 2014: 38) of knowers is evident in inclusive education as we have seen increasing specialisation of the privileged knower. Consider the development of categories of knowers (following Maton 2010a) in inclusive education:

| | | |
|---|---|---|
| *(Dis)ability* | – | Children with disabilities |
| *Type of disability* | – | Children with intellectual disabilities |
| *Race* | – | Black children with intellectual disabilities |
| *Type of school* | – | Black children with intellectual disabilities in regular high schools |
| *Country* | – | Black children with intellectual disabilities in regular high schools in South Africa |

The same progression could be wrangled for teachers and parents as other specialised knowers of inclusive education. The claim to knowledge of inclusive education by those directly impacted by inclusion and exclusion is evident in the number of studies that 'give voice' to these knowers.[7] The specificity of knowers is potentially boundless, offering entrants to the field the opportunity to claim expertise regarding the voice and experience of particular client knower groups.

The second group of 'knowers' in inclusive education are those working in the intellectual field where a hierarchy of knowers is constructed through the conceptualisation of an 'ideal knower' at the apex of the hierarchy (Maton 2010b). Because it is a knower code, entrants to the intellectual field increasingly have to acquire the legitimate 'aptitudes, attitudes and dispositions' (Maton 2010b: 163) to become knowers. Put differently, newcomers to the field of inclusive education do not have access to specialised procedures and recognised practices in order that they might produce recognised knowledge, as they might in a knowledge code. *Who* makes knowledge claims is important in the legitimising of this knowledge. Perhaps the most telling indication that inclusive education is a knower code is the proliferation (even surfeit) of studies into attitudinal and dispositional factors relevant to inclusion. Being inclusive is valued more highly than possessing knowledge of inclusion. There are those who are acknowledged in the field as being higher in the hierarchy of knowers, and their understandings of inclusive education dominate the field.[8] This does not mean that inclusive education is knowledge-free but, as I will explain, its knowledge structure is horizontal.

Knowledge structures, according to Bernstein (2000) may be hierarchical or horizontal. Hierarchical knowledge, typified by the natural sciences, is built as initial theories are integrated into or replaced by subsequent theories with more compelling explanatory powers. Acquisition of this knowledge is strictly sequential, requiring the acquirer to master first principles in order to understand those that follow. Horizontal knowledge, by contrast, consists of a series of specialised 'languages', each with its own mode of interrogation and 'criteria for the construction and circulation of texts' (Bernstein 2000: 161). Horizontal knowledge is built by the accretion of languages which offer new perspectives and which potentially challenge existing languages. Acquisition tends to be cumulative. Inclusive education knowledge is clearly not hierarchical but is rather constituted by a number of languages and thus represents a horizontal knowledge structure. Following Chen and Derewianka (2009), who identified a number of languages in the field of knowledge production in language education, one can suggest possible constituent languages of inclusive education. Slee (2011: 62–3), for example, argues for 'clusters of influence that have contributed differentially to the inception and growth of the field'. Included in his list of influences are special education, with its origins in medicine and psychology; critical theories, including disability theories; curriculum, pedagogy; and assessment and teacher education. While there is little doubt that these have influenced inclusive education, they could constitute the Bernsteinian languages of inclusive education. There are other possibilities, too. The constituent languages of inclusive education might also be the spectrum of research interests and researchers that Allan and Slee (2008) propose: special education research, school improvement/reform, disability activism and critical research.

The 'languages' listed here as potentially constituting inclusive education meet Bernstein's criteria for languages in a horizontal knowledge structure. They 'make different and often opposing assumptions' (Bernstein 2000: 162) and there is the need for ongoing defence of and challenge to other languages, particularly as new languages challenge the hegemony of the old. So the language of disability theory, which promotes a social model of disability, challenges the language of special education which rests on diagnosis, intervention and treatment for individuals. The language of special education which argues for special pedagogies and unique knowledge for children with disabilities is challenged by the language of inclusive pedagogies, which speaks of teaching and learning for all. If inclusive education is a horizontal knowledge structure with a number of constituent languages, all of which offer competing theoretical approaches, then the inclusion wars can be embraced rather than resolved. Inclusive education really is inclusive, as new perspectives and new speakers are welcomed to join the jostling and jockeying.

While appealing, inclusive education as a horizontal knowledge structure in Bernstein's terms is not a perfect fit. Not the least problem is Bernstein's own assertion that it is the 'specialised disciplines' that are either vertical or horizontal knowledge structures (Bernstein 2000: 261). With education not necessarily recognised as a discipline, inclusive education cannot begin to claim disciplinary status. Then, the clusters of influence that I cast as languages that constitute inclusive education could be regarded as fields or even knowledge structures in their own right.[9] Bernstein is quite specific that the languages of a horizontal knowledge structure are the -isms, like functionalism, structuralism and Marxism in sociology.

So the claim to a horizontal knowledge structure by inclusive education is a bit too pretentious, and we need to look elsewhere to find a language to best describe inclusive education knowledge.

The second strand of LCT that offers a lens onto inclusive education knowledge is that of *semantics*, and the key concepts of semantic gravity and semantic density included in this strand. Semantic gravity refers to the extent to which meaning is related to the context in which it is created, and semantic gravity may be stronger or weaker. Semantic density, which might also be weaker or stronger, relates to the degree to which abstract meanings are made independent of context and condensed within concepts and symbols (Maton 2011). Semantic gravity and density can be placed on intersecting axes and considered in the field of knowledge production (Maton 2011) and the field where knowledge is recontextualised, i.e. texts and curricula (Shay 2013). Practical knowledge can be identified where there is weak semantic density, but strong semantic gravity; professional knowledge is found in the quadrant of strong semantic density *and* gravity; and theoretical knowledge is characterised by strong semantic density but weak semantic gravity (Shay 2013). These distinctions offer a useful framework for considering the knowledge of inclusive education both in the field of knowledge production and the recontextualising field.

Inclusive education is characterised by particularly strong semantic gravity and relatively weak semantic density. This has not gone unnoticed by scholars of inclusive education, with Armstrong et al. (2011: 37) noting the 'theoretical vacuum' in which inclusive education currently sits. The semantic gravity of inclusive education is evidenced in the field of knowledge production in various ways. The most obvious is the repeated assertion that inclusive education must be contextually defined, and that its meaning must be made in the context where it is imagined or implemented. This assertion has been made by prominent scholars (for example, Ballard (1999), Booth (1996) and Forlin (1997)) who represent 'first-generation' (Kozleski *et al.* (2011)) inclusive education efforts. It has become a caveat of much inclusive education research in the past two decades that the findings cannot be generalised. As a result, the knowledge produced is only deemed meaningful in a particular context. Beyond contextual specificity, semantic gravity is also seen in research about certain learners or teachers (specialised knowers) under specific conditions. Again, claims for the abstractability of knowledge produced are minimal and meanings become not just context dependent but context bound (Bernstein 2000). These meanings 'lack the power of relation outside a context because they are totally consumed by that context' (Bernstein 2000: 30). Research in inclusive education often shows a preference for small-scale case studies where social, economic and historical determinants of context are seen as salient in the interpretation of results. The consequence of this is that in the field of knowledge production, semantic gravity is emphasised, such that inclusive education is strongly positioned as a practical knowledge. This is not to suggest that there is no semantic density in inclusive education. As I discussed in Chapter 1, the *epistēmē* discourse of inclusive education is where conceptual work is being done and where 'a theory of inclusive schooling' (Slee 2011: 62) might be developing.

The strong semantic gravity of inclusive education extends to the recontextualising field, that is the field where knowledge is recontextualised to become a pedagogic discourse (i.e. curricula and texts). The pedagogic recontextualising field comprises recontextualising agents, like teacher educators, textbook writers and curriculum designers, who select knowledge from the field of knowledge production or the field of practice, and reorganise it to form a pedagogic or instructional discourse for the purpose of 'transmission and acquisition' (Bernstein 2000: 32). The semantic gravity of inclusive education in the recontextualising field is evidenced by the production of curricula and texts which emphasise pedagogical approaches appropriate in certain contexts and with narrowly defined categories of learners. Significantly, the concepts presented are often derived not from theory, but from practice (Shay 2013). This knowledge is the codified 'knowledge-in-practice' (Cochran-Smith and Lytle 1999: 262) of expert inclusive teachers. Textbooks written to support the implementation of inclusive education emphasise knowledge derived from practice, with one explicitly stating that the authors 'learnt many of the principles and practices' that they present from interactions with 'peers who work in inclusive education' (Bornman and Rose 2010: x). Other textbooks present case studies and 'real world' scenarios from which they derive the principles and concepts of inclusive education.

There are various ways to account for the strength of the semantic gravity of inclusive education in the recontextualising field. The first is that where there is strong semantic gravity in the field of knowledge production, this will be reflected in the recontextualising field. In other words, we should expect strong semantic gravity in a pedagogic discourse recontextualised from a field where the knowledge produced is characterised by strong semantic gravity. The second is to recognise where knowledge has been recontextualised not from the field of knowledge production, but from the field of practice, that is from various educational contexts. The extraction of knowledge from the field of practice entails 're-contextualization of context-embedded practices into a set of principles or procedures, even concepts, for these practices' (Shay 2013: 573). Semantic density is necessarily limited where practice, rather than theory, generates the concepts to be studied.[10] Finally, we should acknowledge the role that ideology plays as a discourse moves from one position to another. There are 'ideological screens' (Bernstein 2000: 115) through which the original discourse of inclusive education must pass as it becomes a new pedagogical discourse of inclusive education. Different ideological positions regarding the form and intent of inclusive education will determine what is selected for transmission. An ideological commitment to the 'what works' or *technē* discourse of inclusive education[11] is likely to predispose recontextualising agents to produce texts and curricula with strong semantic gravity and which emphasise practical knowledge.

To take the 'field' of inclusive education forward, its knowledge needs to be shifted from an emphasis on (principled) practical knowledge, to be enacted in particular contexts or with particular groups of learners. LCT offers the conceptual potential for 'knowledge progression' (Shay 2013: 576) in inclusive education through strengthening its semantic density while not losing its semantic gravity. In the recontextualising field, inclusive education could be shifted from its current position as a practical knowledge with minimal abstractability and repositioned as a professional knowledge where conceptually informed judgments are made in response to the complexity of learner diversity in classrooms. Professional judgment requires theoretical knowledge that is not context bound (Shalem 2014). This theoretical knowledge needs to be developed in the field of knowledge production in inclusive education (if this is, in fact, possible), or it needs to be appropriated from other cognate fields.

## Inclusive education is a/n …?

In this and the previous chapter, I have considered inclusive education as a discourse, an ideology and a field. In the next chapter, I refer to inclusive education as a concept. Perhaps it could also be a domain, a principle or a value. The issue is, as Allan and Slee (2008: 2) say, an 'absence of proper critical debate on the *nature* of inclusive education' (emphasis mine), which leads to 'a fuzzy conceptualisation of inclusive education'. In concluding, I would suggest that the challenge for those engaging with inclusive education at any level is that it has not only many different (and contradictory) meanings, but also many different (and contradictory) natures. It is not possible to say that it should be one or another, because it does appear simultaneously to be all of them. Starting as a 'term' in the late 1980s (Allan and Slee 2008), inclusion has transmogrified into something of a behemoth with multiple and concurrent identities. Each of these identities is appropriated (or vilified) by different people with vested interests and for various purposes.[12] Instead of arguing for the priority of one of these identities, perhaps the way forward is to acknowledge their simultaneous existence (perhaps as a constellation (Maton 2014)) and to seek to work productively within the tension that their combination presents. This combination of identities does confound attempts to settle on meaning and frustrates endeavours to make conceptualisations of inclusive education less 'fuzzy', as the next chapter illustrates.

## Notes

1 This is not to recognise that there are other important contributors to a theory of ideology, nor to suggest that Althusser's work has not been critiqued and developed by others.
2 The prevalence of religious terminology in writing about inclusive education should not go unnoticed. Allan and Slee (2008) report that Alan Dyson saw that for some people, 'inclusion had the air of a religion' (35). This is significant in relation to the Althusserian conception of ideology as seen to represent an imaginary relationship with the real conditions of existence and is illustrated by the workings of religion (Althusser 1970/2012). Inclusive education also has 'professional ideologists' (Althusser 1970/2012: 118), those individuals who Althusser sees as responsible for the domination and exploitation of people through a false representation of the world. For Althusser, these are the priests and despots, but the professional ideologists of inclusive education could be seen as those who author, preside over and sustain the representation of an imaginary inclusive reality.

3  See the discussion on learner need in the next chapter.
4  Trope in the form of metaphor is another strategy in this mode, and one to which I devote Chapter 4 of this book.
5  Causton and Tracy-Bronson (2014) are concerned with speech pathologists, Kellegrew and Allen (1996) with occupational therapists, and Engelbrecht (2004) with educational psychologists.
6  With reference to the literacy wars where competing paradigms of literacy teaching (e.g. phonics versus whole language) have polarised the field (Roy 2005). Allan (2013: 1250) also talks about 'turf wars' when working with ideology in inclusive education.
7  Chapter 8 of this book explores voice research in inclusive education in some detail and considers some of the knowledge about inclusive education that different knowers offer to the field.
8  This is explored further in Chapter 3.
9  Maton's (2014) semantic structure of constellations possibly offers a more generative way of thinking of inclusive education as it comprises a 'semantic structure of stances chosen from a potential array, arranged into patterns, condensed with meanings and charged with valuations' (154). This, though, is the subject of another publication.
10  Consider, for example, two inclusive pedagogical strategies often taught as part of inclusive education: cooperative learning and differentiated instruction. The former is largely derived from theoretical principles – social interdependence theory and various social learning theories. The principles of the latter are mostly derived from the logic of practice.
11  See Chapter 1.
12  For those (like myself) who have institutional space to protect, the identity of inclusive education as a field is very important. Others, perhaps, who are invested in the preservation of separate special education would emphasise the ideological nature of inclusive education.

## References

Ainscow, M. (2005) 'Developing inclusive education systems: what are the levers for change?', *Journal of Educational Change*, 6 (2): 109–24.
Allan, J. (2013) 'Including ideology', *International Journal of Inclusive Education*, 17 (12): 124152.
Allan, J. and Slee, R. (2008) *Doing Inclusive Education Research*. Rotterdam: Sense Publishers.
Althusser, L. (1970/2012) 'Ideology and ideological state apparatuses', in S. Žižek (ed.), *Mapping Ideology*. London: Verso, pp. 100–40.
Armstrong, D., Armstrong, A. C. and Spandagou, I. (2011) 'Inclusion: by choice or by chance?', *International Journal of Inclusive Education*, 15 (1): 29–39.
Ballard, K. (1999) *Inclusive Education: International Voices on Disability and Justice*. London: Falmer Press.
Bender, W. N. and Mathes, M. Y. (1995) 'Students with ADHD in the inclusive classroom: a hierarchical approach to strategy selection', *Intervention in School and Clinic*, 30 (4): 226–34.
Benjamin, S., Nind, M., Hall, K., Collins, J. and Sheehy, K. (2003) 'Moments of inclusion and exclusion: pupils negotiating classroom contexts', *British Journal of Sociology of Education*, 24: 547–58.
Bernstein, B. (2000) *Pedagogy, Symbolic Control and Identity: Theory, Research and Critique*, revised edn. Lanham, MD: Rowman & Littlefield.
Bhopal, K. (2004) 'Gypsy Travellers and education: changing needs and changing perceptions', *British Journal of Educational Studies*, 52 (1): 47–64.
Blommaert, J. (2005) *Discourse: A Critical Introduction*. Cambridge: Cambridge University Press.

Booth, T. (1996) 'A perspective on inclusion from England', *Cambridge Journal of Education*, 6 (1): 87–99.
Bornman, J. and Rose, R. (2010) *Believe That All Can Achieve*. Pretoria: Van Schaik.
Bourdieu, P. and Eagleton, T. (2012) 'Doxa and common life: an interview', in S. Žižek (ed.), *Mapping Ideology*. London: Verso, pp. 265–77.
Brantlinger, E. (1997) 'Using ideology: cases of nonrecognition of the politics of research and practice in special education', *Review of Educational Research*, 67 (4): 425–59.
Brantlinger, E. (2006) 'The big glossies: how textbooks structure (special) education', in E. Brantlinger (ed.), *Who Benefits from Special Education? Remediating (Fixing) Other People's Children*. Mahwah, NJ: Lawrence Erlbaum Associates, pp. 45–76.
Chen, H. and Derewianka, B. (2009) 'Binaries and beyond: a Bernsteinian perspective on change in literacy education', *Research Papers in Education*, 24 (2): 223–45.
Cochran-Smith, M. and Lytle, S. (1999) 'Relationships of knowledge and practice: teacher learning in communities', *Review of Research in Education*, 24: 249–305.
Causton, J. and Tracy-Bronson, C. (2014) *The Speech-Language Pathologist's Handbook for Inclusive School Practices*. Baltimore, MD: Paul Brookes.
Dyson, A. (1999) 'Inclusion and inclusions: theories and discourses in inclusive education', in H. Daniels and P. Garner (eds), *World Yearbook of Education: Inclusive Education*. London: Kogan Page, pp. 36–53.
Eagleton, T. (1994) 'Introduction', in T. Eagleton (ed.), *Ideology*. London: Longman, pp. 1–20.
Eagleton, T. (2011) *Why Marx Was Right*. New Haven, CT: Yale University Press.
Engelbrecht, P. (2004) 'Changing roles for educational psychologists within inclusive education in South Africa', *School Psychology International*, 25 (1): 20–9.
Florian, L. and Rouse, M. (2009) 'The inclusive practice project in Scotland: teacher education for inclusive education', *Teaching and Teacher Education*, 25 (4): 594–601.
Forlin, C. (1997) 'Inclusive education in Australia', *Special Education Perspectives*, 6 (1): 21–6.
Forlin, C. (2006) 'Inclusive education in Australia ten years after Salamanca', *European Journal of Psychology of Education*, 21 (3): 265–77.
Frost, J. L. (2009) *A History of Children's Play and Play Environments*. New York: Routledge.
Furlong, J. (2013) *Education – An Anatomy of the Discipline: Rescuing the University Project?* London: Routledge.
Gonsalves, R. (2007) 'Hysterical blindness and the ideology of denial', in L. Bartolomé (ed.), *Ideologies in Education: Unmasking the Trap of Teacher Neutrality*. New York: Peter Lang, pp. 3–27.
Goodley, D. (2007) 'Towards socially just pedagogies: Deleuzoguattarian critical disability studies', *International Journal of Inclusive Education*, 11 (3): 317–34.
Graham, L. J. and Slee, R. (2008) 'An illusory interiority: interrogating the discourse/s of inclusion. *Educational Philosophy and Theory*, 40 (2): 277–93.
Gramsci, A. (1971/1999) *Selections from the Prison Notebooks*, eds and trans. Q. Hoare and G. Smith. London: Electric Book Company.
Janks, H. (2010) *Literacy and Power*. New York: Routledge.
Kavale, K. A. and Forness, S. R. (2000) 'History, rhetoric, and reality: analysis of the inclusion debate', *Remedial and Special Education*, 21 (5): 279–96.
Kavale, K. A. and Mostert, M. P. (2003) 'River of ideology, islands of evidence', *Exceptionality*, 11 (4): 191–208.
Kellegrew, D. H. and Allen, D. (1996) 'Occupational therapy in full-inclusion classrooms: a case study from the Moorpark model', *American Journal of Occupational Therapy*, 50 (9): 718–24.
Kisanji, J. (1998) 'The march towards inclusive education in non-Western countries: retracing the steps', *International Journal of Inclusive Education*, 2 (1): 55–72.

Kozleski, E. B., Artiles, A. J. and Waitoller, F. R. (2011) 'Introduction: equity in inclusive education', in A. J. Artiles, E. B. Kozleski and F. R. Waitoller (eds), *Inclusive Education: Examining Equity on Five Continents*. Cambridge, MA: Harvard Education Press, pp. 1–14.

Liasidou, A. (2012) *Inclusive Education, Politics and Policymaking*. New York: Continuum.

Lynch, S. L. and Irvine, A. N. (2009) 'Inclusive education and best practice for children with autism spectrum disorder: an integrated approach', *International Journal of Inclusive Education*, 13 (8): 845–59.

McCall, Z. and Skrtic, T. M. (2009) 'Intersectional needs politics: a policy frame for the wicked problem of disproportionality', *Multiple Voices*, 11: 3–23.

Maton, K. (2005) 'A question of autonomy: Bourdieu's field approach and higher education policy', *Journal of Education Policy*, 20 (6): 687–704.

Maton, K. (2010a) 'Analysing knowledge claims and practices: languages of legitimation', in K. Maton and R. Moore (eds), *Social Realism, Knowledge and the Sociology of Education. Coalitions of the Mind*. London: Continuum, pp. 35–59.

Maton, K. (2010b) 'Canons and progress in the arts and humanities: Knowers and Gazes', in K. Maton and R. Moore (eds), *Social Realism, Knowledge and the Sociology of Education. Coalitions of the Mind*. London: Continuum, pp. 154–78.

Maton, K. (2011) 'Theories and things: the semantics of disciplinarity', in F. Christie and K. Maton (eds), *Disciplinarity: Systemic Functional and Sociological Perspectives*. London: Continuum, pp. 62–84.

Maton, K. (2014) *Knowledge and Knowers*. London: Routledge.

Norwich, B. (2014) 'SEN policy research forum: Policy Paper. Research in special needs and inclusive education: the interface with policy and practice'. Accessed from: http://www2.warwick.ac.uk/fac/soc/cedar/better/reportspublications/sen_research_policy_paper_senprf_march_2014.pdf.

Paliokosta, P. and Blandford, S. (2010) 'Inclusion in school: a policy, ideology or lived experience? Similar findings in diverse school cultures', *Support for learning*, 25 (4): 179–86.

Popkewitz, T. and Lindblad, S. (2000) 'Educational governance and social inclusion and exclusion: some conceptual difficulties and problematics in policy and research', *Discourse: Studies in the Cultural Politics of Education*, 21 (1): 5–44.

Roy, K. (2005) 'On sense and nonsense: looking beyond the literacy wars', *Journal of Philosophy of Education*, 39 (1): 99–111.

Shalem, Y. (2014) 'What binds professional judgment?', in M. Young and J. Muller (eds), *Knowledge, Expertise and the Professions*. Abingdon: Routledge, pp. 93–105.

Shay, S. (2013) 'Conceptualizing curriculum differentiation in higher education: a sociology of knowledge point of view', *British Journal of Sociology of Education*, 34 (4): 563–82.

Singal, N. (2005) 'Mapping the field of inclusive education: a review of the Indian literature', *International Journal of Inclusive Education*, 9 (4): 331–50.

Slee, R. (2009) 'Audio interview with Roger Slee, Editor, *International Journal of Inclusive Education*, at the Institute of Education, London'. Accessed from: www.educationarena.com/pdf/rslee_transcript.pdf.

Slee, R. (2010) 'A cheese-slicer by any other name? Shredding the sociology of inclusion', in M. Apple, S. J. Ball and L. A. Gandin (eds), *The Routledge International Handbook of the Sociology of Education*. Abingdon: Routledge, pp. 99–108.

Slee, R. (2011) *The Irregular School*. London: Routledge.

Soodak, L. C. (2003) 'Classroom management in inclusive settings', *Theory into Practice*, 42 (4): 327–33.

Taylor, S. and Sidhu, R. K. (2011) 'Supporting refugee students in schools: what constitutes inclusive education?', *International Journal of Inclusive Education*, 16 (1): 39–56.

Thompson, J. (1990) *Ideology and Modern Culture*. Cambridge: Polity Press.
UK Parliament (2006) 'Select Committee on Education and Skills Third Report. Formal Minutes of the meeting of Wednesday 21 June 2006'. Accessed from: http://www.publications.parliament.uk/pa/cm200506/cmselect/cmeduski/478/47813.htm.
UNESCO (1994) *The Salamanca Statement and Framework for Action*. Paris: UNESCO.
United Nations (UN) (2006) *Convention of the Rights of Persons with Disabilities and Optional Protocol*. Accessed from: http://www.un.org/disabilities/countries.asp?navid=12andpid=166#S.
Wilce, H. (2006) 'Special-needs education: does mainstream inclusion work?' Accessed from http://www.independent.co.uk/news/education/education-news/specialneeds-education-does-mainstream-inclusion-work-470960.html.
Young, I. M. (1990) *Justice and the Politics of Difference*. Princeton, NJ: Princeton University Press.
Zanoni, P., Janssens, M., Benschop, Y. and Nkomo, S.M. (2010) 'Unpacking diversity, grasping inequality: rethinking difference through critical perspectives', *Organization*, 17: 9–29.
Žižek, S. (2012) 'Introduction', in S. Žižek (ed.), *Mapping Ideology*. London: Verso, pp. 1–33.

# 3

# THE MEANING OF INCLUSIVE EDUCATION

### An inclusion class for inclusion kids

Some years ago, when inclusive education was just becoming known in South Africa, a colleague told me about her husband's new job. He had been appointed in an independent high school that had taken a policy decision to pursue 'inclusion'. The school had a reputation for stringent academic entry requirements and exceptional matriculation results. Now, the school was looking to 'include' learners from remedial or special primary schools, and others who previously would not have met the minimum entry requirements. My colleague explained (with no apparent sense of irony) that her husband had been assigned to the 'inclusion class' and would be responsible for the 'inclusion kids'. In the interests of providing 'support' in a smaller class with handpicked teachers, this school had decided to contain all the learners admitted in terms of the new inclusion policy in one class. I am convinced that the school devised this arrangement with the expectation that it would give these learners the best possible chance of success in this hitherto exclusionary educational environment. But whether or not this counts as 'inclusive education' or 'inclusion' is debatable, depending on what inclusive education or inclusion means.

### What meaning means

The desire to define or settle on meaning is natural and necessary. We wouldn't make much progress in human interaction if we did not have shared understandings of what words mean in various contexts. And, where words have contested or multiple meanings, we recognise the need to define exactly how it is that we are using a word. Language is inextricably linked with thought and meaning. Vygotsky's important contribution to the understanding of the relationship between words and meanings was in showing that words do not derive meanings from their repeated association with objects. Instead, words and thought develop together. Language does not only allow us to express what we think, it also determines how we think. But word meaning is not only a matter of thought and speech, it is also a matter of communication and social interchange (Vygotsky 1986). As a result, meanings vary across different contexts, and words are used for different purposes. In other words, meaning is situated. Meaning is also negotiated. Humpty Dumpty was wrong in thinking that when using a word, 'It means just what I choose it to mean – neither more nor less' (Carroll 1988: 113). Meanings are not made by individuals alone but, as Gee (2008: 10) reminds us, they are '… ultimately rooted in negotiation between different social practices with different interests by people who share or seek to share some common ground'. Power is always involved in the negotiation of meaning, as those with status or influence can dominate the negotiation and enforce their meanings.

## What 'inclusive education' means

Understanding what is meant by 'inclusive education' requires acknowledging that inclusive education does not exist apart from our construction of it. It is not something 'out there', waiting to be found and needing description or explication. The term 'inclusive education' does not have a fixed association with a particular object. Its meaning is not stable and, like all other words, must be regarded as being in a constant state of evolution. The meaning of inclusive education is made in/by/through its discursive community or communities, so 'inclusive education' means what the discursive community/ies says it means. But, as indicated in the previous chapter, inclusive education has become something of a 'broad church' (Allan and Slee 2008: 99), and the singularity of the term belies the breadth of (potentially contradictory) positions.

There has long been an argument that the situated meaning of inclusive education must be taken into account in its analysis. Kozleski *et al.* (2011: 4) maintain that

> … inclusive education has largely ignored the complex histories and sociocultural conditions of developed and developing nations that shape how inclusive agendas are defined and implemented.

These authors argue that for developing countries, access and completion is the focus of education, whereas for developed countries, participation and outcomes for diverse groups would be more of a concern. This acknowledges that inclusive education must be articulated within the possibilities and constraints of particular contexts. While this argument has merit, and draws attention to the very real contextual issues that impact the way inclusive education is conceptualised and realised, this position is not unproblematic. It potentially sets up two tiers of meaning of inclusive education. There is a gold standard for learners in developed countries, where participation and outcomes constitute the agenda for inclusive education, but learners in developing countries must be satisfied with a lesser agenda, because access and completion are still the priorities of these education systems. This is paternalism, suggesting that developing countries (made poor by the legacies of colonialism and the impact of globalisation) cannot or should not be expected to aspire to the same standard of inclusivity expected in developed countries. Put differently, what is deemed an unquestionable educational minimum in an (over-)privileged context (i.e. access for all to well-functioning schools with adequate resources and tuition of an acceptable quality) potentially becomes an issue of 'inclusive education' in an un(der)-privileged context. So while acknowledging the situatedness of meaning there must also be a recognition that meanings are bounded. There are limits to how far an elasticity of meaning (Slee 2011) can stretch, before it snaps and the meaning is lost. But this then begs the question of who gets to decide on the limits of what inclusive education can mean.

The meaning of 'inclusive education' is not completely relative, even though it may be negotiated and determined by the discourse community. There are those who can exercise their power to promote their meanings of inclusive education. This power is enacted in various ways, like the gatekeeping by editors of journals and their preferred reviewers and (non-)endorsement of conferences through (non-)attendance by 'big names'. These big names in inclusive education constitute the 'canon',[1] that list of authors (or 'ideal knowers'[2]) whose status in the field gives them the power to dominate the discourse. But even these canonical writers offer a bewildering array of perspectives, enough to challenge the novice to identify various 'camps' and work out how (not) to be implicated in one or other (Allan and Slee 2008).

Before considering what inclusive education might mean by looking at how it can be defined, it is worth considering the synonymous use of 'inclusion' and 'inclusive education'. South Africa's *White Paper Six* (DoE 2001) uses the terms interchangeably, as do many scholars in the field (Anderson *et al.* 2014; Graham and Jahnukainen 2011). Inclusion offers a useful contraction of 'inclusive education' and can make for easier expression, particularly when inclusive education is coupled with another aspect of education, like teacher education. Inclusion is, however, a generic word made imprecise by its multiple meanings and applications across fields like economics, health and politics. It is a term of 'extreme abstraction' (Abbott 1988: 103) which, as Shalem (2014: 96) notes, has such wide applicability that 'when recruited into practice' it works like 'a metaphor and not like a concept'. 'Inclusion' is also problematic as a nominalisation of the verb 'include'.[3] There are at least two good reasons for preferring 'inclusive education' over 'inclusion'. The first is that 'inclusive education' is potentially distinctive and marks the concept as being academic knowledge exclusive to the professional knowledge of education (Shalem 2014). The second is that it keeps education firmly in focus. There is no doubt that the affective climate of a school and classroom plays a crucial role in enabling learning. But without foregrounding 'education', inclusion can become merely an issue of values and attitudes, and ways of securing access and belonging. The educational focus is potentially lost, with 'inclusion' deemed successful if all learners *feel* welcome. Instead, I would argue, the success of 'inclusion' needs to be measured in terms of rigorous *educational* outcomes for all learners. But while the term 'inclusion' is problematic, so too is 'inclusive education', particularly when its grammar is closely examined.

When the adjective 'inclusive' is appended to the noun 'education', there are two possibilities. The first is that 'inclusive' works as an epithet and the second is that it works as a classifier (Halliday and Matthiessen 2004). If 'inclusive' is an epithet, it may be regarded as an experiential epithet, in which case it indicates a quality of the noun 'education'. This embeds inclusiveness as a characteristic of this type of education and, significantly, suggests the potential for definition relative to some norm (Halliday and Matthiessen 2004). In other words, we should be able to define what characterises inclusive education relative to anything else, and inclusive education should be recognisable. In functional linguistic terms, this means that the information necessary to identify this particular kind of education is contained in the epithet 'inclusive'. But, definitiveness does not sit well with the multiple and contested possibilities of what 'inclusive' may mean.

The second possibility is that 'inclusive' may work as a classifier, in which case it is identifying a subclass of education. It is in this sense that 'inclusive education' may distinguish itself as a field, distinct, for example, from 'language education' or 'ICT education'. It may also serve to differentiate inclusive education from special education or regular education, showing that these are distinctive types of education. If 'inclusive' is a classifier, though, the rules of functional linguistics do not allow for degrees of comparison or intensity (Halliday and Matthiessen 2004). So it is not possible, in this sense, to have 'more' or 'very' inclusive education. This, in turn, is problematic for a definition of inclusive education as a (gradual) process towards increasing inclusivity. These linguistic distinctions begin to suggest why inclusive education, despite its ideological appeal, falters when hard pressed for definition.

## A progression in definitions

Writers cannot assume or negotiate a shared meaning directly with their readers, but they can try to make their meanings clear. For this reason, writers often define their terms at the outset of a piece of writing. Over the past decades, various scholars have offered their definitions or understandings of what inclusive education is or should be. Rather than arbitrarily selecting some of these authors and discussing what each has offered to developing the meaning of inclusive education, I have, for this section, adopted McNiff's (2008) idea of narrativising one's learning by critically tracing my own attempts to encapsulate what inclusive education might mean. Ellis (2004: 42), an author who champions personal narrative in research, commented, 'I can trace my own transition through the terms I favoured over time.' The terms I have favoured track developments in South African education and also reflect my own trajectory from school teacher and leader and part-time postgraduate student to academic and teacher educator in higher education.

In 2002, when I presented a master's research report, inclusive education was relatively new to South Africa. Before 1994 and the advent of democracy, education here was segregated both on the basis of race and (dis)ability. The Constitution of 1996 (Republic of South Africa (RSA) 1996a) enshrined equality and human rights, including the right to basic education and freedom from discrimination, for all South Africans and it forms one of the legislative imperatives for inclusive education in this country. The South African Schools Act of the same year (RSA 1996b) outlawed discrimination in schools on the basis of race and made provision that where it is 'reasonably practicable', learners with 'special education needs' should be served in the mainstream and relevant support should be provided for these learners (section 12(4)). After a period of consultation, *White Paper Six: Special Needs Education* was published by the Department of Education (DoE) in 2001. *The White Paper* provides a policy framework for the implementation of inclusive education in this country and outlines a 20-year strategic plan to achieve its goals. In this White Paper, inclusive education is positioned simultaneously as an issue of disability and special need, but also more broadly as concerned with all barriers to learning that learners may experience.

Inclusive education was not unknown in South Africa at the time of the publication of *White Paper Six*. The independent sector was already showing interest in inclusive education with some independent schools positioning themselves as leaders in this regard. In the state sector, many schools had become inclusive by default, since prior to 1994 there were relatively few special schools for black learners. The quality of education afforded to learners with disabilities in these mainstream schools was, however, not always satisfactory. Against this background, I defined inclusion in my master's research report thus:

> **Definition one**
>
> Inclusion in South Africa ... should refer to all efforts that are made to improve schools to make them accessible to all, and responsive to the learning needs of all. (Walton 2002: 19)

In the four years between this definition and the next, various policy documents were published which served to 'flesh out' *White Paper Six*. The outcomes-based curriculum introduced in 2002 proclaimed inclusivity as a foundational principle (DoE 2002) and specific guidelines were issued for curriculum adaptation and assessment for inclusion. By 2006 there was growing research interest in inclusive education, with evidence emerging of state and independent schools intentionally pursuing more inclusive policies and practices. It is against this background that I suggested a more complex definition of inclusive education in my doctoral thesis. I had concluded from a review of the international literature that definitions of inclusive education tended either to emphasise access, belonging and participation in the general classroom for all learners with an underlying culture that values diversity, or to focus more on the organisational implications of inclusive education with an

## Definition two

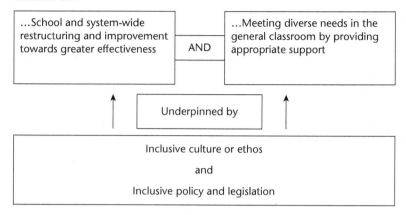

**FIGURE 3.1** Definition two
*Source*: Walton (2006: 33).

emphasis on school restructuring and improvement and the role of policy and legislation, or to stress support for learning and define inclusion in terms of the ways in which support is facilitated at various levels (Walton 2006). I presented my synthesis of these views as a definition in diagrammatic form, as shown in Figure 3.1.

By 2010 another tranche of Department of Education guidelines for inclusive education had been published and a major curriculum revision was underway. I had moved into higher education and dutifully began to submit journal articles for review. And reviewers wanted definitions. In an article published in a South African journal, I settled on the following definition:

## Definition three

Inclusive education is … concerned with achieving equity by identifying and addressing direct and indirect impediments to access, participation and belonging in school cultures, facilities and curricula. This is not achieved by attempts at normalising or assimilation, but by the radical reconstruction of schools and schooling to meet the learning needs of a diverse learner population. (Walton 2011b: 85)

In the face of various attempts to define inclusive education by scholars in the field, Slee (2010: 105) asserts that, 'The project of inclusive education may not be best served by pressing for intellectual foreclosure on its definition.' Adjudicating among definitions in order to arrive at a normative definition of inclusive education is less useful than an analysis of definitions. Such an analysis potentially reveals perspectives and priorities through what is said, what is omitted and how the definition is constructed. A critical analysis of how I have constituted the three definitions reveals a shift in the educational agenda I have associated with inclusive education and how I have defined inclusive education with various combinations of attributes. It is noteworthy, however, that in none of these definitions is disability or special need mentioned, a position that reflects a 'broad' definition of inclusive education (Ainscow *et al.* 2006) and potentially concerns itself with the many identity markers that are correlated with educational exclusion, such as poverty, gender, language, migrant status and sexual orientation.

## *A shift in agenda from access to equity*

The shift in agenda is seen most clearly in the juxtaposition of the first and the third definitions. The first definition is limited to *access*, reflecting the priority of the educational access and completion agenda of developing countries that Kozleski *et al.* (2011) describe. It is problematic that this first definition implies that access equals inclusion, which it patently does not. The reports of the Consortium for Research into Equity, Access and Transformation in Education show that in many developing countries, including South Africa, near universal access to primary education has been achieved, but that a significant percentage of learners in schools are in fact silently excluded (Lewin 2009) from quality education. Many children and young people who are 'included' in schools experience marginalisation and exclusion, and are at risk of repeating years and ultimately dropping out of school. This leads Motala and Deacon (2011: n.p.) to state that 'Lack of *meaningful* access has become a defining feature of the South African schooling system' (emphasis mine).

By the third definition *equity* rather than access is linked with inclusive education, for good reason. South Africa has the unenviable reputation of being the most unequal country in the world. The extremes of inequality are felt in education as exclusion from schooling, and epistemological and other marginalisation within schools is inextricably linked with wider social and economic exclusions. Poverty, rurality and disability are predictors of educational exclusion in South Africa (Fleisch *et al.* 2012), making it important that inclusive education is positioned as an issue of equity (Kozleski *et al.* 2011). Equality and equity are terms that are often used synonymously. Distinguishing them, however, is valuable, with equality viewed as 'group based and quantitative' and equity as group or individual based, qualitative and 'tied to notions of justice' (Secada 1989: 23). Put differently, equality treats everyone the same, but equity recognises that equal treatment does not address the social and historical disadvantage that certain individuals and groups experience. So without providing the means for full participation and achievement, offering access to all is a necessarily limited endeavour. But caution must also be exercised, lest the meaning of equity be reduced to compensatory measures for previously excluded groups, without an examination of the underlying structures that engender and perpetuate inequity.

## Shifts in the boundaries of the definition of inclusive education

Definitions are boundary markers for a concept. They indicate what can and cannot be legitimately regarded as constituting a concept. Across the three definitions, the boundaries of inclusive education change. This occurs through shifts in the attributes that constitute the concept and the complexification of the rules for definition. Four possible rules determine the definition of concepts. These are, according to Klein (2011), affirmation (the concept must have the one attribute), negation (the concept must not have the attribute), conjunction (the concept must have two or more attributes) and disjunction (the concept must have both or either of the attributes). These rules and the constituent attributes signal the boundaries of the concept being defined. Those who define inclusive education combine potential attributes of inclusive education according to these rules to try and fix its meaning.

### Shifts in constituent attributes

All three of my definitions are similar in that they refer to changes in schools and schooling, and present an indication of what inclusive education entails. But the attributes that constitute the definitions are different. This section problematises some of the constituent attributes of the definitions and shows how they change over time. First is the shift from school improvement in the first definition to restructuring, improvement and effectiveness in the second definition and finally to the radical reconstruction of schools and schooling in the third definition. Second, I show how the focus of inclusive education shifts in the three definitions from responsiveness to the learning needs of all, to meeting diverse needs and providing support in the general classroom, to identifying and addressing exclusionary practices and pressures. The first shift is represented in Figure 3.2.

The reference to improving schools in the first definition reflects the interest in school effectiveness and improvement that was prevalent at the time and which continues today. Scholars who can be identified with school improvement and reform on the spectrum of inclusive education researchers (Allan and Slee 2008) feature prominently in South African research into inclusive education[4] and in South African textbooks for inclusive education.[5] There is good reason for school improvement to remain an important dimension of inclusive education. First, inclusive education needs to be seen as a school improvement endeavour, particularly since there are parents, teachers and even learners who regard inclusive education as potentially

FIGURE 3.2  Change in school and schooling

contributing to what they perceive as a lowering of standards. Concern has been expressed that teachers' attention will be diverted to those regarded as having 'additional support needs' and that the pace of learning will be slower, to the detriment of 'regular' learners. Second, education in South Africa is in dire need of improvement. While enrolment in the compulsory years of schooling (from age 7 to 15) is encouraging (about 97 per cent (Fleisch *et al.* 2012)), participation of learners aged 16 to 18 tapers off to about 86 per cent (Meny-Gibert and Russell 2012). Learner achievement remains low in relation not only to developed countries, but also to comparably developing countries (Taylor *et al.* 2013).

Despite the affordances of the idea, improvement potentially limits inclusive education. To improve is to get better at or increase the value of what is already being done. The starting point for improvement is the status quo. For inclusive education, the status quo is not a good place to begin, given the entrenched and systemic pressures towards exclusion. Conceptualising inclusive education as a school improvement project potentially limits it to doing better at what we have always done. In keeping with the *technē* discourse of inclusive education,[6] improvement offers tweaking at the edge of practice to make it more efficient but not necessarily transforming the system at its foundations. A South African comparison is apposite. The advent of democracy brought the expectation of an inclusive society, equity, equality and freedom from discrimination. Twenty years later, with millions of South Africans still living in abject poverty, social unrest attests to the failure of the 'rainbow nation' dream. Antjie Krog, a South African poet and writer, explains the importance of distinguishing change from transformation:

> Change and transformation are not the same thing. You may appoint a new manager, or get a new name for your firm or your country, without changing direction, without changing 'the firmament'. Things have been changed but not transformed. Transformation means that the same unit undergoes an internal change. Replacing white people with black people is therefore not transformation in itself... If black people replace white people but the same structures, systems, visions and attitudes are retained you merely have change.
> 
> *(Krog 2003: 126)*

Improvement offers the possibility of change. But inclusive education needs transformation of 'the firmament' of education. The second definition implicitly recognises that improvement is not sufficient and introduces restructuring and effectiveness.

Introducing restructuring into the second definition goes some way towards indicating that the way education is currently conceived and constructed cannot be inclusive and that we require fundamental change to the way we do things. Slee (2011: 157) puts it well when he says that 'we need to rethink school architecture'. Both schools and systems are mentioned in this definition as being in need of restructuring because I had come across a number of schools in South Africa intentionally and systematically working to dismantle exclusionary policies and practices, only to be thwarted or frustrated by systemic constraints. Restructuring offers more expectation of transformation than the mere improvement of the first definition. But added to this second definition is 'effectiveness', a term which, like improvement, is potentially problematic in the pursuit of inclusive education.

Given the dysfunction of much of South Africa's schooling system, it could be expected that the idea of school effectiveness would grip South African educational thought.[7] School effectiveness has also been linked with inclusive education, both internationally (Avramidis *et al.* 2002; Waldron *et al.* 2011) and in South Africa (Makoelle 2014). School effectiveness research has been concerned to find predictors and indicators of 'effective' schools to serve as prescriptions for school improvement. I do not wish to digress into a review of the contestations about the nature and effect of research into school effectiveness, but I do want to problematise it in relation to inclusive education. Two points are worth mentioning. The first is the ease with which the language of effectiveness, with its lists, measures and descriptors, has seeped into the language of inclusive education. Research in the field has yielded a bumper harvest of indicators and predictors of 'successful' or 'effective' inclusive education (see, for example, Ainscow (2005), Booth and Ainscow (2002) and Walton (2011a)). UNESCO (2005: 31) provides 'checklists' for the 'incorporation of inclusive approaches' and South Africa has goals and milestones for the implementation of inclusive education (DBE 2011). This languages inclusive education as a series of technical interventions which can be ordered, ticked off and measured.

School effectiveness may also be problematic for inclusive education in that learners are likely to be excluded in the drive to meet the indicators for effectiveness. In Chapter 1, I referred to a newspaper report on a Johannesburg school that took the decision no longer to enrol d/Deaf learners on account of the cost implications. In this situation, 'effective' financial management trumped inclusion. Similarly, when school effectiveness is measured by learner achievement on standardised national assessments, including matriculation exams, pressures towards exclusion increase. In South Africa, the '… pressure on schools to perform in the high-stakes Matric exams may result in their pushing out learners who are particularly weak and unlikely to succeed' (Meny-Gibert and Russell 2012: 45). Exclusion is thus seen as a prerequisite for systemic efficiency (Dorling 2011).

The third definition introduces the adjective 'radical' and shifts from restructuring to reconstruction. A sign that nouns have lost their intensity is that writers need to supplement them with adjectives and the use of the term 'radical' in a definition of inclusive education is noteworthy. The title of a new book, *Radical Inclusive Education* (Greenstein 2016) signals that 'inclusive education' has lost its original radical intent and the term can no longer be relied upon to convey the extent of its counter-hegemonic origins. The addition of the adjective 'radical' in this title now indicates the possibility of at least two types of inclusive education: radical inclusive education and mainstream inclusive education. In true mainstreaming fashion, inclusive education has been forced to assimilate into a dominant educational order, and welcomed, on condition that it adapts itself to the expectations of the mainstream and does not disrupt the status quo. So while restructuring might suggest a change in the way in

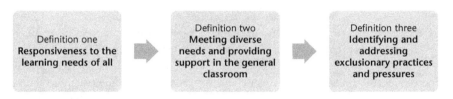

**FIGURE 3.3** Shifts in what inclusive education entails

which educational structures are configured, the 'reconstruction' of this third definition suggests that inclusive education demands a return to the drawing board and a completely new way of thinking and doing education.

The second shift is concerned with what inclusive education entails and is represented diagrammatically in Figure 3.3.

The final clause of the first definition states that inclusive education entails schools being responsive to the learning needs of all. This captures an attempt to make schools, rather than learners and their parents, responsible for making the changes necessary to ensure effective learning. 'Responsive' has some value in how inclusive education can be defined, because it challenges the one-size-fits-all, this-is-the-way-we-have-always-done-it policies and practices that typify many schools. But 'being responsive' is problematic in the sense that it positions schools and teachers as needing to respond to 'needs' as and when they arise, rather than proactively orientating teaching towards learning for all. The South African school that 'accommodates' a learner with spina bifida and others with 'learning barriers' by providing daily 'extra support' could be regarded as being responsive.[8] But the extra effort that the school is reported (by Keating (2006)) as continually 'trying' to make suggests that the school, while willing to respond to these individuals, is not fundamentally committed to inclusivity.

The second definition provides more nuance to a responsiveness to the learning needs of all in saying that inclusive education is meeting diverse needs in the general classroom by providing appropriate support. This is given equal weight and concurrent importance with restructuring, improvement and effectiveness. In the previous chapter I noted a concern with the use of the word 'diverse', which is usually constituted as different from some norm. Here I focus on the word 'needs' in this definition and in the language of inclusive education in general. While denoting nothing more than requirements, the word 'needs', particularly in the context of education, is loaded with connotations. Even when 'special' is dropped as an explicit adjective, the ghost of 'special' hovers over needs, and 'needs' is most often used now where 'special needs' would have been used in the past. The intention of its use in the definition is to embrace needs beyond traditional 'special' needs, like the needs of children who experience trauma, or children who head households. This is certainly implied by my reference to 'diverse' needs. But 'needs' is still bound to wider associations of lack or deficit, and the division of people into those who have needs and those who meet needs (Sapon-Shevin 2007). To be one with needs or needy is to be in the position of a supplicant, and to have many needs is to be pitied or scorned.

In this second definition, learners have been erased so that needs seem to be present apart from the people who have them. The disembodiment of needs paves the way for the language of disorders, syndromes and other conditions which can be described and categorised outside the individual's experience of them. Instead of a pedagogical responsiveness to diverse learners who would come to school with a constellation of characteristics that might impact their learning, this definition focuses on their needs. Thus cast, the need, not the learner, is met in the classroom.

The reference to the provision of appropriate support as an essential component of inclusion reflects the influence at the time of the concern that learners were or could be irresponsibly placed or retained in mainstream schools that were unable to provide the learning, physical, emotional or behavioural support that these learners were deemed to require. 'Support' remains one of the most frequently used words in the various South African guidelines for implementing inclusive education. Like 'needs', 'support' is also indicative of deficit. Providing support is associated with doing something for others based on the assumption that they cannot do it for themselves (Mason 2002). In South Africa, 'support' and 'needs' are often coupled and then 'additional' is appended to give 'additional support needs' (DBE 2014: vii; Walton et al. 2014: 320). The double deficit of 'support' and 'need' is compounded by 'additional', which signifies that the learners so designated require something extra that is not usually provided by the education system. Described thus, these learners are signalled as being different from their peers for whom the schooling provision is sufficient. It is an indicator that the system is designed for most learners, with additions required for some learners. When learners are repeatedly described as having 'additional support needs' there is little wonder that some teachers view inclusive teaching as an 'additional stressor' (Eloff and Kgwete 2007: 354) for their professional practice.

Locating inclusion specifically in the general (or ordinary) classroom in this second definition was, and still is, a bold and contentious statement in the South African context. *White Paper Six* (DoE 2001) is clear that in this country, special schools will remain an important part of an inclusive education system. Special schools will have a role as resource centres and will also enrol learners deemed to have moderate or high support needs.[9] The special school system in South Africa is a legacy of pre-democracy schooling, with a well-resourced special education system set up to serve mainly white and, to a limited extent, Indian and coloured children. The only special schools for black children were set up by missionary or philanthropic organisations. Now, our special schools are filled to capacity by children of all races, and some teachers in these schools are not convinced of the wisdom or viability of inclusive schooling for learners with 'special needs' (Ngwenya 2007). Special school enrolment has increased significantly in the years since the publication of *White Paper Six* (Walton 2015), with one of South Africa's provincial departments of education noting that a 'great number of learners' are 'unnecessarily' referred to special schools (Gauteng Department of Education 2011: 12). Despite this, the numbers of children and young people who are out of school because of disability remains stubbornly high, with 22.1 per cent of children with disabilities not in school (Fleisch *et al.* 2012). While referral to a special school remains an option whenever a learner's support needs are deemed to exceed a school's capacity to meet those needs, being included is always tentative and conditional. By confining my definition to the general classroom, I signalled a rejection of the coupling of special education and inclusive education that is made in South African policy.

The third definition makes the starting point of inclusion not school improvement or the provision of support but the identification and elimination of exclusionary practices and pressures. In other words, pervasive and sedimented exclusion must be recognised before meeting the learning needs of a diverse learner population can begin. In South Africa, as in many other countries, a surfeit of studies have explored teachers' attitudes towards inclusive education, with many[10] concluding that a positive disposition towards inclusive education is a prerequisite for the implementation of the idea. It is about time that we explored the attitudes of teachers and school managers to various taken-for-granted practices that, in effect, pose impediments to access, participation and belonging. These may include retention (making learners repeat a year), streaming (class grouping by ability), pull-out learner support and rewarding some learners with prizes for their achievement. The investment of teachers, school managers and even parents in preserving these practices is likely to be a significant factor that prevents the transformation needed to achieve inclusivity. While teachers and school managers may feel positive about the idea of inclusive education, they may continue to perpetuate exclusionary practices in the belief that these practices are neutral, if not beneficial, in their effect.

While the third definition points to the need to identify and address various impediments to access, it fails to signal the exercise of power that engenders and sustains these impediments. The overt and covert impediments to access, participation and belonging have become entirely commonplace, so that it is difficult to imagine an education system that could function without sorting learners and filtering out the weak, the stragglers and those with 'barriers' or 'challenges'. And power is exercised to maintain the privilege and position of the already powerful. So identifying and addressing impediments to access cannot take place without critically engaging with the question of who benefits from their perpetuation.

One of the (many) challenges of defining inclusive education is that its constituent attributes represent concepts which are contested in their own right. So potential meanings proliferate, depending on how the constituent concepts are defined. The proliferation of meanings also occurs as definitions are complexified through the addition of attributes (the rule of conjunction) and the negation of attributes (the rule of negation).

## Complexification of definition rules

The first of the three definitions is a simple one of affirmation. It states that inclusive education is about efforts that are made to improve schools in terms of accessibility and responsiveness. The second definition uses the rule of conjunction and is composed visually in textboxes to emphasise the concurrent importance of two aspects of inclusive education, i.e. school and systemic restructuring and meeting diverse needs. These two aspects are visually balanced but clearly separate. Further complexity is added by introducing inclusive culture and policy in a textbox underneath the statements about school and systemic restructuring and meeting diverse needs. Unidirectional arrows (problematically) suggest that culture and policy only influence school and systemic restructuring and meeting diverse needs but imply that the reverse is not true. The separation of various aspects of 'inclusion' in this second definition into discrete textboxes, each firmly bordered, is a visual indication that each aspect is sealed from the others. The parts are emphasised rather than the whole. The sharp angles of the textboxes, their linear positioning and the strong lines and borders work together to make inclusion a precise and tidy concept, inorganic, and rationally ordered (Albers 2007). While the aspects of 'inclusion' may have been separated in this visual for ease of discussion, they are, in fact, not easily and neatly separable, and pursuing inclusivity in education is much more 'messy' (Walton and Nel 2012: 6) and organic than this diagram implies.

The third definition is the only one in which negation is used in addition to conjunction in defining the concept. The introduction of negation here is a statement that if normalising or assimilation are present, then what is being described is not inclusive education. Negation offers an alternative to the attempts to define what inclusive education is. Instead of quibbling about what inclusive education is, or should, or could be, perhaps we might be more able to say what inclusive education is not. Slee (2011), who has suggested that precision in definition might not be necessary, is also categorical in terms of what inclusive education is *not*. It is not, he says, '… achieved through charitable dispensations to excluded minorities' and it is not 'about the movement of people from their tenancy on the social margins into unchanging institutions' (107). Others have used negation to say that inclusive education is not 'a set of decontextualized skills used only with disabled students but rather a commitment to critical pedagogy and social justice …' (Lawrence-Brown and Sapon-Shevin 2014: x) and it is not 'about admitting previously excluded learners into untransformed schools' (Walton et al. 2014). These statements of negation are attempts to ensure that inclusive education is not 'tamed' (Slee 2009) to the point that an 'inclusion class' for 'inclusion kids' can actually be regarded as inclusive education.

While this retrospective analysis of definitions is indicative of developments in my own scholarship, it is also illustrative of how language builds things as it defines. Various lexical and syntactical choices make some things significant and others not (Gee 2011). What is deemed most significant in these definitions is signalled through what is positioned as the theme (first part) of sentences rather than the rheme (what follows). The absence of disability or special need in these definitions signals that this identity marker is not significant in these conceptions of inclusive education. Other noteworthy linguistic turns in these definitions include the use of the passive voice in the first definition ('efforts that are made') and the accretion of present participles in the second and third definitions which together avoid signalling a subject who is responsible for carrying out the actions. Similar analyses can be made of other scholars' definitions of inclusive education, revealing different ways in which inclusive education is languaged.

## Accents

The quest for definitions is frustrating because definitions prove to be not very definitive. But definitions are very informative, and offer a way to understand the development of the priorities and perspectives of those who are at work languaging inclusive education through their efforts to fix meaning. Accents work as a useful metaphor to account for these different priorities and perspectives. Any one language is spoken with many different accents. These accents reflect regional origins, and also, in the case of second-language speakers, home-language origins. People mostly don't think that they speak their home language with an accent – accents are usually recognised as a feature of others' speech. So, the language of inclusive education can be found to be strongly accented by psychology, or sociology, or special education, or other fields from which people come to inclusive education. The first two definitions presented in this chapter, for example, are strongly accented by school improvement/effectiveness. This reflects both my personal circumstances – at the time of writing these definitions I was a school manager and came to inclusive education from the academic field of organisational leadership. Mostly, though, people are likely to think that they speak (or write) a 'pure' form of inclusive education and are thus able to detect (and scorn) the accents of others. The challenge of accents is that they can impede understanding by others who are not familiar with the accent. So if the language of inclusive education is spoken with a very strong special education accent, it might be difficult to recognise by those who speak it with a strong critical sociology accent. The question is, how heavily may the language of inclusive education be accented before it can no longer be regarded as inclusive education but as some other dialect?

## What inclusive education means depends on what inclusive education is

As inclusive education has become mainstreamed in recent years, the demand for definitions seems to have diminished. The assumption of a shared understanding has resulted in fewer journal articles explicitly defining the term. Whether or not this trend matters depends entirely on what inclusive education is. If it is an 'umbrella' or 'banner' (Slee 2011) under which a wide variety of definitions, understandings and meanings can cluster, then it can afford to be inclusive. If it is a discourse, as suggested in Chapter 1, then the term will evolve and mean what the discourse community makes it mean – the purists may rail against the shifts in meaning but, as with all semantic change, their/our efforts are likely to prove futile. If it is an ideology, as suggested in Chapter 2, or a value or a principle, the debate about what it means is interesting but a matter for philosophers. If, however, inclusive education is a field of research and/or practice (also in Chapter 2) then the boundary matters. Even if it is a very large field and the boundary is generous, there must be a limit, and continuing efforts to settle that limit are important to the development of the field itself.

## Notes

1 What counts as canonical will obviously be contested. What is canonical to one may be apocryphal to another and heresy to a third.
2 See Chapter 2 for a discussion on ideal knowers.
3 See Chapter 2 for further discussion on the nominalisation of the word inclusion.
4 See, for example, Engelbrecht *et al.* (2006) and Oswald (2010).
5 See Chapter 5 of this book.
6 Discussed in Chapter 1.
7 See, for example, Botha (2010), Pretorius (2014) and Taylor *et al.* (2013).
8 Refer to Chapter 1 for newspaper reports on the efforts that some schools make.
9 Disability diagnosis is not the basis on which learners might secure enrolment in a special school. Instead, the level of support that learners are deemed to need is the determinant of special school admission.
10 See, for example, Avramidis and Norwich (2002), Parasuram (2006) and Savolainen *et al.* (2011).

## References

Abbott, A. (1988) *The System of Professions*. Chicago: University of Chicago Press.
Ainscow, M. (2005) 'Developing inclusive education systems: what are the levers for change?', *Journal of Educational Change*, 6 (2): 109–24.
Ainscow, M., Booth, T., Dyson, A. with Farrell, P., Frankham, J., Gallannaugh, F., Howes, A. and Smith, R. (2006) *Improving Schools, Developing Inclusion*. London: Routledge.
Albers, P. (2007) 'Visual discourse analysis: an introduction to the analysis of school-generated visual texts', in D. W. Rowe, R. T. Jiminez, D. L. Compton, D. K. Dickinson, Y. Kim, K. M. Leander and V. J. Risko (eds), *56th Yearbook of the National Reading Conference*. Oak Creek, WI: NRC, pp. 81–95.
Allan, J. and Slee, R. (2008) *Doing Inclusive Education Research*. Rotterdam: Sense Publishers.
Anderson, J., Boyle, C. and Deppeler, J. (2014) 'The ecology of inclusive education', in H. Zhang, P. Chan, and C. Boyle (eds), *Equality in Education*. Rotterdam: Sense Publishers, pp. 23–34.
Avramidis, E. and Norwich, B. (2002) 'Teachers' attitudes towards integration/inclusion: a review of the literature', *European Journal of Special Needs Education*, 17 (2): 129–47.
Avramidis, E., Bayliss, P. and Burden, R. (2002) 'Inclusion in action: an in-depth case study of an effective inclusive secondary school in the south-west of England', *International Journal of Inclusive Education*, 6 (2): 143–63.
Booth, T. and Ainscow, M. (2002) *Index for Inclusion: Developing Learning and Participation in Schools*. Manchester: Centre for Studies in Inclusive Education.
Botha, R. J. (2010) 'School effectiveness: conceptualising divergent assessment approaches', *South African Journal of Education*, 30 (4): 605–20.
Carroll, L. (1988) *Through the Looking Glass*.Little Alice Edition. London: Macmillan.
Department of Basic Education (DBE) (2011) *Action Plan to 2014. Towards the Realisation of Schooling 2025*. Pretoria: Government Printers.
Department of Basic Education (DBE) (2014) *Policy on Screening, Identification, Assessment and Support*. Pretoria: Department of Basic Education.

Department of Education (DoE) (2001) *White Paper Six: Special Needs Education.* Pretoria: Department of Education.
Department of Education (DoE) (2002) *Revised National Curriculum Statement: Grades R – 9 (Schools): Overview.* Pretoria: Department of Education.
Dorling, D. (2011) *Injustice. Why Social Inequality Persists.* Bristol: Policy Press.
Ellis, C. (2004) *The Ethnographic I: A Methodological Novel About Autoethnography.* Walnut Creek, CA: AltaMira Press.
Eloff, I. and Kgwete, L. K. (2007) 'South African teachers' voices on support in inclusive education', *Childhood Education*, 83 (6): 351–5.
Engelbrecht, P., Oswald, M. and Forlin, C. (2006) 'Promoting the implementation of inclusive education in primary schools in South Africa', *British Journal of Special Education*, 33 (3): 121–9.
Fleisch, B., Shindler, J. and Perry, H. (2012) 'Who is out of school? Evidence from the Statistics South Africa Community Survey', *International Journal of Educational Development*, 32 (4): 529–36.
Gauteng Department of Education (2011) *Inclusion Strategy for Early Identification and Support Provisioning for Learners Experiencing Barriers to Learning and Development 2011–2015.* Johannesburg: Gauteng Department of Education.
Gee, J. (2008) *Social Linguistics and Literacies: Ideology in Discourses*, 3rd edn. London: Routledge.
Gee, J. (2011) *An Introduction to Discourse Analysis*, 3rd edn. New York and Abingdon: Routledge
Graham, L. J. and Jahnukainen, M. (2011) 'Wherefore art thou, inclusion? Analysing the development of inclusive education in New South Wales, Alberta and Finland', *Journal of Education Policy*, 26 (2): 263–88.
Greenstein, A. (2016) *Radical Inclusive Education.* London: Routledge.
Halliday, M. and Matthiessen, M. (2004) *An Introduction to Functional Grammar*, 3rd edn. London: Arnold.
Keating, C. (2006) 'Kamielah finds niche at mainstream school'. Retrieved from: http://www.iol.co.za/news/south-africa/kamielah-finds-niche-at-mainstream-school-1.291982?ot=inmsa.ArticlePrintPageLayout.ot.
Klein, S. (2011) *Learning. Principles and Applications*, 6th edn. Thousand Oaks, CA: Sage.
Kozleski, E. B., Artiles, A. J. and Waitoller, F. R. (2011) 'Introduction: equity in inclusive education', in A. J. Artiles, E. B. Kozleski and F. R. Waitoller (eds), *Inclusive Education: Examining Equity on Five Continents.* Cambridge, MA: Harvard Education Press, pp. 1–14.
Krog, A. (2003) *A Change of Tongue.* Johannesburg: Random House.
Lawrence-Brown, D. and Sapon-Shevin, M. (2014) *Condition Critical: Key Principles for Equitable and Inclusive Education.* New York: Teachers College Press.
Lewin, K. M. (2009) 'Access to education in sub-Saharan Africa: patterns, problems and possibilities', *Comparative Education*, 45 (2): 151–74.
McNiff, J. (2008) 'The significance of "I" in educational research and the responsibility of intellectuals', *South African Journal of Education*, 28: 351–64.
Makoelle, T. M. (2014) 'School effectiveness and inclusion: cases of selected secondary schools in the Free State, South Africa', *International Journal of Educational Science*, 7 (1): 131–40.
Mason, J. (2002) *Researching Your Own Practice: The Discipline of Noticing.* London: RoutledgeFalmer.
Maton, K. (2009) 'Cumulative and segmented learning: exploring the role of curriculum structures in knowledge-building', *British Journal of Sociology of Education*, 30 (1): 43–57.
Meny-Gibert, S. and Russell, B. (2012) 'South Africa's school-going culture? Findings from the Social Surveys Africa-Centre for Applied Legal Studies Access to Education Survey',

in S. Motala, V. Dieltiens and Y. Sayed (eds), *Finding Place and Keeping Pace*. Cape Town: HSRC Press, pp. 28–47.

Motala, S. and Deacon, R. (2011) *Parental Participation and Meaningful Access in South African Schools*, CREATE South Africa Policy Brief 4. Accessed from: http://www.create-rpc.org/pdf_documents/South_Africa_Policy_Brief_4.pdf.

Ngwenya, P. (2007) Perceptions of Teachers in Special Schools Towards Inclusive Education'. Unpublished Master of Education Research Essay, University of Johannesburg. Accessed from; https://ujdigispace.uj.ac.za/handle/10210/2552.

Oswald, M. (2010) 'Teacher Learning During the Implementation of the Index for Inclusion in a Primary School'. Unpublished doctoral dissertation, University of Stellenbosch, Stellenbosch, South Africa.

Parasuram, K. (2006) 'Variables that affect teachers' attitudes towards disability and inclusive education in Mumbai, India', *Disability and Society*, 21 (3): 231–42.

Pretorius, S. (2014) 'Educators' perceptions of school effectiveness and dysfunctional schools in South Africa', *Journal of Social Science*, 40 (1): 51–64.

Republic of South Africa (RSA) (1996a) *The Constitution of the Republic of South Africa, 1996*. Act No. 108 of 1996, in *Government Gazette*, 378 (17678). Cape Town: Government Printer.

Republic of South Africa (RSA) (1996b) *South African Schools Act, 1996*. Act No. 84 of 1996, in *Government Gazette*, 377 (17579). Cape Town: Government Printer.

Sapon-Shevin, M. (2007) *Widening the Classroom Circle*. Boston: Beacon.

Savolainen, H., Engelbrecht, P., Nel, M. and Malinen, O. P. (2011) 'Understanding teachers' attitudes and self-efficacy in inclusive education: implications for pre-service and in-service teacher education', *European Journal of Special Needs Education*, 27 (1): 51–68.

Secada, W. G. (1989) 'Agenda setting, enlightened self-interest, and equity in mathematics education', *Peabody Journal of Education*, 66 (2): 22–56.

Shalem, Y. (2014) 'What binds professional judgment? The case of teaching', in M. Young and J. Muller (eds), *Knowledge, Expertise and the Professions*. Abingdon: Routledge, pp. 93–105.

Slee, R. (2009) Audio interview with Roger Slee, Editor, International Journal of Inclusive Education, at the Institute of Education, London. Accessed from: http://www.educationarena.com/pdf/rslee_transcript.pdf.

Slee, R. (2011) *The Irregular School*. London: Routledge.

Taylor, N., van der Berg, S. and Mabogoane, T. (2013) 'Context, theory, design', in N. Taylor, S. Van der Berg and T. Mabogoane (eds), *Creating Effective Schools*. Cape Town: Pearson, pp. 1–30.

Thompson, J. (1990) *Ideology and modern culture*. Cambridge: Polity Press.

UNESCO (2005) *Guidelines for Inclusion: Ensuring Access to Education for All*. Paris: UNESCO.

Vygotsky, L. (1986) *Thought and Language*, trans. rev. and ed. Alex Kozulin. Cambridge, MA: MIT Press.

Waldron, N., McLeskey, J. and Redd, L. (2011) 'Setting the direction: the role of the principal in developing an effective, inclusive school', *Journal of Special Education Leadership*, 24 (2): 51–60.

Walton, E. (2002) 'The Role of Education Managers in Implementing a Policy of Inclusion in Independent Christian Schools'. Unpublished MEd Research Report, University of South Africa, Pretoria.

Walton, E. (2006) 'The Extent and Practice of Inclusion in Independent Schools (ISASA Members) in South Africa'. Unpublished DEd Thesis, University of South Africa, Pretoria.

Walton, E. (2011a) 'Getting inclusion right in South Africa', *Intervention in School and Clinic*, 46 (4): 240–5.

Walton, E. (2011b) 'They discluded me: the possibilities and limitations of children's participation in inclusion research in South Africa', *Perspectives in Education*, 29 (1): 83–92.

Walton, E. (2015) 'Working towards education for all in Gauteng', in F. Maringe and M. Prew (eds), *Twenty Years of Education Transformation in Gauteng 1994 to 2014: An Independent Review*. Somerset West: African Minds for the Gauteng Department of Education, pp. 210–17.

Walton, E. and Nel, N. (2012) 'What counts as inclusion?', *Africa Education Review*, 9 (1): 1–26.

Walton, E., Nel, N. M., Muller, H. and Lebeloane, O. (2014) '"You can train us until we are blue in our faces, we are still going to struggle": teacher professional learning in a full-service school', *Education as Change*, 18 (2): 319–33.

# 4

# METAPHORS THAT MATTER IN INCLUSIVE EDUCATION[1]

## We don't worry about Wandile

I was at a primary school in Johannesburg to observe and evaluate a lesson given by a pre-service teacher (I'll call her Stacey) doing her practicum. It was a grade one lesson on numeracy, and Stacey had prepared an elaborate game of 'bingo' to drill number bonds. As I settled in to watch the lesson and write my comments, I noticed one boy (I will call him Wandile) was not assigned a partner with whom to work. Instead, he was added to a pair to make a triad. The number of learners in the class was not even so this didn't immediately strike me as problematic. But as the game got underway it became clear that Wandile was not participating with his peers in working out the sums given and he kept leaving his seat and wandering around the classroom. Stacey began to reprimand him, and the game was punctuated with injunctions to Wandile to 'sit down', 'leave the other learners' and 'be quiet'. Her irritation with Wandile and his behaviour was obvious, and she became increasingly frustrated that Wandile was jeopardising the smooth running of her game and potentially compromising my evaluation of her teaching ability. Finally, about ten minutes before the end of the lesson, Wandile went back to his desk, put his head on his arms, put his thumb in his mouth and watched the rest of the game until the bell rang to signal the end of the lesson.

As we began the post-observation conference, I asked Stacey to tell me about Wandile. This took her by surprise, as she clearly expected me to prioritise discussion about the content of the lesson and its delivery. 'Oh, Wandile', she replied. 'There's something wrong with him and he's on a waiting list for a special school. My supervising teacher told me that I don't have to worry about him except to ensure he doesn't bother the other learners.' I didn't push the point and reviewed other aspects of her lesson. Before leaving, though, I caught up with the supervising teacher and, after making some small talk about Stacey's progress, I asked about Wandile. I admit (rather to my shame) that I wondered if perhaps Stacey was making an excuse to me for her neglect of Wandile during the lesson. The supervising teacher assured me in the identical words that 'There is something wrong with Wandile' and that his name was indeed on a waiting list for one of the special schools in the area. In light of that, they 'don't worry about him so long as he doesn't disrupt the other learners'. The supervising teacher had instructed Stacey accordingly. I then asked a question that elicited the answer that prompted this work:

> 'OK, but what about inclusive education?'
> The teacher confidently answered, 'That's a long-term goal of the department. We are not really concerned about it here.'

And in one metaphor for inclusive education – a goal – this teacher had neatly exonerated herself and her school from any pedagogical responsibility for Wandile and could continue with business as usual. For Wandile and others like him, the choice and use of the goal metaphor is a 'highly consequential decision' (Sfard 1998: 5) because it has enabled a particular way of thinking and consequent actions. This incident, then, led me to look more closely at the workings of metaphor for inclusive education in South Africa, with a particular focus on how these metaphors may shape how inclusive education is conceptualised and realised or resisted.

## About metaphors

For many people, metaphor exists as a dim memory from high-school poetry classes and yet metaphor pervades much of what we say and shapes how we think, with Sfard (1998: 5) observing that '… we live by the metaphors we use'. Metaphors, says Fairclough (1992: 194), 'structure the way we think and the way we act, and our systems of knowledge and belief, in a pervasive and fundamental way', and therefore our choice of metaphor will determine how we construct or define reality (Lakoff and Johnson 2003). Our capacity for thinking about something is constrained or enabled by the metaphors available to us and the development of formal or scientific concepts is often mediated through the use of metaphor (Cameron 2003: 33). We often express new or complex concepts in terms of physical experience as a 'resource-saving technique for interpreting the world' (Schmitt 2005: 366) and the repeated use of particular metaphors leads to a 'collective bias' (Deignan 2005: 24) in our understanding of concepts. Metaphors also influence and determine action. For this reason, 'How we think metaphorically matters' (Lakoff and Johnson 2003: 243).

Metaphors have engaged the interest of scholars since the time of Aristotle (Ricœur 1975) and there are various ways of thinking about how metaphor works linguistically, cognitively and discursively. My approach to metaphor draws on cognitive and discourse theories of metaphor. The crux of cognitive metaphor theory is that 'the locus of metaphor is not in language at all, but in the way we conceptualize one mental domain in terms of another' (Lakoff 1993: 203). Thus cognitive mapping rather than linguistic feature is seen as the focus of metaphor study with the metaphorical linguistic expression seen as the means to study the nature of the metaphorical concepts. Lakoff and Johnson have made a significant contribution to metaphor theory through their description of various kinds of metaphors (for example, structural, orientational and ontological metaphors) and their emphasis, based on empirical findings, on the central role that metaphor plays in abstract thought. Of particular relevance to my work on metaphors for inclusive education in South Africa is the observation that metaphorical concepts have the potential to highlight and to hide aspects of a concept (Lakoff and Johnson 2003; Danforth and Kim 2008). The cognitive approach to metaphor analysis allows researchers to identify metaphorical language, use this to reconstitute conceptual metaphors and then analyse the conceptual mappings to discover their assumptions and limitations (Cameron 2003). Cognitive metaphor analysis has opened many fruitful lines of enquiry within education, and within the broad field of special education. Danforth and Naraian (2007), for example, have investigated the use of the machine metaphor in autism research, Danforth (2007) has explored metaphors used to frame Emotional Behavioural Disorder in American public schools, and Danforth and Kim (2008) have done a preliminary analysis of metaphors in writing about ADHD and the implications of this for inclusive education. However, analysis that focuses only on the conceptual mappings of metaphor neglects the complex and dynamic discourse contexts in which metaphors are used.

A discourse perspective suggests that the selection and use of metaphor reflects the complex interaction of personal, linguistic, cognitive, affective and socio-cultural variables across time (Gibbs and Cameron 2008). Thus the impact of metaphor use should be considered beyond the ideational (that is helping to explain something complex or abstract in terms of something more familiar or concrete). Affect and attitude should also be considered as they play an important role in the emergence and entrenchment of particular metaphors (Cameron 2003; Cameron and Deignan 2006; Deignan 2005). Certain metaphors also become conventionalised through repeated use in specific socio-cultural groups and discourse communities and dynamically shape, encode and reflect the histories, discourse models and ideological positions of these groups or communities (Deignan 2005; Gee 2005; Gibbs and Cameron 2008).

## *Metaphors at work in inclusive education*

How and what we think about inclusion or inclusive education is largely enabled and constrained by metaphors. Inclusive education is neither a physical entity nor a clearly defined scientific concept, and is thus well positioned to be mediated by metaphor. A discourse community determines our understanding of inclusive education in a dynamic and interactive process that includes conceptualising and theorising, practice, reflection and research on practice. The metaphors used in this process help to construct inclusion knowledge and inclusive education becomes whatever we, the discourse community (authoritatively or repeatedly), say it is. In turn, the ways we think about inclusive education will determine the way we enact inclusive education (Brantlinger 2006). Because inclusive education is a complex concept, metaphors are used by members of the discourse community to describe or explain inclusive education and its effects. As examples, Booth (1996: 89) thinks of inclusive education as 'an unending set of processes, rather than a state', and Sapon-Shevin (2007) titles her book as *Widening the Circle: The Power of Inclusive Classrooms*. A religious metaphor is invoked by Armstrong *et al.* (2011) who note that 'the panacea of "inclusion" masks many *sins*' (30) and that the 'inclusion of diversity' is 'an *evangelical belief*' (33) (italics mine) that is spread in the developing world. Slee (2011: 155) likens inclusive education to a Trojan horse as it has entered the citadel of education, only to disgorge the enemy troops that maintain 'the structures, processes and values of regular and special education alike'. A final example is the evocative and sustained metaphor of inclusive education as fashion, described by Armstrong *et al.* (2010: vii). Here inclusive education as fashion has its origins in haute couture imagination, is 'mass produced for the high street' and ultimately finds itself in the world of 'cheap replicas and reproductions'.

South Africa comes relatively late to inclusive education and is eager to share the 'fashion'. Its conceptualisation here reflects the influence of the international community through scholarship and United Nations initiatives, but also defers to the unique historical and educational context here. Metaphors play no small part in this conceptualisation and the analysis that follows is intended to challenge the 'normative implications' (Sfard 1989: 8) of prevalent and pervasive metaphors.

## Metaphor analysis

I set out to identify the metaphors used for inclusive education in South Africa and to analyse[2] these metaphors with a particular focus on possible implications for how inclusive education could be conceived and practised here. I drew on Schmitt's (2005) systematic metaphor analysis, which is a step-by-step approach that facilitates 'a systematic reflection of the metaphors in which, and through which, we perceive, speak, think, and act' (Schmitt 2005: 369). Beginning with *White Paper Six* (Department of Education (DoE) 2001) as this country's seminal and directional document on inclusive education, I identified metaphorical items used for inclusive education, and then looked for these in subsequent departmental publications and academic writing. These metaphorical items were grouped into conceptual metaphors of inclusive education as goal, building, process and hospitality. I focused on these with an exploration of the strengths and resources that the metaphors offer, together with the deficits or limits of the metaphor and the actions that the metaphor may motivate (Schmitt 2005: 375–8). Table 4.1 in the appendix to this chapter shows metaphorical items with examples given from policies or academic writing. It shows how these have been clustered as conceptual metaphors, which informed my analysis.

Drawing on a discourse perspective, I reflected on the affective or socio-cultural dimension of the metaphors by showing possible South African associations of metaphorical items. These contextual links may help to explain why these particular metaphor clusters (and not others) have become entrenched in inclusion discourse in this country. It must be borne in mind that metaphor use is not static, and it should be expected that over time we shall see shifts in metaphors for inclusive education. But for now, this is how South Africa uses metaphors for inclusive education.

## South African metaphors for inclusive education

The sections that follow discuss each of the identified conceptual metaphors for inclusive education in South Africa. It is important to note that I am not imputing sinister motives to those who use metaphors which I find problematic, nor am I suggesting that the users of these metaphors are deliberately undermining the inclusion effort. Instead, I am concerned, like Sfard (1989: 9), with the way in which those who harness metaphors can 'shape the practice' and ultimately what the cumulative effect of various metaphors may be for inclusive education in South Africa.

### *Inclusive education is a goal*

The teacher who identified inclusive education as a goal in the opening anecdote of this chapter was reflecting a metaphor cluster used in South Africa's *White Paper Six* (DoE 2001). In this document, inclusive education or inclusion is a 'policy goal' (4 and 22) which is extrapolated into various long-term goals and short- to medium-term goals. The word 'goal' probably originated from the Middle English word 'gol', which meant boundary, and its modern literal understanding denotes the object of a ball game, either the act of scoring or the structure to which the ball is projected. In popular personal or business discourse, a goal denotes an aim or something that is strived for. In either case, the goal is an ideal state or achievement, not immediately attainable, and usually requires some effort or overcoming of obstacles to attain. Invoking the goal metaphor for inclusive education is a means to indicate that the current state of education is far from being inclusive, and thus plans and effort must be made to make education inclusive at some future date. These are not invalid sentiments. Educational exclusion is obdurate and will require well planned and intentional measures to dismantle. Given the interests vested in the perpetuation of educational exclusion, inclusive education is not likely to be immediately achieved and a long-term view is both practical and necessary. The goal metaphor, if extended to the idea of a team working together for a common purpose, resonates with the emphasis on collaboration found in much writing about inclusive education (see, for example, Deng (2010) and Miles and Ainscow (2011)). Just like various team members have particular positions on a field with particular roles to play in achieving a goal, inclusive education is more likely to become a reality as parents, teachers, teacher educators, education managers, professional and other support personnel work together to resist exclusion.

Despite what the goal metaphor contributes to understanding inclusive education and the likely uptake of such a metaphor in a country (like South Africa) where soccer is popular, it is a problematic metaphor for two reasons. The first is that there are immediate and pressing needs of children in South Africa (and other countries) to access quality education. There are varying estimates of the numbers of South African learners who are out of school. Fleisch *et al.* (2012) reported from the 2007 community survey that there were 386,069 children in the 7–15 year age group out of school, of which 57,952 had never attended school. The Department of Basic Education (DBE) in South Africa estimates 200,000 children and young people out of school. Poverty and disability/special need are identified as the most common reasons for this (DBE 2011b). Each individual represented in these numbers is a real life that, like Wandile, is affected because inclusive education is conceived of as a goal instead of an urgent priority. This lack of urgency is reflected in Wildeman and Nomdo's (2007: 3, 18) account of the non-implementation of inclusive education in South Africa. They indicate that what gets done is determined by available capacity and note that 'special needs education (or inclusive education) does not top the agenda of provincial education issues'.

The second concern I have with inclusive education as a goal is that it is seen as something that is 'some idealised final state' (Allan 2007: 48). This is reinforced by the metaphorical items allied to the goal – inclusive education as a 'vision' or as an 'ideal'. *White Paper Six* speaks quite often of inclusive education as a vision, and authors in South Africa (e.g. Prinsloo 2001) and internationally (e.g. Leeman and Volman (2001)) say inclusive education is an ideal. These somewhat ephemeral metaphors make inclusive education something out of the realm of the possible, worth striving for but ultimately unattainable. This is reinforced by inclusive education being the object of a 'quest', a metaphor also used in both South African (Ncube *et al.* 2012) and international (Leeman and Volman 2001) literature. Quests in popular discourse are mythical searches for some rare and precious object, often one which has magical or supernatural powers (like the Holy Grail, the object of King Arthur's quest, or the Arkenstone of Thrain, sought in Tolkien's *The Hobbit*). Some other-worldly strength is presumed to be needed to succeed in the quest, as it involves overcoming impossible obstacles. Inclusive education, positioned as the object of a quest, thus becomes something shrouded in mystery, potentially powerful but unlikely to be found by mere mortals. Invoking the items in this metaphorical cluster allows us to live comfortably with educational exclusion, having safely languaged ourselves into believing and behaving as if inclusive education is desirable but unrealistic, worth pursuing but a dream nonetheless. These shortcomings of the goal metaphor are compounded by the next metaphor, that of buildings.

## *Inclusive education is a building*

South African policy documents make extensive use of building metaphors to describe the realisation and implementation of inclusive education. In fact, the subtitle of *White Paper Six* is 'Special needs education/*Building* an inclusive education and training system' (emphasis mine). Throughout this White Paper, we learn that inclusive education is to be built and foundations, frameworks and structures are allied metaphors for various aspects of the inclusive education system. The building metaphor has certain traction in conceptualising inclusive education. First, from a discourse perspective, building and buildings are associated with transformation in South Africa, with millions of houses having been built for people in the twenty years since democracy. Second, there are many characteristics of buildings that are usefully transferred to the concept of inclusive education. These include the fact that inclusive education was not well known in South Africa when it was introduced in *White Paper Six* and so buildings capture the idea of creating something new. Building also speaks of plans, a systematic approach, the application of skill and effort, and the creation of something permanent and protective. All of these are pertinent to the transformation of an education system to become inclusive.

Like the goal metaphor, however, the building metaphor is also counterproductive to inclusive education in some ways. I raise two concerns, drawing on Thompson's (1990) schema of the workings of ideology.[3] The first is that the building metaphor makes inclusive education a 'thing' rather than an action. In other words, it is reified. South Africa is by no means unique in this tendency, as inclusive education worldwide has become an 'it', a thing to be examined, debated and defined as if it exists independently of our making. The nominalisation of inclusive education has been discussed in Chapter 2 of this volume and does not bear repeating here, except to note the way the building metaphor buttresses this tendency. Linked to this, though, is passivisation, another way that Thompson (1990) notes that ideology works. In *White Paper Six*, there is a noticeable lack of any individual or human agency in the building of inclusive education. Where the verb 'to build' is in the active voice, the subject is usually the amorphous 'Ministry' or the equally unspecified 'we' or 'the Department of Education'. Sometimes, though, when building an inclusive education system is described, the passive voice is used, as in 'an inclusive education and training system is organised …' or 'These actions will be undertaken' (DoE 2001: 16, 28). Together, nominalisation and passivisation 'delete actors and agency and … represent processes as things or events which take place in the absence of a subject who produces them' (Thompson 1990: 14). So we are left with the impression that it is both everybody's and nobody's responsibility for building inclusive education. Compounding this are statements in *White Paper Six* (DoE 2001) that reduce people into 'resources' and 'capacities'. For example, '… [W]e will evaluate carefully what resources we already have within the system and how these existing *resources* and *capacities* can be strengthened and transformed so that they can contribute to the building of an inclusive system' (16) or 'Classroom educators will be our *primary resource* for achieving our goal of an inclusive education and training system' (18) (italics mine). Given these abstractions, it is clear why Wandile's teacher felt that inclusive education was the responsibility of the department, and that she felt no personal responsibility for action.

## *Inclusive education is a process*

In this metaphorical cluster, I have included movement, journey and steps together with process as they seem conceptually similar in intent and effect. Internationally, process metaphors are common in defining inclusive education (for example, Booth (1996) and Pijl and Frissen (2009)). Process metaphors compensate for some of the shortcomings of the goal metaphor in that they reject positioning inclusive education as an ideal state of affairs to be achieved at some future date. Instead, they assert that the process of achieving inclusive education is in fact what inclusive education is. It could also be worded thus: inclusive education is not the destination, it is the journey to the destination. Process metaphors, I would suggest, have discursive resonance for two reasons. In South Africa, as I would imagine in other countries, journeys are a common experience as people traverse the country and its borders to visit scattered families. Second, process metaphors are common for a number of human experiences, including grieving, healing and change. So it is not difficult to absorb inclusive education as a process too, especially when we realise that achieving the kinds of change we want takes time, and that people can find change difficult, particularly if it threatens their professional identities. But, as with goals and buildings, process metaphors shape our thinking about inclusive education in ways that might prove counterproductive.

First, the process metaphor implies linearity. Extended to inclusive education, this suggests that progression towards inclusivity is an incremental, forward moving trajectory. It suggests that comparisons can be made across time and place – we are or are not more inclusive than we were yesterday, or than the school down the road. In fact, resisting exclusion and embracing inclusion is messy and contradictory, and 'progress' isn't always easy to measure. Learners may participate and feel that they belong in some classes and not others. They may be thoroughly integrated in a social circle, but experience epistemological marginalisation in lessons. They may experience exclusion even though they are 'included'. Benjamin *et al.* (2003: 547) call this 'moments of inclusion and exclusion' as they note how inclusion and exclusion are enacted moment by moment by teachers and learners. Two South African examples illustrate this. First, we have an independent education system with some schools which are accessible only to the affluent, and also some religiously exclusive schools. Many of these schools would claim to be inclusive, or at least to be making progress to becoming inclusive schools, as they increasingly admit learners who they would regard as having 'special' or 'additional support' needs (Walton *et al.* 2009). As a result, inclusion and exclusion coexist, as they did in a state school in the Durban area. Sookrajh *et al.* (2005) described research in a primary school which, unlike its neighbours, admitted a number of 'refugee' children. These learners had been displaced by conflict in places like the Democratic Republic of Congo and had come to South Africa. The school that 'included' them made various provisions for their support, including extra English classes while the rest of the school was assembled. This gesture, while ostensibly benign and initiated in response to the needs of these learners, in fact served to marginalise the 'refugee' learners and perpetuate their exclusion from their peer group. These contradictions expose the conceptual limitations of linear metaphors for inclusion. Linearity conceals the intersecting and multiple layers of experiences of inclusion and exclusion.

Second, the process metaphor potentially encourages a broad, diluted and very elastic idea about inclusive education. I wonder, is it good enough that a school 'includes' learners who might previously have expected to attend a special school and sets them up in a separate class for 'aid' or 'remediation' or 'bridging'? Is some effort towards inclusion better than none? If any steps towards inclusion count as inclusive education, then perhaps we have set our sights too low. On the other hand, if we do not acknowledge and encourage all moves towards greater inclusivity, we risk alienating people who may be valiantly resisting exclusionary practices in their contexts. Not only does the process metaphor allow for a very generous concept of inclusive education, it can also be used to exonerate. 'We're not there yet' was one principal's response to the parents of a child with Down's syndrome seeking admission to a Johannesburg school. The principal was able to deflect criticism by locating the school on the inclusion journey, but rationalise exclusion in terms of limited progress thus far. A high school, faced with an admission request from a learner whose educational difficulties may have compromised the school's unblemished record in the national matriculation results, recommended that the parents approach a neighbouring school. The neighbouring school was 'further down the inclusion path', so apparently better equipped to support the learner. My sense of this is that it is little more than an excuse to keep academically 'undesirable' learners at bay in a competitive and marketised educational environment.

A final word about inclusive education as process, and perhaps its use in the following way is idiosyncratic. A South African teacher explained her understanding of inclusive education as 'what we do after we have assessed a learner, and found that he or she has a barrier to learning. Then we start inclusive education.' By this she meant the (unwieldy) processes required by our inclusive education policy to identify 'support needs' and come up with a support plan, involving parents, school and district support structures and other professionals.[4] In this teacher's experience, inclusive education was not an encompassing systemic orientation, but it was the process that was invoked when a learner experienced some scholastic difficulty. I don't know how widespread this use of inclusive education as process is, and my account here is hearsay and outside a research context. What I do know is that at least for some teachers, inclusive education is nothing more than a technical and administrative process that they 'do' for certain learners.

## *Inclusive education as hospitality*

The term 'hospitality' does not appear in any of the literature used in metaphor analysis but is used as a conceptual metaphor to cluster the metaphorical items of welcome, accommodation, service and catering. This metaphor is the most pervasive in the language of inclusive education and is usually used with benign intention. I will argue, however, that this metaphor may be the most pernicious of them all. Hospitality is generally seen as a positive thing, both in domestic and commercial contexts. It is associated with an invitation to share space and company, welcome, and the provision of food and/or accommodation. Tourism is an important sector of the South African economy and the industry is keen to present South Africans as warm and welcoming, famous for their hospitality.[5] It is within this discursive context that the following statement is made in the *Guidelines for Inclusive Teaching and Learning*: 'Learners who experience barriers to learning as a result of disability should be *welcomed* in ordinary school environments' (DBE 2010: 13) (italics mine). This echoes another policy in which an example of 'positive support' for 'learners who have been identified by the teacher as experiencing challenges in the learning process' is given as 'an open and welcoming school ethos which allows children to feel welcome and valued' (DoE 2008a: 14). However benevolent these statements may appear, the hospitality metaphor must be problematised, particularly in terms of how certain learners are positioned by the metaphor as guests in a system that has to accommodate them, serve them and cater for their needs.

The hospitality metaphor sets up the education system as a gracious host, now expanding its capacity to receive and 'accommodate' previously unwelcome guests, i.e. those deemed to experience barriers to learning or represent diverse learning needs. A sentence in the Minister's introduction to *White Paper Six* is telling in this regard:

> Let us work together to nurture our people with disabilities so that they also experience the full excitement and the joy of learning, and to provide them, and our nation, with a solid foundation for lifelong learning and development.
>
> *(DoE 2001: 4)*

It is noteworthy that in this statement, people with disabilities are clearly 'they' and 'them' as opposed to 'us' and are thus othered. People with disabilities are also positioned as children who need the caring work of 'nurture' and are the passive recipients of provision. The use of the word 'also' in this statement acknowledges the educational marginalisation of people with disabilities, but the statement as a whole perpetuates the idea that inclusive education is what is being done for a particular group of people. Subsequent policy documents further entrench the hospitality metaphor through the use of the term 'cater'. It seems that schools do not specifically 'cater' for 'regular' learners, but learners deemed to need additional support or identified as experiencing barriers to learning must be 'catered' for. This catering, according to the *Guidelines for Inclusive Teaching and Learning* (DBE 2010a), could be through cooperative learning, differentiated teaching and multi-modal instruction. It is interesting that this document moves from advising teachers about catering for diverse learners to catering for 'barriers to learning', thus excising the learner entirely. The capacity of a school to 'cater' for learners with higher levels of 'support needs' determines the extent to which it would be inclusive (DoE 2008). Thus inclusion remains conditional on a school's ability to cater for any particular learner's needs, and should these needs exceed the school's capacity, then processes begin to find a school better equipped to meet these needs.

Accommodation works as a metaphorical item in similar ways. To accommodate is to make room or to make place for another and is often a concession. Various South African policy documents speak of the 'accommodation' of diversity, different learning needs and learners who experience barriers to learning in an inclusive education system (for example, DoE 2001, 2008; DBE 2010a). Implicit in these constructions is that diversity, different learning 'needs'[6] and learners who experience barriers to learning require special arrangements to be made so that they can have some space within the system. Fundamentally, the system does not change; it is just rearranged. The education system as it is currently constructed thus represents the norm and, like a host making accommodation and catering arrangements for invited guests, determines the support needs of learners and 'accommodates' them accordingly. The focus remains on the individual and on the various accommodations that must be made because of identified learning and support needs or differences. It is then not surprising that South African teachers perceive the inclusion of certain learners to be an additional responsibility (Eloff and Kgwete 2007; Ladbrook 2009), given that they are tasked with making accommodations rather than improving teaching.

The hospitality metaphor has the potential to contribute to the domestication of inclusive education, making it a benign if not paternalistic endeavour rather than a radical idea with 'insurrectionary power' (Slee 2009). I argue here (and elsewhere (Walton, in progress)), that inclusive education imagined as hospitality is doomed to failure, as the system as we currently know it is premised on exclusion through mechanisms such as one-size-fits-all and lock-stepped curricula and standardised assessment. Making various arrangements, like assessment 'concessions' and curriculum modifications for individual learners in order to patch them into the system, is ultimately unworkable as the strong pressures for exclusion that are inherent in the system are, in the end, likely to prevail.

My concerns about the hospitality metaphor rest on the discursive uptake of the metaphor, and I have suggested that in South Africa there may be good reason to suggest positive associations with hospitality. Conversely, though, the hospitality metaphor for inclusive education may end up being self-defeating if seen in the light of the sporadic but ongoing xenophobic violence that occurs in South Africa. These incidents seem to suggest that hospitality in this country is extended to visitors and community members, but not necessarily to foreigners who come and live in this country. The reasons for xenophobic attacks vary but include the perception that foreigners take jobs and compete for limited services and resources, leaving less for South Africans. Echoes of these reasons are found in the sentiments of some teachers when considering inclusive education. With classrooms in many schools crowded and low teacher-to-learner ratios, additional learners, representing 'additional support needs', may not be welcomed in classrooms where human and material resources are already stretched thinly. In this regard, Engelbrecht (2006: 260) documents 'discriminatory practices towards "outsiders" and those who are "different"', noting that '... children with disabilities ... are viewed by both teachers and learners as "different"' and that 'they are bullied'. With regard to limited resources, Loebenstein (2005: 146) reports a teacher as saying, 'How does the department expect that we have inclusive education when we have such large class sizes? ... [W]e can't even give the attention to the students who need a little extra attention.' In my work in South African schools, I have heard parents complain that learners with disabilities in inclusive classrooms take up more than their fair share of teachers' time and attention, and therefore they resist inclusive education. I thus suggest that South African's ambivalence about hospitality, especially when it comes to sharing resources with those who are perceived to be outsiders, limits the value of the metaphor in this country.

## Concluding observations

In this chapter, I have attempted to show that inclusive education in South Africa is described by metaphor, and at the same time the metaphors we use determine how we think about, and therefore practise, inclusion. The limitations inherent in any one metaphor used in connection with a target are often overcome by other metaphors used for that target. We could therefore expect that the limitations of the goal metaphor, which locates the realisation of inclusion in a future time, should be offset by the process metaphor, which makes inclusion the ongoing and incremental reduction of exclusionary pressures and practices. In South Africa, however, both these metaphors and that of inclusion as building can be seen to work against positioning inclusion as an urgent imperative for classroom teachers, education managers and department officials. Compounding this, the hospitality metaphors have the potential to reduce our thinking about inclusive education to a question of whether or how previously excluded learners can now be accommodated in a largely unreconstructed education system. So, after my analysis of four dominant metaphors for inclusive education, I find that these metaphors are not merely inadequate, but potentially counterproductive in the inclusive endeavour in this country. New metaphors that address the scandal of exclusion in our schools are needed in the South African construction of the concept of inclusive education. These new metaphors need to be aggressive, demanding and urgent if they are to make up for the shortfalls of our current metaphors.

Danforth and Kim (2008: 61), writing in the context of ADHD metaphors, suggest intentionally cultivating alternative metaphors that contain the elements that we find missing in the conventionalised metaphors. I suggest that we could co-opt aspects of the language of the struggle against apartheid with its passion, commitment and radical critique of the existing system to frame inclusion discourse. Those opposing apartheid rejected the limited participation offered in the homeland system or the tri-cameral parliament of 1984, and refused to compromise until full racial equality and universal suffrage was achieved. It is perhaps time for more militant metaphors that challenge our thinking about who can belong in South African schools, who decides and whose interests are served by these decisions.

## Appendix

**TABLE 4.1** Conceptual metaphors, metaphorical items and their sources

| Conceptual metaphor | Metaphorical item | Source | Context |
|---|---|---|---|
| INCLUSIVE EDUCATION IS A GOAL | Goal | *White Paper Six* (DoE 2001) | 'our policy goal of inclusion' (pp. 2, 22) 'our goal of an inclusive education and training system' (p. 18) 'our long-term goal of an inclusive education and training system' (p. 45) |
| | | Prinsloo (2001) | 'South Africa has set a firm foot on the road towards realizing this goal … [of] providing quality education for all learners within the mainstream of education' (p. 344) |
| | | Naicker (2005) | 'The social goal, which is inextricably linked with the educational goal, provides a platform for creating inclusive spaces in South African educational institutions' (p. 250) |
| | | *Guidelines* (DoE 2009) | Everyone at schools is responsible for the education of each learner and for introducing reasonable accommodations which are 'in keeping with the goals of full inclusion' (p. 7) |
| | Vision | *White Paper Six* (DoE 2001) | '[T]he education and training system should promote education for all and foster the development of inclusive and supportive centres of learning … The principles guiding the broad strategies to achieve this vision include …' (p. 6) 'The vision and goals outlined in this White Paper reflect a 20-year developmental perspective' (p. 45) |
| | | Pottas (2004) | '… the vision for inclusive education' (p. 71) |
| | | Engelbrecht (2009) | '… the vision of an educational system that not only recognises the wide diversity of children's educational needs but also expects schools to meet these diverse needs' (p. 111) |
| | | *Guidelines* (DoE 2009) | 'A full-service school seeks to embrace the vision of a society for all' (p. 7) |
| | Ideal | Prinsloo (2001) | '… realising the ideals of inclusive education' (p. 345) |
| | | Sukhraj (2006) | '… inclusive education would indeed be the ideal' (p. 1) |

| | | |
|---|---|---|
| | *White Paper Six* (DoE 2001) | 'The White Paper … lists the key steps to be taken in establishing an inclusive education and training system for South Africa' (p. 5) |
| | Prinsloo (2001) | 'South Africa has set a firm foot on the road towards realizing this goal … [of] providing quality education for all learners within the mainstream of education' (p. 344) |
| | UWC (2002) | 'Inclusion is never a static outcome. It is an objective that is constantly being worked towards. This means that the emphasis should be on identifying the signs that indicate we are "on the way" …' (p. 151) |
| Journey/steps | Swart *et al.* (2004) | 'the journey towards inclusive education' (p. 105) |
| | Engelbrecht and Swanepoel (2009) | 'Inclusive education: a never-ending journey' (title of prescribed textbook for postgraduate students at the University of Pretoria) |
| INCLUSIVE EDUCATION IS A PROCESS | Motshegka (2010a) | 'the department has already introduced several steps to address the capacity of ordinary schools to include learners with disabilities' |
| | Motshegka (2010b) | 'The Department is taking gradual steps to ensure that there are sufficient schools with the required, structural and communication accessibility for children and youth with disabilities' |
| Process | *White Paper Six* (DoE 2001) | '… a realistic and effective implementation process that moves responsibly towards the development of a system that accommodates and respects diversity …' (p. 12) |
| | Donald *et al.* (2002) | 'full implementation [of inclusive education] will be a long-term process' (p. 298) |
| | Engelbrecht *et al.* (2006) | 'Achieving an inclusive school community … implies a process' (p. 122) |
| | *Guidelines* (DoE 2009) | 'Inclusion should … be seen as a process rather than an event' (p. 8) |
| | Green and Engelbrecht (2007) | 'the movement towards inclusive education' (p. 8) |
| Movement towards | Inclusive Education Directorate (DoE 2008b) | 'Moving ahead with inclusion in South Africa' (newsletter headline) |

*(continued)*

**TABLE 4.1** Conceptual metaphors, metaphorical items and their sources (Continued)

| Conceptual metaphor | Metaphorical item | Source | Context |
|---|---|---|---|
| | Build(ing) | *White Paper Six* (DoE 2001) | 'build[ing] an inclusive education and training system' (pp. 4, 6, 16, 17, 30, 32, 50) |
| | | Swart and Oswald (2008) | 'building inclusive learning communities' (p. 104) |
| | | Ngcobo and Muthukrishna (2008) | 'This requires communities to build a school environment in which the needs of every child are accommodated' (p. 36) |
| | | *Guidelines* (DoE 2009) | 'building an inclusive education system' (p. 1) |
| | | | 'building an inclusive environment' (p. 16) |
| INCLUSIVE EDUCATION IS A BUILDING | Foundations | *White Paper Six* (DoE 2001) | 'laying the foundations of the inclusive education and training system' (p. 46) |
| | Structures | *White Paper Six* (DoE, 2001) | 'The White Paper proposes a mix of institutional structures … to meet the challenges of provision within an inclusive system' (p. 38) |
| | | | 'Inclusive education and training is about … enabling education structures' (p. 16) |
| | Framework | *White Paper Six* (DoE 2001) | 'policy framework for establishing an inclusive education and training system' (p. 23) |
| | | Engelbrecht and Swanepoel (2009) | 'accommodation within an inclusive education and training framework' (p. 25) |
| | | *Guidelines* (DoE 2009) | 'the inclusion education framework' (p. 68) |
| | | | 'The guidelines … are designed to provide a practical framework for education settings to become inclusive institutions' (p. 2) |

| | | | |
|---|---|---|---|
| INCLUSIVE EDUCATION IS HOSPITALITY | Accommodate | *White Paper Six* (DoE, 2001) | 'learners who experience mild to moderate disabilities can be adequately accommodated within mainstream education' (p. 24) |
| | | | 'their [learners with disabilities] accommodation within an inclusive education and training framework' (p. 25) |
| | | | 'the accommodation of diversity in our schools' (p. 31) |
| | | | 'Full-service schools will ... accommodate the diverse range of learning needs' (p. 48) |
| | | Swart et al. (2004) Engelbrecht (2006) | 'where the parents and the school successfully learned to accommodate the child together' (p. 89) |
| | | | '... basic rights of all South African children to be accommodated in inclusive school communities' (p. 261) |
| | | Swart and Oswald (2008) | '...developing an identity as an inclusive teacher requires ... learning how to accommodate the diverse learning needs of pupils' (p.92) |
| | | *Guidelines* (DoE, 2009) | 'include learners with disabilities and ... accommodate them' (p.3) |
| | | *Guidelines* (DoE, 2011a) | 'reasonable accommodation of individuals' requirements' (p.5) |
| | | | 'All schools are required to offer the same curriculum to learners while simultaneously ensuring variations in mode of delivery and assessment processes to accommodate all learners'. |
| | | Williams et al. (2009) | 'Schools are expected to adjust in order to accommodate and adopt a sense of ownership regarding all learners' (p. 199) |
| | Serve | *White Paper Six* (DoE, 2001) | '... improvement of special schools and settings for the learners that they serve...' (p. 20) |
| | | Walton et al. (2009) | '...inclusive practices that enable them to meet the learning needs of the children they serve' (p. 110) |
| | Cater | *White Paper Six* (DoE, 2001) | '... school management is obliged to ensure that the learners ... are adequately catered for ...' (p. 20) |
| | | SIAS (DoE, 2008a) | 'The extent to which schools are able to become inclusive schools will have an impact in the long term on the levels of support needs that they will be able to cater for...' (p. 20) |
| | | Vosloo (2009) | 'very few sports programmes in the mainstream schools and the relevant communities that catered for them' (p. 27) |
| | Welcome | DoE (2005) | 'Learners who experience barriers to learning as a result of disability should be welcomed in ordinary school environments' (p. 11) |
| | | *Guidelines* (DoE 2009) | 'Full-service institutions promote cultures that truly welcome diversity and address all exclusionary pressures' (p. 18) |

## Notes

1 This chapter is based on the following journal article which is used with kind permission of the co-author and the publisher: E. Walton and G. Lloyd (2011) 'Metaphors matter: an analysis of metaphors used for inclusive education in South Africa', *Acta Academica*, 43 (3): 1–30.
2 For a full account of the metaphor analysis, please see the article on which this chapter is based.
3 Thompson's modes of the operation of ideology are explored in more detail in Chapter 2.
4 This is reflected in the SIAS process, discussed in Chapter 1.
5 See the following websites for examples of the promotion of South Africans as hospitable: http://www.exploresouthafrica.net/culture/; http://www.southafrica.info/2010/tourism-131109.htm.
6 'Needs' is problematised in Chapter 3.

## References

Allan, J. (2007) *Rethinking Inclusive Education*. Dordrecht: Springer.
Armstrong, C., Armstrong, D. and Spandagou, I. (2010) *Inclusive Education: International Policy and Practice*. London: Sage.
Armstrong, D., Armstrong, A. and Spandagou, I. (2011) 'Inclusion: by choice or by chance?', *International Journal of Inclusive Education*, 15 (1): 29–39.
Benjamin, S., Nind, M., Hall, K., Collins, J. and Sheehy, J. (2003) 'Moments of inclusion and exclusion: pupils negotiating classroom contexts', *British Journal of Sociology of Education*, 24 (5): 547–58.
Booth, T. (1996) 'A perspective on inclusion from England', *Cambridge Journal of Education*, 6 (1): 87–99.
Brantlinger, E. (2006) 'The big glossies: how textbooks structure (special) education', in E. Brantlinger (ed.), *Who Benefits from Special Education? Remediating (Fixing) Other People's Children*. Mahwah, NJ: Lawrence Erlbaum Associates, pp. 45–76.
Cameron, L. (2003) *Metaphor in Educational Discourse*. London: Continuum.
Cameron, L. and Deignan, A. (2006) 'The emergence of metaphor in discourse', *Applied Linguistics*, 27 (4): 671–90.
Danforth, S. (2007) 'Disability as metaphor: examining the conceptual framing of Emotional Behavioral Disorder in American public education', *Educational Studies*, 42 (1): 8–27.
Danforth, S. and Kim, T. (2008) 'Tracing the metaphors of ADHD: a preliminary analysis with implications for inclusive education', *International Journal of Inclusive Education*, 12 (1): 49–64.
Danforth, S. and Naraian, S. (2007) 'Use of the machine metaphor within autism research', *Journal of Developmental and Physical Disabilities*, 19: 273–90.
Deignan, A. (2005) *Metaphor and Corpus Linguistics*. Amsterdam: John Benjamins.
Deng, M. (2010) 'Developing inclusive approaches to teaching and learning', in R. Rose (ed.), *Confronting Obstacles to Inclusion*. Abingdon: Routledge, pp. 203–12.
Department of Basic Education (DBE) (2010) *Guidelines for Inclusive Teaching and Learning*. Pretoria: Department of Basic Education.
Department of Basic Education (DBE) (2011a) *Guidelines for Responding to Learner Diversity in the Classroom*. Pretoria: Government Printers.
Department of Basic Education (DBE) (2011b) *Action Plan to 2014. Towards the Realisation of Schooling 2025*. Pretoria: Government Printers.
Department of Education (DoE) (2001) *Education White Paper Six: Special Needs Education: Building an Inclusive Education and Training System*. Pretoria: Department of Education.

Department of Education (DoE) (2005) *Curriculum Adaptation Guidelines of the Revised National Curriculum Statement.* Pretoria: Department of Education.

Department of Education (DoE) (2008a) *National Strategy on Screening, Identification, Assessment and Support.* Pretoria: Department of Education.

Department of Education (DoE) (2008b) *Inclusion Today.* Newsletter of the Directorate: Inclusive Education, 1(1).

Department of Education (DoE) (2009) *Guidelines for Full-Service/Inclusive Schools.* Pretoria: Department of Education.

Donald, D., Lazarus, S. and Lolwana, P. (2002) *Educational Psychology in Social Context*, 2nd edn. Cape Town: Oxford Southern Africa.

Eloff, I. and Kgwete, L. (2007) 'South African teachers' voices on support in inclusive education', *Childhood Education*, 83 (6): 351–5.

Engelbrecht, A. and Swanepoel, H. (2009) *Inclusive Education: A Never Ending Journey.* Silverton, South Africa: Corporate Assessment Solutions.

Engelbrecht, P. (2006) 'The implementation of inclusive education in South Africa after ten years of democracy', *European Journal of Psychology of Education*, 21 (3): 253–64.

Engelbrecht, P. (2009) 'Inclusive psychology and social transformation: responding to the challenges of the new South Africa', in P. Hick, R. Kershner and P. Farrell (eds), *Psychology for Inclusive Education.* Abingdon: Routledge, pp. 108–16.

Engelbrecht, P., Oswald, M. and Forlin, C. (2006) 'Promoting the implementation of inclusive education in primary schools in South Africa', *British Journal of Special Education*, 33 (3): 121–9.

Fairclough, N. (1992) *Discourse and Social Change.* Cambridge: Polity Press.

Fleisch, B., Schindler, J. and Perry, H. (2012) 'Who is out of school? Evidence from the Statistics South Africa Community Survey', *International Journal of Educational Development*, 32: 529–36.

Gee, J. (2005) *An Introduction to Discourse Analysis Theory and Method*, 2nd edn. New York: Routledge.

Gibbs, R. and Cameron, L. (2008) 'The social-cognitive dynamics of metaphor performance', *Cognitive Systems Research*, 9: 64–75.

Green, L. and Engelbrecht, P. (2007) 'An introduction to inclusive education', in P. Engelbrecht and L. Green (eds), *Responding to the Challenges of Inclusive Education in Southern Africa.* Pretoria: Van Schaik, pp. 2–9.

Ladbrook, M. (2009) 'Challenges Experienced by Educators in the Implementation of Inclusive Education in Primary Schools in South Africa'. Unpublished MEd dissertation, University of South Africa, Pretoria.

Lakoff, G. (1993) 'The contemporary theory of metaphor', in A. Ortony (ed.), *Metaphor and Thought*, 2nd edn. Cambridge: Cambridge University Press, pp. 202–51.

Lakoff, G. and Johnson, M. (2003) *Metaphors We Live By.* Chicago: Chicago University Press.

Leeman, Y. and Volman, M. (2001) 'Inclusive education: recipe book or quest', *International Journal of Inclusive Education*, 5 (4): 367–79.

Loebenstein, H. (2005) 'Support for Learners with Intellectual Disabilities in the Transition to Secondary School'. Unpublished PhD (Specialised Education) thesis, Stellenbosch University, Stellenbosch.

Miles, S. and Ainscow, M. (2011) 'Learning through inquiry', in S. Miles and M. Ainscow (eds), *Responding to Diversity in Schools.* Abingdon: Routledge, pp. 159–82.

Motshegka, A. (2010a) National Council of Provinces: Reply to question 91 asked by Mr M. J. R. de Villiers (Democratic Alliance – Western Cape) (Internal Question Paper: 5-2010).

Motshegka, A. (2010b) Reply to question 526 asked by Mrs P. C. Duncan (Democratic Alliance).

Naicker, S. (2005) 'Inclusive education in South Africa: an emerging pedagogy of possibility', in D. Mitchell (ed.), *Contextualizing Inclusive Education.* Abingdon: Routledge, pp. 230–52.

Ncube, M., Shimeles, A. and Verdier-Chouchane, A. (2012) *South Africa's Quest for Inclusive Development*, Working Paper Series No 150. Tunis: African Development Bank.

Ngcobo, J. and Muthukrishna, Z. (2008) 'Teachers' dominant discourses of inclusion and disability', in S. Gabel and S. Danforth (eds), *Disability and the Politics of Education: An International Reader*. New York: Peter Lang, pp. 19–14.

Pijl, S. and Frissen, P. (2009) 'What policy makers can do to make education inclusive', *Educational Management Administration Leadership*, 37 (3): 366–77.

Pottas, L. (2004) 'Inclusive Education in South Africa: The Challenges Posed to the Teacher of the Child with a Hearing Loss'. Unpublished DPhil (Communication Pathology) thesis, Department of Communication Pathology, Faculty of Humanities, University of Pretoria, Pretoria.

Prinsloo, E. (2001) 'Working towards inclusive education in South African classrooms', *South African Journal of Education*, 21 (4): 344–8.

Ricœur, P. (1975) *The Rule of Metaphor: The Creation of Meaning in Language*. London: Routledge.

Sapon-Shevin, M. (2007) *Widening the Circle: The Power of Inclusive Classrooms*. Boston: Beacon.

Schmitt, R. (2005) 'Systematic metaphor analysis as a method of qualitative research', *Qualitative Report*, 10 (2): 358–94.

Sfard, A. (1998) 'On two metaphors for learning and the dangers of choosing just one', *Educational Researcher*, 27 (2): 4–13.

Slee, R. (2009) Audio interview with Roger Slee, Editor, *International Journal of Inclusive Education*, at the Institute of Education, London. Accessed from: http://www.educationarena.com/pdf/rslee_transcript.pdf.

Slee, R. (2011) *The Irregular School*. London: Routledge.

Sookrajh, R., Gopal, N. and Maharaj, B. (2005) 'Interrogating inclusionary and exclusionary practices: learners of war and flight', *Perspectives in Education*, 23 (1): 2–13.

Sukhraj, P. (2006) *The Implementation and Challenges to Inclusive Education Policy and Practice in South Africa*. Paper delivered at a Conference of the International Council on Education of Visually Impaired Persons, Kuala Lumpur, Malaysia, 16–21 July.

Swart, E. and Oswald, M. (2008) 'How teachers navigate their learning in developing inclusive learning communities', *Education as Change*, 12 (2): 91–108.

Swart, E., Engelbrecht, P., Eloff, I., Pettipher, R. and Oswald, M. (2004) 'Developing inclusive school communities: voices of parents of children with disabilities', *Education as Change*, 8 (1): 80–108.

Thompson, J. (1990) *Ideology and Modern Culture*. Cambridge: Polity Press.

UWC (University of the Western Cape) (2002) *Resource and Training Programme for Educator Development: Building an Inclusive Education and Training System. End-term National Quality Evaluation. Final Report*. Cape Town: Education Policy Unity, University of the Western Cape.

Vosloo, S. (2009) 'The functioning of primary school learners with paraplegia/paraparesis in mainstream schools in the Western Cape, South Africa. An exploratory study', *Disability and Rehabilitation* 31 (1): 23–31.

Walton, E. (in progress) 'Inclusive education: a tame solution to a wicked problem?', in D. Mahlo, N. Pasha and G. Dei (eds), *Inclusive Education in African Contexts: A Critical Reader*.

Walton, E. and Lloyd, G. (2011) 'Metaphors matter: an analysis of metaphors used for inclusive education in South Africa', *Acta Academica*, 43 (3): 1–30.

Walton, E., Nel, N., Hugo, A. and Muller, H. (2009) 'The extent and practice of inclusion in independent schools (ISASA members) in Southern Africa', *South African Journal of Education*, 29 (1): 105–26.

Wildeman, R. and Nomdo, C. (2007) *Implementation of Inclusive Education: How Far Are We?* Occasional Papers, IDASA – Budget Information Service.

# 5
# INCLUSIVE EDUCATION ON THE (UNIVERSITY) LIBRARY SHELF

## On the library shelf

In an assignment I set for students a few years ago, an undergraduate, pre-service teacher confidently discussed the importance of responding to the educational needs of the 'sub-normal' in South African schools. He explained how 'the retarded' needed assessment to find out what they were capable of, and that despite people thinking it was a waste of resources, these children could be 'trained' with appropriate educational interventions. With a mixture of surprise and horror, I went to his reference list to discover that this diligent pre-service teacher had thought to read beyond the prescribed and recommended texts for the course on inclusive education. He had gone to the university library, browsed the collection and taken out a book[1] written in the early 1950s and used this to inform his writing. It seemed as if he regarded the book as a more reliable and scholarly source than the compilation of recent journal articles and chapters provided in a reading pack. The authority of the book had apparently trumped all the critique of discourses of individual deficit that had been taught in lectures. I was surprised to see that this, and other similar books, were in fact available in the library and I wondered if they shouldn't be withdrawn. However, South Africa has a long history of censorship, which has had a negative impact on scholarship (Merrett 1994) and advocating for the banning of books is decidedly unappealing. My disquiet at the outdated and offensive language of these books, though, was the impetus to think further about current books available to pre-service teachers. I began to consider that although the language has changed, some of the fundamental assumptions about 'different' learners might not have changed much at all.

Teacher education for inclusive education seems to be primarily concerned with learner diversity, the challenges this presents in the classroom and the ways teachers should respond to these challenges. In this chapter, I will show how these ideas predominate in textbooks available for teacher education for inclusive education in

South Africa. I begin by briefly reflecting on inclusive education as it has become a pedagogic discourse, recontextualised from the field of knowledge production. My focus then narrows to a critical engagement with some of South Africa's textbooks[2] on inclusive education. I use these to exemplify a pedagogic discourse that both creates and reflects certain ways of talking about learner difference, and about inclusive education more generally. I conclude by arguing for textbooks that force a gaze on the exclusionary pressures and practices that are endemic to schooling to disrupt the single story that 'different learners' represent a challenge to teachers and a burden to the system.

## Inclusive education in teacher education

The published international literature on research in teacher education for inclusive education mostly concerns itself either with describing innovative curricula and pedagogies or making a case for the impact of courses on teachers' knowledge, skills, attitudes and sense of self-efficacy. Within this body of literature, there is little account of how inclusive education knowledge comes to be pedagogised. Pedagogising knowledge is achieved as recontextualising agents (like teacher educators and textbook writers) select knowledge from the field of specialist knowledge production and render it in a form (usually curricula and texts) that is accessible to non-specialists (Bernstein 2000). This process, maintains Singh (2002: 575), has implications for

> ... 'what' knowledge is available to be converted into pedagogic communication, 'who' ... will undertake the work of pedagogising knowledge, and 'how' this knowledge is transformed into pedagogic forms.

The pedagogic form of the textbook is the focus of this chapter, and I consider textbook writers as recontextualising agents. Bernstein (2000: 115) makes it clear that when a discourse moves from its original site in the field of knowledge production to its new pedagogical site, it passes through 'ideological screens'. Recontextualising agents have 'practising ideologies' (Bernstein 2000: 33), which will influence what is selected from the field of knowledge production, and how it is presented to those who must acquire this knowledge. Ideologies among recontextualising agents may well be discordant, as they are among those producing knowledge in the field. However, while competing ideologies might make for interesting debates among academic peers in journals, power relations in the recontextualising field will determine which perspectives dominate in teacher education courses and texts (Bernstein 2000). In South Africa, as I will show, a perspective informed by the discipline of psychology dominates in teacher education textbooks.

According to Bernstein's schema, the recontextualising field consists of a Pedagogic Recontextualising Field (PRF) and an Official Recontextualising Field (ORF). The latter is 'created and dominated by the state for the construction and surveillance of state pedagogic discourse' (Bernstein 2000: 115). The ORF also has ideological positions and will struggle with the PRF for control of the field.

In South Africa, the ORF asserts its dominance through legislation that determines the structure and content of teacher education qualifications. With regard to pre-service teacher education, *The Minimum Requirements for Teacher Education Qualifications* (RSA 2011) notes that 'inclusive education forms an important aspect of both general pedagogical knowledge and specialised pedagogical content knowledge' (11) and that the basic competencies for beginner teachers include being able to understand diversity 'in order to teach in a manner that includes all learners' (56). Teacher education institutions must show that they meet the minimum requirements and equip novice teachers with the basic competencies. It is likely, then, that textbooks that support this imperative are more likely to be prescribed. So it is in the commercial interests of the publisher to ensure that its textbook writers align their content (to some degree) with the demands of the ORF. As inclusive education takes the pedagogic form of a textbook, the influence of the ORF is seen in the extent to which legislative or policy directives determine or shape the pedagogic discourses.

## The contribution of textbooks

Over the years, various scholars have looked closely at how inclusive education and special education are constructed and represented in textbooks. Rice (2005), for example, analysed extracts from introductory textbooks on special and inclusive education, and found that pre-service teachers are likely to be exposed to a traditional view of special education with a limited account of the possibilities of full inclusion. Brantlinger (2006) details the ways in which special education textbooks structure disability, claim expert authority and present a sanitised and ideal vision of classroom practice. More recently, Black-Hawkins (2012) examined commercially produced texts aimed at the in-service teacher market. She found that the message of these texts reinforced the idea that inclusive practices were for certain learners only, representing 'add-on provision' and offering 'quick-fix solutions' (513).

Any examination of textbooks must begin with an acknowledgement of the complex terrain of textbook production. Apple and Christian-Smith (1991: 1–2) remind us that textbooks

> ... are at once the results of political, economic, and cultural activities, battles, and compromises. They are conceived, designed, and authored by real people with real interests. They are published within the political and economic constraints of markets, resources and power.

These realities must be acknowledged in considering how inclusive education has opened possibilities for higher education textbook publishers. With legislative imperatives for inclusive education in teacher education, and a preponderance of studies showing teachers' beliefs that they need 'training' for inclusive classrooms, there is significant market opportunity for the publication of textbooks. All of South Africa's major education textbook publishers in higher education now have titles that specifically address inclusive education and these compete for places on the prescribed and recommended textbook lists at universities. Having said this, the South African higher education market is relatively small and the student population is not affluent. Many students cannot afford a phalanx of textbooks, and many do not purchase textbooks at all, relying on library copies and judicious borrowing. So while there are opportunities for publishers, there are also significant market constraints. These observations serve as a prelude to two comments that need to be made before proceeding with my analysis of three inclusive education textbooks.

First, the relationship between commissioning editors who must deliver a marketable book to the publisher and the textbook writers is complex. In order to get a textbook onto the shelves, textbook writers are likely to have to make concessions and compromises to align their work with brand expectations. Thus individual writers may not necessarily have preferred some of the approaches or conventions required by their publishers.[3] Second, for South African authors, textbook writing is not acknowledged by the Department of Higher Education as a scholarly output, so textbook writing is not a means to advance an academic career. There are, however, royalties for textbook writers and this may serve as an incentive for lecturers to prescribe books that they write, or contribute to, or edit. So while Apple and Christian-Smith (1991) note that there is no guarantee that the content of textbooks is actually taught in classes, many South African courses in inclusive education would, in fact, be closely linked to the textbooks. There is certainly no guarantee that what is taught is actually learned. But a case can be made that the cumulative effect of the dominating discourse of inclusive education in textbooks is likely to be expressed and enacted in universities and schools across the country.

## South African textbooks on inclusive education

I have chosen to focus my analysis on three South African textbooks on inclusive education: *Believe That All Can Achieve* (Bornman and Rose 2010), *Addressing Barriers to Learning* (Landsberg et al. 2011) and *Making Inclusive Education Work in Classrooms* (Pienaar and Raymond 2013). My selection was made on the basis that all three texts have been published within three years of each other and are, at the time of writing, still in print. While inclusive education can be found as a chapter in other South African education textbooks, these three volumes are devoted exclusively to the topic. My focus is on three aspects of the textbooks: how they imagine their audience; how inclusive education is presented in the first chapters; and how learner difference is constructed and its implications for pedagogy. My intention is not in any way to denigrate the work of my colleagues in the field, or to be unnecessarily critical. Instead, I want to present the effect of language and semiotic patterns across these texts to show general features of the pedagogic discourse.

### *Designing the audience*

Audience design studies the ways in which the writers of texts and the texts themselves imagine and situate their audiences (Thieme 2010). Every time language is used, including in the writing of textbooks, the conversational partner is taken into account (Horton and Gerrig 2005). This is evident in each of the three textbooks as the preface writers imagine their audiences in expressing their 'hopes', 'vision' and 'dream' for their books. All three books are designed for practitioner use and explicitly designate their intended readers as 'educators' (Lansberg et al. 2011: vii), 'peers who work in the field of inclusive education' (Bornman and Rose 2010: x) and 'teachers, teachers in training, parents and community members' (Pienaar and Raymond, 2013: vii). To justify the pedagogic intent of these textbooks, reader 'need' must be established. To this end, the prefaces articulate various needs that the readers would have, including the need for understanding the value and possibilities of inclusive education, the need to appreciate how learners are different, and the need to know various pedagogic strategies that might be effective in teaching for all. At the outset, then, all three textbooks implicitly align themselves with the rhetoric of teacher un(der)preparedness for inclusive education with the assumption that it is within the power of the (trained, knowledgeable and skilled) teacher to implement inclusive education. Readers are thus imagined as generally unknowledgeable, and various linguistic and stylistic devices continue throughout the books to reinforce this construction.

The authority of the textbook authors relative to their readers is written into the texts in different ways. Details of authors and contributors at the beginning of each book show their university affiliations and/or qualifications in the field, indicating their expertise in teacher education and inclusive education. Two of the three texts are presented in columns, mirroring the authority of religious texts, and they all make use of scientific-looking diagrams, flow charts and tables. Most of the content sections (i.e. not the textboxes or other call-out features) are written in the third person using the indicative mood, which reinforces the idea that the reader needs information (Janks 2010) and the writer has the authority to provide this information. The present tense predominates in these texts, indicating 'timeless truths and absolute certainty' (Janks 2010: 75). Few personal pronouns are found in the content sections and the authors are made mostly invisible by this linguistic device. The 'truth' thus presented seems to come from no human agent. In the few cases where 'we' is used, it is not clear if the writer means to include the reader in 'we' or not. It is more likely that 'we' refers to the scholarly community of which the writer, but not the reader, is a part. The authority of the text is further asserted by reference to other authorities (often international experts), policy and United Nations initiatives. Medical, psychological and other technical language is used throughout the texts and two of the three texts assure readers that they are presenting 'evidence-based' practices and techniques. Contestations about the topics in the field of knowledge production are sometimes mentioned but mostly neglected. Together, these features reflect pedagogised knowledge of inclusive education and learner diversity characterised by certainty, objectivity and scientific accuracy.

The reader is addressed by the textbook writers in various textboxes. These are visually distinct from the main content, have their own headings (like 'activity', 'stop and reflect' or 'think about'), and employ different linguistic features. These textboxes contain either commands for actions, thought or discussion or questions for reflection, application or discussion. The imperative mood assumes the writers' authority and right to tell others what to do (Janks 2010). So readers of these texts are instructed to 'Make a list' (Bornman and Rose 2010: 87), 'Write down a short explanation' (Prinsloo 2011: 45) or 'Consider your own experiences' (Moletsane 2013: 74). Sometimes questions are asked, such that the readers' own knowledge and experience is seen as a legitimate contribution, as in 'What other strategies can you think of?' (Bornman and Rose 2010: 87), and 'What does this mean to you in your context?' (Pienaar 2013: 42). This call for contextual or personal application sets up a binary between theoretical and personal practical knowledge. Theoretical knowledge, which is principled, abstractable and generalisable over contexts, is provided by the (expert) textbook writer, and practical knowledge, which is both contingent and contextually dependent, is elicited from the (lay) reader. The use of the second person pronoun in many of these directions or questions stands in contrast to the rest of the text where verbs are generally unmarked for person. This reinforces the pedagogical authority of the writer in relation to the reader, in that the writer has the power to address the reader using the personal pronoun, but does not reveal him or herself through personal pronouns. The word 'you' does not indicate number, so it is not clear if the activities are imagined as private or communal tasks for readers.

The readers of these texts are thus assumed to be, and constructed as, initiates needing information and instruction. As teachers (or 'teachers in training'), they would be familiar with the format of textbooks from their work in schools and would recognise many of the conventions of textbook language and layout. Readers of these books, then, are positioned as adult 'learners' (in the South African sense of schoolgoers), needing explicit guidance on how to navigate and respond to the information in the text. Mention does need to be made of Bornman and Rose (2010) who seem to aim for a more proximal relationship with their readers. Their preface states that they are writing for 'peers' and 'colleagues' and they make frequent use of rhetorical questions within the content sections of their texts. This gives their text a more conversational tone than the other two books. It also does not have beginning and end of chapter formalities, like learning outcomes, questions to guide or assess reading and summaries that the others do. These features set it slightly apart among the three texts. However, there are remarkable similarities among the three texts under consideration when it comes to introducing readers to the idea of inclusive education.

## *Inclusive education explained*

After a short preamble, all three books take section 1.2 to answer 'What is inclusive education?' (Ntombela and Raymond 2013: 3), 'What is inclusion?' (Swart and Pettipher 2011: 3) and 'Understanding inclusion' (Bornman and Rose 2010: 6). All three immediately point to the difficulty of definitions and multiplicity of meanings of their terms. They also all use words with negative connotations in their first introduction of the concept. Variously, inclusion or inclusive education is 'a slippery concept' (Ntombela and Raymond, 2013: 3), a 'buzzword' or a 'cliché' (Swart and Pettipher 2011: 3) and a concept causing 'bewilderment' (Bornman and Rose 2010: 6). While these appellations may be apposite in the broad discourse of inclusive education, the effect of foregrounding these in an initial introduction sets up inclusive education as a problematic concept. All do go on to speak about human rights, diversity and the need for the education system to be responsive to all learners, so it is clear that the writers all support the idea of inclusive education. But first impressions linger, and there are many tacit and explicit reminders to readers of all three books of the challenge that inclusive education represents. Delays in the implementation of institutional support structures are described by Landsberg (2011: 74) and are attributed to lack of training and funding and 'lack of commitment of personnel'. Bornman and Rose (2010) mention lack of training in differentiated teaching, lack of support and resources and negative attitudes to disability. Ntombela and Raymond (2013: 11) devote an entire section to 'Highlights and *challenges*' (emphasis mine) in the implementation of inclusive education. I have argued elsewhere (Walton, in progress) and reiterate here that in naming inclusive education as the problem, we potentially lose focus on the problem of pervasive and endemic educational exclusion.

In their introductions to inclusive education, three distinct sources of information are foregrounded, each reflecting a distinct orientation to inclusive education knowledge. The first, exemplified in *Addressing Barriers to Learning* (Landsberg *et al.* 2011), is that the field of knowledge production is identified as the source of understanding inclusive education. The authors of this chapter, Swart and Pettipher, draw extensively on some of the 'big names' and seminal writers in the field to define inclusive education. In so doing, they derive their understandings and definitions of inclusive education from authoritative scholars like Alan Dyson, Mel Ainscow, Lani Florian, Alfredo Artiles and others. The textbook writers extract and synthesise context-independent ideas and indicate principles of inclusive education that are articulated internationally. Readers are thus given an indication that there is a wider field of scholarship from which the understanding of inclusive education is derived, and that there are (at least some) generalisable and abstractable concepts that arise from research in the field. I detect 'ideological screens' that filter what is selected from the field of knowledge production for the purpose of transmission (Bernstein 2000). So Swart and Pettipher have selected constructions of inclusive education mainly from writers in the broad 'school improvement' (Allan and Slee 2008: 16) tradition of inclusive education research internationally. They do not introduce dissenting voices from special education research, nor do they draw much from scholars in disability activism or critical research, which are other positions on the spectrum of inclusive education research (Allan and Slee 2008). This is not to say there is not 'truth' in what they present, simply that it is partial (Bernstein 2000). Importantly, though, the principle of recontextualising that structures the transmission in the textbooks is 'invisible' at the level of the acquirer (Bernstein 2000: 164). This means that textbook readers are not likely to be aware of the ideologies that inform selection or even that selection has taken place.

Instead of drawing on the field of knowledge production, writers of *Making Inclusive Education Work in Classrooms* (2013) go straight to policy to define inclusive education. Ntombela and Raymond (2013: 3) laud the South African education department for being 'bold enough to come up with its own definition of what it is trying to develop' by taking contextual issues into consideration. These writers then present to their readers the definition of an inclusive education system provided in *Education White Paper Six* (DoE 2001) and then discuss this in a further three paragraphs. While all the textbooks under consideration embed the official discourse (i.e. policy) in their texts, this one aligns itself with the current policy early and unambiguously, making the policy the determinant of what inclusive education is and how it should be implemented. This could be regarded as problematic on a number of levels. Policy is known to be contradictory (Liasidou 2012) and scholars have documented the paradigmatic contradictions inherent in South African policy on inclusive education (Donohue and Bornman 2014; Pather 2011). As the textbook writers' voice segues into policy provisions, the readers are positioned less as professionals whose practice needs to be informed by the principles of inclusivity, and more as policy implementers.

The foregrounding of South African policy in defining inclusive education serves to reinforce the semantic gravity of inclusive education.[4] In other words, contextual relevance is signalled as most important. This view is also evident in Bornman and Rose's understanding of inclusive education. Technically, this is not discussed in their section 1.2 on 'understanding inclusion', where they suggest that the focus of inclusive education should be on '… increasing participation by the removal of barriers … in order for the children to reach their full potential' (Bornman and Rose 2010: 6). This definition is not explicitly derived from the field of knowledge production, nor from policy, but is asserted by the authors. It is in the following section that they reveal their advocacy of a 'narrative approach' to emphasise 'the human understanding of inclusion' (8). In their preface, these writers report that they share many 'true narratives' (x) elicited from the role-players (parents, teachers and therapists) that they have encountered in their personal and professional lives. Teachers have been asked 'to tell their own stories about inclusion' which, the writers say, give 'access to personal and idiosyncratic understanding' (8). Thus, before Chapter 1 is even introduced, the reader is presented with a lengthy account, written in the first person, of a teacher's encounter with a parent of a 'slow learner' called Rachel. The parent is seeking access to this school because it is 'a happy school', where teachers like to work and where parents are not scared to speak to teachers. The narrator is sure that Rachel would be happy, and grow and learn new skills in this school, as it 'is called an inclusion school' (5). I will return to a concern I want to raise about the tone and content of 'case studies' that permeate all three texts. Here, I want to draw attention to the fact that this happily ending tale sets the stage for the textbook writers' valorisation of an anecdotal, individual and experiential understanding of inclusive education. If a policy focus strengthens the semantic gravity of the concept of inclusive education, then this individual focus grounds it entirely in personal experience and contextual specificities. In this view, inclusive education is not just understood differently across contexts, each individual can legitimately claim an 'idiosyncratic' understanding of inclusion, and it potentially means anything to anyone.

An individual commitment to inclusive education is clearly what Bornman and Rose (2010) want to promote through their narrative approach. They argue that inclusion should not 'simply' be driven by external processes, but it should be 'something that impacts on individual lives' (8). This resonates with Allan's (2005: 293) injunction that inclusive education is not something we do to a discrete population of children, but is 'something we must do to ourselves'. I do not dispute the importance of critical personal reflection and also the value of reading accounts of individual experiences with inclusive practices. Nor do Bornman and Rose base their book entirely on individual understandings of inclusive education. They also draw from the field of knowledge production and refer to policy. But, their early and explicit advocacy of a narrative approach which emphasises 'life stories and unravelling beliefs, rather than focusing only on knowledge and skills' (Bornman and Rose 2010: 8), foregrounds the importance they place on a personal practical knowledge of inclusive teaching.

All three textbooks attempt to orientate their readers to an understanding of inclusive education, but each emphasises a different source to inform this understanding. There are other commonalities across all the introductory chapters and I suggest that these can be seen as 'gateway' issues in the presentation of inclusive education. I use the term 'gateway' to indicate the issues that the writers of the three textbooks regard as the 'way in' to introduce inclusive education and the salient ideas that direct a gaze onto the field. The gateway issues foregrounded across these textbooks are: learner diversity, linked to 'barriers to learning'; Bronfenbrenner and bio-ecological or systemic approaches to understanding learners in context; the South African history and policy landscape of inclusive education; and the various 'needs' of an inclusive education system. These include professional development, collaborative relationships, school and systemic reform, and changed beliefs and attitudes, particularly towards learners with disabilities. Two of the three books also introduce readers to the international experience of inclusive education with reference to United Nations initiatives, and explicate the distinction between mainstreaming/integration and inclusion. Table 5.1 summarises how the first chapters of each of the three books address these gateway issues. There is no doubt that these issues can be regarded as important in the development of inclusion at all levels of the education system, and that all of these issues can be grounded in the international and South African literature on inclusive education.

My concern is not with these issues in and of themselves, but with the fact that they form the gateway into inclusive education for readers and thus provide a very particular perspective on the terrain. Many people who know about South Africa know about (and perhaps have visited) the Kruger National Park. A common question asked of visitors to the park is 'Which gate did you go in?' The reason for this

**TABLE 5.1** 'Gateway issues' in inclusive education textbooks

| Textbooks | *Making Inclusive Education Work in Classrooms* (Pienaar and Raymond 2013) | *Addressing Barriers to Learning* (Landsberg et al. 2011) | *Believe That All Can Achieve* (Bornman and Rose 2010) |
|---|---|---|---|
| **Gateway issues:** | | | |
| Learner diversity and barriers to learning | Barriers to learning and development listed with reference to White Paper Six. Linked to the problematic construction of LSEN (Learners with Special Educational Needs). | Barriers to learning discussed from a 'systemic perspective' (19) and with reference to a change in terminology from 'special needs'. | Advocates the celebration of diversity and a 'salad bowl' rather than 'melting pot' metaphor to reflect society. Barriers to learning briefly mentioned, with readers directed to Chapter 2. |
| Bronfenbrenner/ bio-ecological or systemic approaches | Not addressed in Chapter 1. Discussed in Chapter 2. | Extensive, detailed and technical discussion. | Extensive discussion, but used with a 'lens' metaphor and linked to role players in inclusive education. |
| South African history and policy on inclusive education | South Africa's trajectory towards inclusive policy outlined, mention of the constitution and focus on White Paper Six. | Extensive discussion of South Africa's history 'from exclusion to inclusion' (18). | One mention of White Paper Six. Draws extensively on and develops the idea of the roles of the teacher as described by the Norms and Standards for Educators. |
| Need for professional development | Indicated as the first challenge of the implementation of inclusive education. | Professional development of educators is discussed as one of six 'implications of inclusion' (20). | Equipping teachers to 'deal with inclusion' is the focus of the section 'How is inclusion currently being addressed?' |
| Need for collaborative partnerships | Discussed as 'community development and partnerships' (13). | Support and collaboration is discussed as one of six 'implications of inclusion' (20) with 'defining characteristics of collaboration' (21). Home-school-community partnerships mentioned with respect to the mesosystem. | Discussed under the subheading of 'Collaborative team approach'. Also, teachers expected to play critical 'collaborative and pastoral roles' (12). Extensive attention given to 'the child in the home context' with guidelines for teachers working with families. |

TABLE 5.1 'Gateway issues' in inclusive education textbooks (Continued)

| Textbooks | *Making Inclusive Education Work in Classrooms* (Pienaar and Raymond 2013) | *Addressing Barriers to Learning* (Landsberg et al. 2011) | *Believe That All Can Achieve* (Bornman and Rose 2010) |
|---|---|---|---|
| Need for school and systemic reform | Discussed in three paragraphs under the heading of 'School and educational system development' (13). | Vision and leadership, and whole school development are discussed as two of the six 'implications of inclusion' (20). | Brief mention of the role of principals and officials in education departments. |
| Beliefs and attitudes | Mention made of the need to shift teacher attitudes through understanding the goals of inclusive education. | Attitudes and values are discussed as a discrete section under 'implications of inclusion' (20). | Mentions the importance of teacher perceptions and attitudes 'to fully understand inclusion' (8). |
| The difference between mainstreaming and inclusion | Presented as given in White Paper Six (DoE 2001). | Extensive discussion with reference to international literature. | Not mentioned. |
| International history and policy on inclusive education | Brief discussion of inclusion in the USA and UK, UNESCO and the Salamanca statement introduced. | Discusses changing paradigms from medical to (bio) social models in 'international context' (4) and provides some detail on the provisions of Salamanca. | Not mentioned. |

question is that there are a number of possible entry points to the park, and each gate brings the visitor into a different landscape, and different configurations of fauna and flora. In other words, the entry gate determines what one sees and how one sees it. The analogy with inclusive education is that a reader's *way in* to the field will, to a large extent, determine how the field is viewed.

The problem with the gateway issues in the three textbooks is that they are second-order (Slee 2011) issues. They concern the resources and reorganisation that inclusive education implies, but they do not commence with the economic, social and political power structures that lead to exclusion in the first place. The exclusion of certain children from schooling or the marginalisation of children within schooling is not the result of unfortunate personal circumstances, but is the result of structures that systematically privilege certain characteristics and ways of being and disprivilege others. Missing from these chapters is a critical account of current educational arrangements with an indication of how they are sustained by those who benefit from them. In the acknowledgement of the international antecedents of inclusive education, for example, globalisation and colonialism are omitted, with no consideration of how global competition and post-colonial challenges translate into exclusionary practices in the race for 'success'. These are first-order issues, which Slee (2011) says need consideration in thinking about inclusive education. They are, however, largely absent from these three textbooks. This is not to suggest that the textbook writers are not personally concerned with educational exclusion, or that they are fundamentally uncritical of the status quo. But, the ideological screens through which the discourses of inclusive education pass as they become pedagogical discourse are mostly psychological rather than sociological.

A glance at the contributing writers across the three volumes shows a preponderance of psychologists, therapeutic personnel and lecturers in psychology departments. This might explain why Bronfenbrenner is selected from the field of knowledge production and given prominence in the pedagogical discourse. In foregrounding Bronfenbrenner and (bio)eco-systemic theories, writers of all three textbooks explicitly distance themselves from a 'medical' orientation to learner difference and disability. They are all concerned to locate the barriers that learners experience in their learning and development in the interaction of the various systems of which the learner is a part. So as much as individual impairment is identified as a barrier to learning, these writers stress the importance of family, community and wider societal, economic and cultural influences on the learner. I suggest that while this is an attempt to move away from a medical account of individual difference, the learner still tends to be viewed as the embodiment of these influences and is pathologised by association. Many of the gateway issues raised in the first chapters of these books are revisited in chapters devoted to their explication – none more so than learner diversity and barriers to learning. In the section that follows, I comment on how learner difference is constructed by the organisation and content of these textbooks.

## *Learner diversity and barriers to learning*

The writers of the three textbooks have looked to the fields of medicine, special education and psychology to select knowledge to be recontextualised in their textbooks. *Addressing Barriers to Learning* (Landsberg *et al.* 2011) finds its antecedents in *Children with Problems: An Orthopedagogical Perspective* (Kapp 1991). Both texts consider in discrete chapters the various problems or barriers that South African children might have, with the more recent volume reflecting more 'acceptable' terminology (e.g. 'Visual impairment' as a chapter heading instead of 'The visually handicapped'), and additional chapters that include the framework of inclusive education. In Landsberg *et al.* (2011), barriers to learning are clustered into categories such as socio-economic barriers, educational barriers, literacy barriers, attitude barriers and disability, with individual chapters dealing separately with issues like second language difficulties, learning impairment, cerebral palsy and autism. What was a special need, problem or handicap in *Children with Problems* is now a barrier in *Addressing Barriers to Learning*. The textbook retains the formula of marking out some basis on which learners might be deemed different in a way that is problematic for education, describing the causes and effects of this difference and indicating pedagogical responses that are appropriate in response to this difference.

In *Believe That All Can Achieve* (Bornman and Rose 2010), discrete chapters invite readers to 'understand' children 'with' challenging behaviour, intellectual disabilities, learning disabilities, physical disabilities, autism spectrum disorders and medical conditions. Definitions and causes of these disabilities, disorders or conditions are provided, along with characteristics of these children and suggestions and strategies for teachers. Pienaar and Raymond's (2013) edited book, *Making Inclusive Education Work in Classrooms*, gives a chapter to 'Understanding barriers to learning' and then a cluster of chapters to describing the differences among 'learners in our classrooms today'. These are framed as 'challenges related to individual differences', 'cognitive and behavioural challenges' and 'sensory, physical and health challenges' (iii–iv). Details given in the chapters about these challenges also include causes, characteristics and their impact on learning. Skidmore (2002) identifies this as a pedagogical discourse of deviance, such that learning difficulties can be explained by individual deficits, and support requires the remediation of these weaknesses.

The implication of this pedagogical discourse is that inclusive education represents a problem *of* learners, and *for* teachers. Whichever of the three books a teacher or teacher-to-be reads, he or she is likely to be getting the message that:

- Categories of difference among learners are absolute and discrete, evidenced by their being chronicled in different chapters and sections.
- Categories of difference are scientific and objective, and are drawn from evidence in the fields of medicine and psychology.
- Difference is measured against normality, and different learners are characterised by what they cannot think, understand or do.
- Understanding categories of difference is a necessary precondition for understanding learners.
- Categories of difference are pedagogically significant, with different categories demanding different pedagogical responses.
- Whatever the causes of these differences, they present a problem to the teacher in the classroom.

South African textbooks are not alone in this construction of difference. Brantlinger's (2006: 63) evaluation of textbook 'glossies' shows that despite lip-service being paid to inclusive education, the traditional special education concerns of 'assessment, identification, classification and remediation' are not dislodged. Black-Hawkins (2012: 510) found that although the texts she studied about inclusive pedagogical practices were not organised around a categorical approach to learners, aspects of content 'reinforce a categorical approach to learning'. In the South African textbooks, all the categories of barriers or learners described are accompanied by directions for teaching strategies or interventions appropriate to that category.

Readers of any one of these three textbooks would discover that there is teaching for all, and there is teaching for some. Each book contains sections (of varying length) on general teaching practices that would support all learners and promote inclusivity. These include universal design for learning, differentiated instruction and scaffolding, approaches to assessment and cooperative learning. While these sections promote inclusive pedagogy as appropriate for all learners, other sections reinforce findings from Black-Hawkins's (2012: 513) textbook analysis that

> ... 'deviant' learners require provision that is different from, or additional to, that which is made available to the majority 'usual' learners in a class.

Each description of a category of learner or barrier to learning in the South African textbooks includes the impact of the 'barrier' or 'challenge' on learning and how teachers should 'address' the barrier or respond pedagogically to the learner. It seems as if certain learners present as problems for teachers, but these problems can be understood and then solved through effective classroom practices. Some of these solutions or strategies are given as suggestions, some as directives and some as 'tips' (Bornman and Rose 2010: 161). There are 'dos' and 'don'ts' (Bornman and Rose 2010: 85), 'ideas' (Jooste and Jooste 2011: 435) and 'guidelines' (Koudstaal 2011: 353), each specific to teaching learners in particular categories. Often the teaching strategies are presented in bullet form, visually indicating a shift in the communication from explaining the concepts to instructing readers on applying them (van Leeuwen 2006). The bullet points create a visual list, giving an impression of things to do. Some of these are similar to the 'quick-fix' solutions found in the textbooks analysed by Black-Hawkins (2012: 513), who says such advice is 'banal, lacking flexibility and depth'. Dednam (2011: 409), for example, lists no fewer than 31 bullet points on 'accommodation of challenging behaviour and ADHD'. These include not letting learners sit near to 'air conditioners, fans, heaters, windows and doors' and seeing that they 'write down their homework'. Bornman and Rose (2010: xi) are explicitly keen to distance their book from quick fixes or 'other short-term solutions'. They do, however, also present lists of strategies, tips, directions and suggestions for teachers.

There are a number of concerns with these category-specific classroom interventions. Not least of these is that it would be an exceptional teacher who could remember, far less implement, all the solutions, ideas and strategies presented for each category of learner. Inclusive teaching in this discourse is technical, with teachers needing to apply a series of skills and strategies to a bounded problem. The category-specific interventions oversimplify learners' lives and identities, and underplay the complexity of classroom dynamics. This is not only evident in the neat lists and bullet points, but also in the scenarios that intersperse these textbooks. Variously introduced as 'case-studies' (Landsberg 2011), 'learners in inclusive classrooms' (Pienaar and Raymond 2013) and anecdotes in 'stop and reflect' (Bornman and Rose 2010) textboxes, these little tales add a human story to the text. They are visually separated from the main text by the outline of the textbox and the language and style of these anecdotes is quite different from that of the main text.

Often, these 'textbox tales' have named actors, making the stories sound more personal and authentic. These anecdotes have illustrative, and thus didactic, intent and their message tends to be simple. For example, Tshidi, Lianne, Lesedi and Lisel (Moletsane 2013) and Joe (Koudstaal 2011) are all introduced with a list of their difficulties and are presented to exemplify various conditions and diagnoses. Other textbox tales follow a washing powder advertisement formula: the display of dirt or a stain, the use of the advertised product and a celebration of the resulting cleanliness. Using this formula, textbox tale writers typically give a brief rendition of the learner's problem, the application of some or other inclusive strategy and a positive outcome. Heinrich, for instance, was bullied. But after watching a school play about bullying, Heinrich confronted the bully who thanked Heinrich for talking to him. And, as a result, 'He vowed to stop bullying, and a year later has become a popular peer' (Bornman and Rose 2010: 55–6). Mattie's teacher decided to try a different strategy to help her with number bonds. After two weeks of using flash cards, her test scores had 'significantly improved' (Raymond 2013: 111). This is not to say that various strategies have no pedagogical impact. But the message of these textbox tales is problematic for various reasons.

While the bullet point lists of strategies oversimplify, these textbox tales tend to be reductionist, sometimes to the point of caricature. Like the idyllic pictures that Brantlinger (2006) reports in special education glossies, they suggest that classroom interactions are straightforward, with selected interventions having immediate and lasting effects. The reality of inclusive classrooms is quite different and a reader might be disappointed to find that not every intervention has a happy ending. Beyond this simplification of classroom complexity, there is a possibly more sinister underlying impression given that the system is ultimately benign, merely requiring a series of bolt-on strategies for certain learners. The textbox tales do not describe the many exclusionary pressures and practices that pervade schools and education systems and which have the potential to render many inclusive strategies ultimately ineffective or unworkable. There is a misplaced optimism about the impact an individual teacher can have in the face of systemic constraints and wider social, economic and political factors which are complicit in the perpetuation of exclusion.

In summary, then, South African teachers and teachers-to-be can access at least three commercially published textbooks to support their learning about inclusive education. These textbooks reflect a selection from the field of knowledge production made with particular ideological screens. As a result, the predominant pedagogic discourse of inclusive education has a psychological orientation. It is also concerned with two main themes – identifying and describing ways in which learners are different; and describing support strategies in response to these differences. Recognition of learner diversity in teacher education for inclusive education is not necessarily problematic. Inclusive pedagogy requires an acknowledgment of learner difference because a one-size-fits-all pedagogy is the precursor to epistemological marginalisation and the 'silent exclusion' that Lewin (2009: 157) describes.

However, the representation of learner diversity in textbooks obscures the fact that diversity and difference are not value neutral. Diversity is constructed by those with the power to pronounce difference and reflects the characteristics that are valorised by the powerful. Textbook writers decide who to describe as different and which differences matter. As such, difference is taken as self-evident, intrinsic and mostly problematic. In this discourse, the classroom contains the problem, such that it is firmly located in the interaction of individual learner and individual teacher.

## New books, old themes

Some of the older books that talk of the 'subnormal' or the 'retarded' have now been consigned to our library store, accessible to scholars but not immediately available to the casual browser. But newer ones take their place. The language in these textbooks is more acceptable, but the ideologies at work as inclusive education knowledge is pedagogised seem to be intact. It may no longer be acceptable to write about the 'subnormal' child, but a reader browsing the library shelves for textbooks about inclusive education would find much to confirm the idea that certain learners are indeed aberrant (for any number of reasons) and pose challenges to the smooth running of a classroom. The reader would also be enjoined to understand these challenges and then 'address' them by implementing a series of (mostly additional) strategies so that the learner might be included.

Our university libraries and prescribed reading lists need textbooks reflecting a pedagogic discourse of inclusive education recontextualised with different ideological screens. Different gateways into the field might force a shift of gaze beyond the classroom walls to locate the 'challenge' of inclusive education in wider issues of global and local inequality. As a result, the 'diverse learner' might not be seen as an additional burden on an already constrained system. But I conclude with the question that a publisher would ask: 'Is there a market for that kind of approach?'

## Notes

1 The book in question is F. Lloyd (1953) *Educating the Sub-normal Child*. London: Methuen.
2 I use the word textbook with some reservation. Text, on its own, suggests something of the interactional dynamics of reader, author and what is written (Apple and Christian-Smith 1991; Black-Hawkins 2012). Here I am deliberately concerned with those texts written with teacher education in mind, and as likely prescribed or recommended texts for teacher education courses at pre-service or in-service level.
3 I myself have written for textbooks and devised 'textbox tales' (which I critique later in this chapter) to meet the publisher's requirements.
4 The semantic gravity of inclusive education is discussed in Chapter 2.

## References

Allan, J. (2005) 'Inclusion as an ethical project', in S. Tremain (ed.), *Foucault and the Government of Disability*. Ann Arbor, MI: University of Michigan Press, pp. 281–97.
Allan, J. and Slee, R. (2008) *Doing Inclusive Education Research*. Rotterdam: Sense Publishers.

Apple, M. and Christian-Smith, L. (1991) 'The politics of the textbook', in M. Apple and L. Christian-Smith (eds), *The Politics of the Textbook*. New York: Routledge, pp. 1–21.

Bernstein, B. (2000) *Pedagogy, Symbolic Control and Identity: Theory, Research and Critique* (revised edn). Lanham, MD: Rowman & Littlefield.

Black-Hawkins, K. (2012) 'Developing inclusive classroom practices: what guidance do commercially published texts offer teachers?', *European Journal of Special Needs Education*, 27 (4): 499–516.

Bornman, J. and Rose, R. (2010) *Believe That All Can Achieve*. Pretoria: Van Schaik.

Brantlinger, E. (1997) 'Using ideology: cases of nonrecognition of the politics of research and practice in special education', *Review of Educational Research*, 67 (4): 425–59.

Brantlinger, E. (2006) 'The big glossies: how textbooks structure (special) education', in E. Brantlinger (ed.), *Who Benefits from Special Education? Remediating (Fixing) Other People's Children*. Mahwah, NJ: Lawrence Erlbaum Associates, pp. 45–76.

Dednam, A. (2011) 'Learning impairment', in E. Landsberg, D. Kruger and E. Swart (eds), *Addressing Barriers to Learning: A South African Perspective*. Pretoria: Van Schaik, pp. 319–47.

Department of Education (DoE) (2001) *Education White Paper Six: Special Needs Education*. Pretoria: Department of Education.

Donohue, D. and Bornman, J. (2014) 'The challenges of realising inclusive education in South Africa', *SA Journal of Education*, 34 (2): 1–14.

Hall, J. T. (1997) *Social Devaluation and Special Education*. London: Jessica Kingsley.

Horton, W. S. and Gerrig, R. J. (2005) 'The impact of memory demands on audience design during language production', *Cognition*, 96 (2): 127–42.

Janks, H. (2010) *Literacy and Power*. New York: Routledge.

Jooste, C. and Jooste, M. (2011) 'Intellectual impairment', in E. Landsberg, D. Kruger and E. Swart (eds), *Addressing Barriers to Learning: A South African Perspective*, 2nd edn. Pretoria: Van Schaik, pp. 418–45.

Kapp, J. A. (ed.) (1991) *Children with Problems*. Pretoria: Van Schaik.

Koudstaal, C. (2011) 'Autism spectrum disorders', in E. Landsberg, D. Kruger and E. Swart (eds), *Addressing Barriers to Learning: A South African Perspective*, 2nd edn. Pretoria: Van Schaik, pp. 341–62.

Landsberg, E. (2011) 'Learning support', in E. Landsberg, D. Kruger and E. Swart (eds), *Addressing Barriers to Learning: A South African Perspective*, 2nd edn. Pretoria: Van Schaik, pp. 69–86.

Landsberg, E., Kruger, D. and Swart, E. (eds) (2011) *Addressing Barriers to Learning: A South African Perspective*, 2nd edn. Pretoria: Van Schaik.

Lewin, K. (2009) 'Access to education in sub Saharan Africa: patterns, problems and possibilities', *Comparative Education*, 45 (2): 151–74.

Liasidou, A. (2012) *Inclusive Education, Politics and Policymaking*. London: Continuum.

Merrett, C. (1994) *A Culture of Censorship. Secrecy and Intellectual Repression in South Africa*. Cape Town: David Philip.

Moletsane, M. (2013) 'Cognitive and behavioural challenges', in C. Pienaar and E. Raymond (eds), *Making Inclusive Education Work in Classrooms*. Cape Town: Pearson, pp. 60–84.

Ntombela, S. and Raymond, E. (2013) 'Inclusive education in South Africa and globally', in C. Pienaar and E. Raymond (eds), *Making Inclusive Education Work in Classrooms*. Cape Town: Pearson, pp. 2–17.

Pather, S. (2011) 'Evidence on inclusion and support for learners with disabilities in mainstream schools in South Africa: off the policy radar?', *International Journal of Inclusive Education*, 15 (10): 1103–17.

Pienaar, C. (2013) 'Challenges related to individual differences', in C. Pienaar and E. Raymond (eds), *Making Inclusive Education Work in Classrooms*. Cape Town: Pearson, pp. 38–59.

Pienaar, C. and Raymond, E. (eds) (2013) *Making Inclusive Education Work in Classrooms*. Cape Town: Pearson.

Prinsloo, E. (2011) 'Socio-economic barriers to learning in contemporary society', in E. Landsberg, D. Kruger and E. Swart (eds), *Addressing Barriers to Learning: A South African Perspective*, 2nd edn. Pretoria: Van Schaik, pp. 29–47.

Raymond, E. (2013) 'Assessment for teaching and learning', in C. Pienaar and E. Raymond (eds), *Making Inclusive Education Work in Classrooms*. Cape Town: Pearson, pp. 108–31.

Rice, N. (2005) 'Guardians of tradition: presentations of inclusion in three introductory special education textbooks', *International Journal of Inclusive Education*, 9 (4): 405–29.

RSA (2011) *The Minimum Requirements for Teacher Education Qualifications*, Government Gazette 34467. Pretoria: Government Printers.

Singh, P. (2002) 'Pedagogising knowledge: Bernstein's theory of the pedagogic device', *British Journal of Sociology of Education*, 23 (4): 571–82.

Skidmore, D. (2002) 'A theoretical model of pedagogical discourse', *Disability, Culture and Education*, 1 (2): 119–31.

Slee, R. (2011) *The Irregular School*. Abingdon: Routledge.

Swart, E. and Pettipher, R. (2011) 'A framework for understanding inclusion', in E. Landsberg, D. Kruger and E. Swart (eds), *Addressing Barriers to Learning: A South African Perspective*, 2nd edn. Pretoria: Van Schaik, pp. 3–26.

Thieme, K. (2010) 'Constitutive rhetoric as an aspect of audience design: the public texts of Canadian suffragists', *Written Communication*, 27 (1): 36–56.

van Leeuwen, T. (2006) 'Towards a semiotics of typography', *Information Design Journal + Document Design*, 14 (2): 139–55.

Walton, E. (in progress) 'Inclusive education: a tame solution to a wicked problem?', in D. Mahlo, N. Pasha and G. Dei (eds), *Inclusive Education in African Contexts: A Critical Reader*. New York: Peter Lang.

# 6
# LANGUAGING ADHD[1]

## Why learners don't listen

'These learners don't listen because they have a sickness called ADHD. It's caused by eating junk food and sweets.' This was proclaimed by Mrs Ndzaba (not her real name), a teacher in a primary school in Johannesburg where I am involved with professional development and research.[2] The school is newly built and serves a poor community, with many children coming from informal settlements. Classes are large, with between 40 and 48 learners in each class. Many of the teachers are deemed 'underqualified', which means that they have a three-year teaching diploma, attained during the time when this was sufficient for foundation phase (grade 1–3) teaching.[3] My work in the school involves the development of Professional Learning Communities (PLCs) in support of the school's status as a 'full-service' or inclusive school. In the context of small groups of teachers discussing the development of listening skills among their foundation phase learners, this conversation caught my ear. The teachers had said that they were struggling to teach when learners misbehave. There had been very productive conversations in the PLC groups about enhancing listening and attention, with a valuable focus on the multilingual background of the learners. This was effectively curtailed as Mrs Ndzaba, who has an additional qualification in special needs education, weighed in on the discussion. Her comment about ADHD drew immediate interest from the five group members, none of whom seemed to have had previous knowledge of ADHD. Mrs Ndzaba (now holding the floor) informed the group that these 'ADHD children' would never listen in class until they were given medicine. It was a problem, she said, peculiar to cities because teachers in rural provinces seldom teach children who are inattentive. The group meeting then closed with general agreement that the teachers needed to be 'workshopped' on the topic of ADHD.

This incident is interesting for different reasons, not least of which is the imagination of classrooms where teachers are working with inattentiveness not as a pathology, but as an expected part of children's learning. Without ADHD as a default explanation for children's behaviour, these teachers had been getting on with the business of teaching and learning. They were clearly concerned with behavioural challenges but saw these challenges as requiring pedagogical responses. Their naivety about ADHD is striking, especially since Gauteng province (where this school is situated) has the highest incidence of ADHD in South Africa. Countrywide, ADHD accounts for 7.54 per cent of the total recorded incidence of disability in special schools, yet it accounts for 10.45 per cent of the incidence of disability in Gauteng (Department of Basic Education (DBE) 2014). It seems likely that the higher incidence of ADHD in Gauteng is related to the fact that the province is the most affluent and urbanised province and medical and psychological services are relatively more available here than in other parts of the country (Walton 2015). This may well confirm Tait's (2010: 22) contention that 'differences in the statistics relating to diagnosis are solely a reflection of social issues'.

Mrs Ndzaba's observation that inattentiveness is unknown in rural areas is not borne out by research. In Limpopo province, which is relatively poor and mostly rural, researchers are confident that ADHD characteristics (though not necessarily medical diagnoses) are evident and comparable with incidence elsewhere. Meyer *et al.* (2004: 132) used the Disruptive Behaviour Disorders (DBDs) rating scale in a study in Limpopo province, and found

> ... surprisingly small cultural differences in the structure and prevalence of ADHD-like behaviour between various South African cultures as well as between South African and other 'Western' cultures.

In her study of teachers from Limpopo, Moodley (2015: 104) reports that teachers in an in-service programme 'indicated inattention and distractibility to be a major behavioural challenge' and linked these behaviours to 'the label of hyperactivity despite not having confirmed medical reports to substantiate their claim'. Unlike the teachers in the Johannesburg school, the teachers in Moodley's sample seem conversant with ADHD, possibly having learned about it during their in-service teacher education programme.

The teachers in Mrs Ndzaba's PLC group qualified as teachers quite some time ago and may not have not been exposed to the various 'upgrading' qualifications or 'training' programmes offered by non-government organisations or provincial education departments (Taylor *et al.* 2013), hence their request to be 'workshopped' about this 'sickness' called ADHD. The noun 'workshop' is found as a verb not only in conversation but also in policy, with one policy document saying that 'therapists or other relevant experts ... will workshop teachers' (Gauteng Department of Education (GDE) 2011: 17). It is well documented that nouns surface in language use as verbs (Clark and Clark 1979). The shift in language from attending a workshop to being workshopped is significant in terms of what it reveals about South African teachers and their experience of professional development through workshops. Teachers who attend (or participate in) a workshop are the subject of the verb, and thus active agents in the material process (Halliday and Matthiessen 2004; Janks 2010) of attending (or participating in) an event. When teachers are workshopped, they lose their agency, and become the passive objects of an action. I do not want to digress here and engage with the complex issues regarding professional development for teachers in South Africa[4] but I do want to highlight the problem of teachers positioning themselves (or being positioned) as the acted upon, rather than the actors in their professional learning. This is compounded by the fact that professional development has increasingly become associated with educational underperformance in South Africa (Gravett 2013), and that teacher incompetence is a well-worn complaint. In this climate, teachers are less likely to question what is presented to them. This is salient when it comes to inclusive education, and to ADHD in particular. As teachers become aware of ADHD in South Africa, they may well move from general thinking that securing learner concentration and attention is pedagogically important, to thinking that securing an ADHD label is pedagogically important. Teachers who read and study further or attend workshops are likely to be exposed to an orthodoxy of ADHD, as my discussion of ADHD in the section that follows shows.

## ADHD in South Africa

Unlike other countries where the waters of ADHD are choppy with debate about this 'condition', ADHD in South Africa is something of a glassy pond, with barely a ripple on the surface. The 'truth' of ADHD is generally uncontested in this country and as a result, ADHD has become an 'over-all "discursive fact"' (Foucault 1976: 11). My intention is to agitate the waters somewhat by interrogating the way in which ADHD is languaged and how this positions the 'child with ADHD' and his or her teacher and parents and the school. This is important because addressing and eliminating exclusion requires that we recognise the power of language to construct and direct our thinking about ourselves and Others. In South Africa, there seems to be overwhelmingly uncritical acceptance that *ADHD is*. Other countries have seen scholars interrogate the diagnostic criteria, discrepancies in rates of diagnosis, the treatment and the purposes that the ADHD label serves (Slee 2010). By contrast, South African literature shows remarkable confidence in the fact or truth of ADHD as a disability (Department of Education (DoE) 2009; Kokot 2006), special need (Du Toit and Forlin 2009) or barrier to learning (Magare *et al.* 2010). With voices of authority, authors use the indicative mood to state what ADHD *is*, for example 'ADHD *is* a universal disease …' (Erasmus 2009: 9) and 'ADHD *is* a challenging condition' (Maema 2009: 90) (emphasis mine). The child 'with ADHD' is described with assurance as 'never organised' (Wilke 2009: xxiv) and 'present[ing] emotional problems, social problems, behaviour problems, learning problems and/or lack of motivation' (Hyam 2009: 81). Where teachers are given guidance for 'managing' (Bornman and Rose 2010: 142) children 'with ADHD', the fact of the condition is first assumed and descriptions of possible interventions and classroom strategies proceed from there (Bornman and Rose 2010, Maema 2009; Staniforth 2009).

The orthodoxy regarding ADHD in the South African literature might be expected given entrenched and conservative epistemologies based on notions of segregated education in this country. The advent of democracy in 1994 saw the abandonment of legalised racially segregated education, and legislation (The South African Schools Act (Republic of South Africa 1996)) and policy (*White Paper Six: Special Needs Education* (DoE 2001)) pave the way for inclusive education. However, separate special schools still exist in South Africa; in fact, they are conceived as part of the inclusive education system. Learners who attend special schools '… have been assessed to be in need of high levels of support' (DoE 2008: 7). Thus the system identifies and sorts learners according to their support needs and 'places' them accordingly. This provision justifies and perpetuates the idea across the system that learners can be categorised according to their deficiencies (what they need) and that meeting the needs of some learners is beyond the capacity of the ordinary school. The policy and rhetoric of inclusion in this country is careful to distance itself from a medical or deficit approach to 'special needs' by emphasising systemic barriers to learning (DoE 2001) and positioning inclusive education as being more than a disability issue. Despite this, textbooks, like the widely prescribed *Addressing Barriers to Learning* (Landsberg et al. 2011) describe, in discrete chapters, the characteristics of various types of barriers to learning and suggest classroom strategies that teachers might use to teach individual children who experience these barriers. As was noted in Chapter 5, the authoritative and depersonalised tone set by 'experts' in the various disabilities in these texts create the epistemic climate for the unquestioning acceptance of a 'disorder' called 'attention deficit and/or hyperactivity'.

Language and thinking are inextricably linked. The language we use reflects the way we think about things, and ways of thinking are made possible by the language we use. Thus, conceptual constructions can be accessed by examining language use but, in turn, language constructs these concepts. As Swain (2006: 97) expresses it: 'Languaging serves to mediate cognition.' Languaging is a term that would be familiar to those in the field of additional language learning, and is useful here because of its emphasis on the way that knowledge is shaped through language. ADHD knowledge has been shaped by language used in different domains. These include the policy domain where ADHD is languaged in policy, guidelines and other government-issued documents. In the professional domain, ADHD is languaged in scholarly writing and research in the academy and through textbooks, workshops and conferences for teachers and other personnel working in schools. ADHD is languaged in the public domain through magazines and newspaper articles, and publically accessible online support groups.

Language constructs ADHD in three distinct categories, which can be identified across all the domains. While drawing on the South African context, I can make no claims for the uniqueness of these categories, with Graham (2008) finding similar patterns in the way in which ADHD is constructed. In the sections that follow, I look at what knowledge about ADHD South Africans in the field of education are likely to encounter and consider how language constructs this knowledge. My reading of texts across the domains suggests that ADHD is a problem in one of three categories: a type of medical disease, a type of behavioural disorder and a type of learning impairment or disability. These categories are not absolute or uncontested. South African education statistics (DBE 2014) list ADHD as a quantifiable disability separate from other behavioural disorders and from learning disabilities. Textbooks in the professional domain, however, make ADHD a subcategory of behavioural or learning disabilities/difficulties. First, though, I want to explore the medical perspective because it seems to be pre-eminent.

## ADHD is a medical disease

The most prevalent conceptual construction of ADHD in South Africa is that it is a disease and thus a type of medical problem. I am deliberately choosing not to engage here with claims about the bio-neurological processes underlying some of the symptoms clustered under the heading of ADHD. Instead, attention is drawn to the fact that medical vocabulary like 'diagnosis', 'symptoms', 'suffer from', 'treatment', 'therapy' and 'disease' is prevalent as ADHD is languaged across all the domains. The medical 'facts' of ADHD are the standard introduction to sections on ADHD in textbooks used by pre-service and in-service teachers. 'Diagnosis' is the first section of *Teaching and ADHD in the Southern African Classroom* (Decaires-Wagner and Picton 2009) with the 'medical perspective' as the first chapter in this volume. The section on ADHD in *The Guidelines for Inclusive Teaching and Learning* (DBE 2010: 94) begins with the statement that 'ADHD is a neurobehavioral disorder of childhood affecting between 3 and 10% of school-age children'. Typically, these opening sections refer to the diagnostic criteria of ADHD from the *Diagnostic and Statistical Manual of Mental Disorders* (DSM) (American Psychiatric Association 2000/2013) and offer the epidemiology of ADHD. The fronting of the medical credentials of ADHD in these texts works to secure the foundational 'truth' of ADHD as an objective, scientifically described disease. It pre-empts challenge by offering facts and figures which seem indisputable, and uses specialised terminology like 'dopamine and noradrenergic systems' (Erasmus 2009: 6) which reminds non-medical people of their relative lack of knowledge. The aetiology of ADHD is sometimes presented in these foundational sections and ranges from neurobiology (DBE 2010) to genetics as well as environmental and dietary factors (Bornman and Rose 2010). These authoritative sections then set the scene for the subsequent use of the words 'symptoms', 'diagnosis' and 'treatment' in the 'management' of ADHD.

As happens in other countries, South African teachers have been 'influenced by the truth-shaping power of the medical authorities and the drug companies' (Tait 2010: 25). Pharmaceutical companies enjoy a presence at various teacher conferences and sometimes sponsor delegate gifts or catering (South African Association for Learning and Educational Differences (SAALED) 2008, 2011). At one of these conferences, a booklet written 'with the intention of improving the understanding of ADHD' (Novartis n.d.) was placed in each delegate's conference bag. This is a multimodal text, where the layout, use of headings and written text work together to lead readers to the inexorable conclusion that medication really is necessary to treat ADHD. Information about the nature, causes and diagnosis of ADHD is followed by a section on possible co-morbid conditions. Significantly, no source for the information is offered and it seems that the reader must accept that the author of the booklet, although not named, is to be trusted. The reader is thus patronised, with the assumption that he or she will uncritically accept the 'science' contained in the booklet. The second half of the booklet is concerned with treatment, with medication being introduced after mention of behaviour modification and diet and nutritional supplements. The third-person, informative writing style of the booklet then gives way to a direct engagement with parents using the second person, moving them from general knowledge about ADHD to challenging them personally. Parents are assured that if their children's education, relationships and personal well-being are 'suffering' then medication is 'probably the most effective form of treatment there is' (Novartis n.d.: 14). After lists of various medications that are available and their possible adverse effects, the readers are offered 'A mother's perspective' (17–18). The mother (who is unnamed) shares 'a success story' of her child who 'was earning a reputation for being a monster'. The child was prescribed medication and ended up as a 'happier little boy' who was 'liked by his teachers and peers'. The narrative of this mother's perspective is in the first person, the effect of which is to stifle questions, as who would dare to contradict the truth of a personal testimony? There is much in this booklet that bears comment, not least the way in which the language and layout of the text constructs parents and teachers as uninformed. This echoes Allan's (2013: 1246) reference to Brantlinger who suggested that parents in disadvantaged contexts are 'made to believe that their child has a medicalized condition'. This, she said, was 'an exercise of power on the powerless'.

Whether through booklets like these or from presentations at conferences or from various textbooks, teachers accumulate wisdom about the 'disease' of ADHD. With knowledge of the 'symptoms' of ADHD, the teacher can 'suspect' that certain children 'have ADHD' (Decaires-Wagner and Picton 2009: 1). Teachers become the examiners of children's behaviour (Foucault 1977), alert to ways in which it might deviate from what is considered 'normal'. Informing teachers of the 'medical perspective' on ADHD, Erasmus (2009) delineates 'normal development' (3) before describing the 'constellation of symptoms' (4) on which a diagnosis is based. Teachers are encouraged by Dednam (2011: 410) to support parents by 'referring them to a neurologist'. They may be given rating scales to document instances of inattention, hyperactivity or impulsivity, or they may be directed to the Screening, Identification, Assessment and Support (SIAS) (DoE 2008) process. The latter entails lengthy documentation of observed characteristics and the outcomes of efforts to provide 'support'. If necessary, additional assessments may be recommended, and a 'diagnostic profile' is drawn up for learners now deemed as having 'additional support needs' (DoE 2008). The child thus becomes a 'case' as he or she is 'described, judged, measured [and] compared with others' (Foucault 1977: 191).

In South Africa, a teacher's recommendation that parents seek medical attention for their child's 'symptoms' is no small matter, particularly in poor communities.

A trip to a hospital or clinic for an evaluation or to fill a repeat script is likely to be costly in terms of transport as well as a day lost from work. Given the relative disempowerment that poor parents feel in their interaction with schools (Smit and Liebenberg 2003), these parents may not question the necessity of such an intervention. I am also aware of parents who fear that if they do not acquiesce to the request to seek medical intervention, their children will not be given the support they need from teachers.

Diagnosis may provide relief for parents (and teachers) who thereby find an acceptable explanation for the child's behaviours and difficulties as well as treatment options (Novartis n.d.; Croock 2009). They are now exonerated from accusations of bad parenting or incompetence when their children's behaviour does not conform to their expectations. Because the child is diseased, she or he can no longer be held responsible as the 'illness' manifests in challenging behaviour or poor school performance. In this regard, the ADHD label could have a protective effect, although the research is ambivalent in this regard (Frederickson 2010). Importantly, if ADHD is a type of medical problem, then medication is the obvious solution. In the international literature, teachers have been criticised for being quick to recommend medication (Snider *et al.* 2003; Stobo 2007) to reduce disruptive behaviour and make classroom control easier (Gottlieb 2002; Phillips 2006). In South Africa, there seems to be comparably less critique of the advocacy for, and use of medication for children with an ADHD diagnosis. Erasmus (2009: 9) assures teachers that 'Combined treatments, including medication, result in improved child and family functioning.' Teachers are enjoined to 'make sure' that learners take their medicine, or 'subtly remind them to take it' by keeping a 'glass or flask of water in [the] classroom for this purpose' (Dednam 2011: 410).

The child with an ADHD diagnosis (or, more commonly, the 'ADHD child') is now marked as not only different, but deviant. We cannot overlook the associations of disease or disorder with notions of abnormality, deficit and deviance. Disease (and disability) is measured against our construction of normalcy and diagnosis effectively divides people into those whose bodies, minds, behaviours and emotions conform to what we have agreed is normal and those who do not so conform. There is thus something wrong with children with ADHD. This view of ADHD as a pathology is shored up by South African authors who language ADHD as a threat (Theron 2009), a burden (Fourie 2009) and a struggle (van Vuuren 2009). I have a final concern about positioning ADHD as a medical problem. This is the potential for homogenising children with ADHD and essentialising their experiences. Many childhood diseases commonly known to parents and teachers have clear symptoms and prognoses, enabling them to predict with some confidence the course and effect of the disease. ADHD is different in this regard. In referring to the (now outdated) DSM-IV criteria, Venter (2006) presents four possible subtypes of ADHD, and a child diagnosed with ADHD would show at least six out of nine possible symptoms of inattention or hyperactivity-impulsivity. This suggests that there will be significant variation among children with an ADHD diagnosis, and yet the various domains show remarkable confidence in recognising 'ADHD child(ren)'

(Perold et al. 2010: 464). Thus languaged, ADHD defines the child's identity. Often, ADHD becomes the child's identity, as the person is erased entirely. Instead of having ADHD, the learner 'is ADHD'. This is typified by a parent's comment on the Facebook page of the Attention Deficit Hyperactivity Support Group of South Africa: '… my son is ADHD' (https://www.facebook.com/ADHASA. ADHD).

Once the central 'fact' of ADHD as a medical disease is established it is then languaged as a behavioural disorder and/or as a learning disability.

## ADHD is a behaviour disorder

Apparently, there is 'a general climate of undisciplined behaviour and an aversion to the acceptance of authority' and a 'rising tide of unruliness' in South African classrooms (Prinsloo and Gasa 2011: 490). It seems that explicitly or implicitly, ADHD is implicated in this problem of challenging behaviour. In fact, the *Guidelines for Inclusive Teaching and Learning* (DBE 2010: 94) suggests the reduction of 'violent behaviours in schools' may be achieved by 'early identification and intervention' of ADHD to 'offset the development of oppositional defiance disorder (ODD) and conduct disorder (CD)'. In the book *Making Inclusive Education Work in Classrooms*, Moletsane (2013: 77) describes 'Attention-deficit/hyperactive disorders (ADHD)' under the heading of 'Challenges related to differences in behavioural functioning'. In this schema, ADHD is clustered with 'emotional or behavioural disorders' and 'autism-spectrum disorders'.[5] Savitz and Jansen (2005) also classify ADHD as a behaviour disorder in their paper on 'Mainstream and remedial school Attention Deficit Hyperactivity Disorder boys'. The way ADHD is languaged as disorderly behaviour in the professional domain offers a bleak picture for teachers. ADHD behaviour is described as 'boisterous' and 'difficult to manage' (Hyam 2009: 81, 83). Teachers are warned that children with ADHD may do unruly things like 'throw tantrums' or 'throw stones' (Steinmann and Botha 2009: 108). ADHD as a behaviour disorder positions the child as requiring management and control by his or her proximal adults. So, classroom teachers have to 'manage' ADHD (Holz and Lessing 2002; Perold et al. 2010) as do doctors (Venter 2006) and parents (Picton 1997). Classroom teachers should seat children with ADHD sensibly, and help them become better organised with 'structured procedures' (Staniforth 2009: 57). Dednam (2011: 409) provides a list of ways in which classroom teachers should address 'challenging behaviour and AD/HD', including applying rules, punishment, organisational techniques and structure. Maema (2009: 91) advocates 'positive discipline' and 'behaviour modification' as a means to develop 'self-discipline'. The behaviour of a 'difficult child' can be improved, according to Hyam (2009: 84), by goal setting, rewards and punishment, and implementing and monitoring a programme.

Whether with the more benign words of 'organisation', 'structure' and 'management' or the more regimental and coercive words of 'discipline', 'control' or 'punish', this language constructs the child as the passive object of adult actions. In Foucauldian terms this is making others' bodies the objects and targets of power and determining the technique, speed and efficiency of how these bodies operate (Foucault 1977). Thus the 'management' of ADHD as a behaviour disorder is a normalising venture intent on constraining and directing, and on enforcing conformity and homogeneity. To this end, South African teachers are enjoined to engage in surveillance (Foucault 1977) by seating children with ADHD where teachers can 'keep constant eye contact' (Staniforth 2009: 57) and to apply penalties through 'immediate and frequent consequences' (Maema 2009: 91) for negative behaviour. ADHD as a behaviour disorder makes the unacceptable or deviant behaviour the focus of the problem. This focus shifts somewhat when ADHD is cast as a learning problem. Behaviours associated with an ADHD diagnosis are still of concern in this category, but their negative impact on teaching and learning is foregrounded. The behaviours are problematic insofar as they constrain learning, both for the learner with an ADHD diagnosis and for his or her classmates.

## ADHD is a learning disability/impairment

Two well-known and often-cited South African books in the professional domain situate ADHD as a learning impairment (Dednam 2011) or learning disability (Bornman and Rose 2010). The first, arguably the most influential text in teacher education for inclusive education in South Africa, is *Addressing Barriers to Learning* (Landsberg et al. 2011[6]). Here, ADHD is presented under the chapter titled 'Learning impairment', with the motivation that special attention needs to be given to 'this disorder' because 'more than 50 per cent of learners with learning impairment experience ADHD' (Dednam 2011: 404). The second book is *Believe That All Can Achieve* (Bornman and Rose 2010), where ADHD is explicitly positioned as a 'type of learning disability', given first place before 'dyslexia, dyscalculia, dysgraphia and dyspraxia' (133).

In situating ADHD as some kind of learning impairment or learning disability, ADHD becomes a barrier to learning for the child thus diagnosed. 'Barriers to learning' has been the term adopted in South Africa to explain why some learners do not succeed at school. The term was designed to replace 'special needs' which has been associated with a medical model of disability and a difference as deficit discourse. *White Paper Six* (DoE 2001) divides barriers into intrinsic barriers that arise from within the learner, including impairments, developmental delays and illness, and extrinsic barriers like family, educational and societal factors that impede access and participation. 'Barriers to learning' or 'learners who experience barriers to learning' are terms that enjoy widespread use in policy (DoE 2008, 2009), in scholarship (Engelbrecht 2006: 255) and in textbooks for teachers (Landsberg et al. 2011). The notion that learners *experience* barriers signals an attempt to avoid locating deficit within the learners. But 'learners who experience barriers to learning' has often become shortened to 'learners with barriers' (Alant and Casey 2005; DBE 2010; GDE 2009) and the barrier is located firmly with the learner once more. ADHD is described as one such barrier to learning (Bizos 2009; Decaires-Wagner 2009; Hattingh and du Plessis 2004; Kokot 2006).

One of the tasks of the inclusive education system is to 'address' barriers to learning that learners experience (DoE 2001). It is not always clear exactly what is meant by 'addressing' a barrier to learning. Addressing is usually understood as either speaking to or writing to but this is not likely to be what those who coined the phrase had in mind. (That is not to say I am not interested in the way in which 'addressing' a barrier might be a way of speaking it into existence.) It seems that 'addressing barriers' is used in the sense of doing something about them – either eliminating them, reducing them or finding ways to circumvent them. While ADHD as a learning disability or impairment still locates the problem firmly within the child, the professional domain is replete with suggestions about what teachers could or should do to promote learning when faced with this 'barrier'. These suggestions range from reducing environmental stimuli (for example, that teachers wear 'soft coloured clothes in … unpatterned material' because learners may focus on the patterns instead of on teachers' faces 'and what they are saying' (Dednam 2011: 409)), to managing classroom behaviour (Hyam 2009) and adapting curriculum, instruction and assessment (Bornman and Rose 2010; Dednam 2011; DBE 2010). These suggestions (or 'Tips for teachers' (Matentjie 2009: 74)) are usually presented as bulleted lists, a format which I argue[7] trivialises the need for considered professional judgment in response to learner differences that are pedagogically significant. Offered as ways in which teachers should modify their approaches, these tips sound like inclusive gestures. However, the way ADHD is languaged in the various domains may not bode well for inclusive education in South Africa.

## Some implications for inclusive education

In this final section, I would like to draw the linguistic construction of these three ADHD categories together to consider how they may impact the inclusion project in South Africa. Identifying three categories is a heuristic device because in naturally occurring discourse these categories overlap, compounding the 'problem' of ADHD. This is well illustrated in the words of an email from ADHASA (The Attention Deficit and Hyperactivity Support Group of Southern Africa). It was sent to encourage teachers to attend a one-day conference:

> Charlie decided that there must be something terribly wrong with her. She had always wanted to be a teacher and had visions of being *the perfect teacher* … and here she was frustrated out of her mind. She had many beautiful children and usually looked forward to her day … until she remembered Logan! Logan was disruptive, disorganized, argumentative, antisocial, didn't do his work, and his books were a disaster. She'd had enough. She couldn't handle his temper outbursts any more. She'd come to the terrible conclusion that there was only one way to survive … and that was to crush him. At the same time she couldn't help feeling a little bit guilty about this child. With mixed feelings she booked to attend the ADHASA Teachers Conference – as far as she was concerned Logan was a spoilt brat and little could be done for him.

She was most surprised to find Logan's symptoms being described – even ridiculous things like walking around the classroom when he was supposed to be sitting; she also realized he wasn't being difficult, that he had social and emotional difficulties. That was just the beginning – it was as if someone had been sitting in the classroom watching them. She also learnt about other children and recognized some of their challenges. Best of all she went home armed with many solutions and strategies.

Charlie had more tools, and they helped many pupils. To her amazement, the child who showed the most improvement was Logan – the greatest surprise was when she recognized how hard he was trying to win her approval. Take this opportunity to make teaching more rewarding and join us at the ADHASA conference …

This vignette captures how children and teachers in South Africa are positioned as ADHD is languaged. The child, Logan, is characterised by his deficits, and he clearly isn't one of the 'beautiful' children in the class. He is the cause of the teacher's frustration and a threat to her survival in the classroom. The beleaguered teacher, Charlie, is promised the following at the conference:

> Understanding why non-verbal cues are important; medications used for ADHD – Ritalin, Strattera, Concerta as well as other medications used over and above them; the link between diet and behaviour; why children with poor social and emotional intelligence struggle to be accepted by others or to make friends; and split sessions to accommodate both Junior School Teachers and High School Teachers on 'Accommodations and Teaching Strategies to Help Students with ADHD'.
>
> *(ADHASA 2014[8])*

The conference concerns itself with the 'problem' of ADHD in medical, behavioural and learning terms, and offers Charlie insight into children's 'symptoms' and 'challenges'. She leaves with 'solutions and strategies' which lead to Logan's improvement and the restoration of teaching as a rewarding endeavour. The story of Charlie and Logan reflects the conventionalised advertising story structure of problem – intervention – happy ending with problem solved, much like the textbox tales described in the previous chapter. Its use of hyperbole in words like 'crush' creates emotive appeal, and needs to be read in the context of the genre of advertising. The story does, however, reflect the child with ADHD languaged as a threat and the teacher as beleaguered and disempowered by her apparent lack of information about ADHD. Expert knowledge, offered here via a conference, makes all the difference, and enables the teacher to return to the battleground of the classroom 'armed' with solutions.

In South Africa, referral to a special school may follow an ADHD diagnosis, given that special education is reserved for learners deemed to have moderate or high support needs. Whether or not the learner remains in the ordinary classroom once a deficit label has been ingrained in thinking and speaking, it is very difficult for individuals to see beyond the negativity that the label connotes (Danforth and Navarro 2001). Roffey (2010: 281) concurs, saying: 'When dominant discourses are negative, it is hard for individuals to counter with a more constructive view of a young person.' We seem to have little restraint in how we language the child with an ADHD diagnosis. Whether it is Logan who is a 'brat', ruining things for the 'perfect teacher', or the unnamed child in the Novartis narrative who was being a 'monster', we do not spare the invective. Nor do we shy away from the scaremongering, by cautioning against the violent behaviours or compounded problems that might accompany delays in identifying ADHD.

As ADHD is languaged in South Africa, teaching and schooling generally escape blame for children's inattention, impulsivity and hyperactivity (given that these behaviours are deemed aberrant). Our language produces the teacher as the harbinger of the 'solution', as if applying a series of tips and tools compensates for the structures of education that work to pathologise, marginalise and ultimately exclude non-conforming learners. In a drive for school improvement in the face of abysmal schooling outcomes for South African learners[9] there is a fast-paced curriculum where the emphasis is on curriculum coverage to the possible detriment of mastery (Kennedy 2004) and on standardised national assessments in key grades every year. This curriculum and these assessments must be implemented in schools where classrooms are crowded and facilities for play and sport are limited. Many teachers cling to the authoritarian roles of the past and have rigid ideas about what constitutes acceptable behaviour. In this context, it is likely that a child who learns or behaves 'against the grain'[10] will be identified as somehow problematic. How better to preserve the status quo than to harness the knowledge of ADHD and language the child as being a burden and having a barrier? Thus the way we do education in South Africa is exempted from critical self-reflection. Inclusive education is reduced to an elaborate series of tips, tools and techniques as we tinker on the edges of our practice to 'include' learners with this disease or disorder or learning disability.

## Notes

1 The acronym ADHD is commonly used as a shortened form for Attention Deficit Hyperactivity Disorder. Sometimes, hyperactivity is bracketed off, to indicate the possibility of an attention deficit without hyperactivity. Sometimes, too, a forward slash precedes hyperactivity for the same reason. I have chosen not to add these additional punctuation marks, unless quoting from a source that does.
2 Details of this project can be found in Walton (under review).
3 A four-year qualification with a degree is now required to qualify as a teacher in any phase in South Africa.
4 Refer to E. Walton, N. M. Nel, H. Muller and L. D. M. Lebeloane (2014) '"You can train us until we are blue in our faces, we are still going to struggle": teacher professional learning in a full-service school', *Education as Change*, 18 (2): 319–33.
5 This is a noteworthy classification decision taken by the textbook authors. In the DSM-V, ADHD is grouped together with autism spectrum disorders under neurodevelopmental disorders. Emotional/behavioural disorders fall under the category of 'disruptive, impulse-control and conduct disorders' in the DSM-V (American Psychiatric Association (APA) 2013).

6 With a more detailed consideration of the role textbooks play in teacher education for inclusive education offered in Chapter 5 of this book, I wish to signal here the influence that the construction of ADHD in *Addressing Barriers to Learning* would have among South African teachers.
7 In Chapter 5.
8 Email correspondence, used with permission.
9 Taylor et al. (2013: 3) say that South Africa 'performs poorly compared with many of its more impoverished neighbours, and very poorly in relation to developing countries in other parts of the world'.
10 With acknowledgment to M. Cochran-Smith (2004) *Walking the Road. Race, Diversity, and Social Justice in Teacher Education*. New York: Teachers College Press.

## References

Alant, E. and Casey, M. (2005) 'Assessment concessions for learners with impairments', *South African Journal of Education*, 25 (3): 185–9.
Allan, J. (2013) 'Including ideology', *International Journal of Inclusive Education*, 17 (12): 1241–52.
American Psychiatric Association (APA) (2000/2013) *Diagnostic and Statistical Manual of Mental Disorders*, 4/5th edn, text revised. Washington, DC: APA.
Bizos, E. (2009) 'Understanding learners with special educational needs', in A. Decaires-Wagner and H. Picton (eds), *Teaching and ADHD in the Southern African Classroom*. Johannesburg: Macmillan, pp. 30–6.
Bornman, J. and Rose, J. (2010) *Believe That All Can Achieve*. Pretoria: Van Schaik.
Brantlinger E. (2006) 'The big glossies: how textbooks structure (special) education', in E. Brantlinger (ed.), *Who Benefits from Special Education? Remediating (Fixing) Other People's Children*. Mahwah, NJ: Lawrence Erlbaum Associates, pp. 45–76.
Clark, E. and Clark, H. (1979) 'When nouns surface as verbs', *Language*, 45 (4): 767–811.
Croock, M. (2009) 'Psycho-educational assessment', in A. Decaires-Wagner and H. Picton (eds), *Teaching and ADHD in the Southern African Classroom*. Johannesburg: Macmillan, pp. 19–23.
Danforth, S. and Navarro, V. (2001) 'Hyper talk: sampling the social construction of ADHD in everyday language', *Anthropology and Education Quarterly*, 32 (2): 167–90.
Decaires-Wagner, A. (2009) 'Developing self esteem', in A. Decaires-Wagner and H. Picton (eds), *Teaching and ADHD in the Southern African Classroom*. Johannesburg: Macmillan, pp. 151–5.
Decaires-Wagner, A. and Picton, H. (2009) 'Section 1: Diagnosis', in A. Decaires-Wagner and H. Picton (eds), *Teaching and ADHD in the Southern African Classroom*. Johannesburg: Macmillan.
Dednam, A. (2011) 'Learning impairment', in E. Landsberg, D. Kruger and E. Swart (eds), *Addressing Barriers to Learning: A South African Perspective*, 2nd edn. Pretoria: Van Schaik, pp. 319–417.
Department of Basic Education (DBE) (2010) *Guidelines for Inclusive Teaching and Learning*. Pretoria: Department of Education.
Department of Basic Education (DBE) (2014) *Education Statistics in South Africa 2012*. Pretoria: Department of Education.
Department of Education (DoE) (2001) *Education White Paper Six: Special Needs Education: Building an Inclusive Education and Training System*. Pretoria: Department of Education.
Department of Education (DoE) (2008) *National Strategy on Identification, Assessment and Support*. Pretoria: Department of Education.
Department of Education (DoE) (2009) *Guidelines for Full-Service/Inclusive Schools*. Pretoria: Department of Education.

Du Toit, P. and Forlin, C. (2009) 'Cultural transformation for inclusion, what is needed? A South African perspective', *School Psychology International*, 30 (6): 644–55.
Engelbrecht, P. (2006) 'The implementation of inclusive education in South Africa after ten years of democracy', *European Journal of Psychology of Education*, 21 (3): 253–64.
Erasmus, J. (2009) 'Attention Deficit Hyperactivity Disorder – the medical perspective', in A. Decaires-Wagner and H. Picton (eds), *Teaching and ADHD in the Southern African Classroom*. Johannesburg: Macmillan, pp. 2–10.
Foucault, M. (1976) *The Will to Knowledge. The History of Sexuality:1*. London: Penguin.
Foucault, M. (1977) *Discipline and Punish*. London: Penguin.
Fourie, J. (2009) 'Stress in children living with ADHD', in A. Decaires-Wagner and H. Picton (eds) *Teaching and ADHD in the Southern African Classroom*. Johannesburg: Macmillan, pp. 156–64.
Frederickson, N. (2010) 'Bullying or befriending? Children's responses to classmates with special needs', *British Journal of Special Education*, 37 (1): 4–12.
Gauteng Department of Education (GDE) (2009) *Circular 20 of 2009: Application on Behalf of a Learner with Barriers to Learning for a Special Concession*. Johannesburg: Gauteng Department of Education.
Gauteng Department of Education (GDE) (2011) *Inclusion Strategy for Early Identification and Support Provisioning for Learners Experiencing Barriers to Learning and Development 2011–2015*. Johannesburg: Gauteng Department of Education.
Gottlieb, S. (2002) '1.6 million elementary school children have ADHD, says report', *British Medical Journal*, 324: 1296.
Graham, L. (2008) 'Drugs, labels and (p)ill-fitting boxes: ADHD and children who are hard to teach', *Discourse: Studies in the Cultural Politics of Education*, 29 (1): 85–106.
Gravett, S. (2013) 'Response to Hilda Borko'. Seminar held at Wits School of Education, 30 July.
Halliday, M. and Matthiessen, M. (2004) *An Introduction to Functional Grammar*, 3rd edn. London: Arnold.
Hattingh, A. and du Plessis, A. (2004) 'Technology education', in I. Eloff and L. Ebersohn (eds), *Keys to Educational Psychology*. Cape Town: UCT Press, pp. 272–88.
Holz, T. and Lessing, A. (2002) 'Reflections on Attention-Deficit Hyperactivity Disorder (ADHD) in an inclusive education system', *Perspectives in Education*, 20 (3): 103–10.
Hyam, M. (2009) 'Managing classroom behavior', in A. Decaires-Wagner and H. Picton (eds), *Teaching and ADHD in the Southern African Classroom*. Johannesburg: Macmillan, pp. 80–7.
Janks, H. (2010) *Literacy and Power*. New York: Routledge.
Kennedy, M. (2004) 'Reform ideals and teachers' practical intentions', *Education Policy Analysis Archives*, 12 (13): 1–38.
Kokot, S. (2006) 'The nature and incidence of barriers to learning among Grade Three learners in Tshwane', *Africa Education Review*, 3 (1 and 2): 134–47.
Landsberg, E., Kruger, D. and Swart, E. (eds) (2011) *Addressing Barriers to Learning. A South African Perspective*, 2nd edn. Pretoria: Van Schaik.
Maema, A. (2009) 'Discipline strategies for children with ADHD', in A. Decaires-Wagner and H. Picton (eds), *Teaching and ADHD in the Southern African Classroom*. Johannesburg: Macmillan, pp. 88–91.
Magare, I., Kitching, A. E and Roos, V. (2010) 'Educators' experiences of inclusive learning contexts: an exploration of competencies', *Perspectives in Education*, 28 (1): 52–63.
Matentjie. T. (2009) 'Cognitive control strategies in the classroom', in A. Decaires-Wagner and H. Picton (eds) *Teaching and ADHD in the Southern African Classroom*. Johannesburg: Macmillan, pp. 70–6.

Meyer, A., Eilertsen, D., Sundet, J., Tshifularo, J. and Sagvolden, T. (2004) 'Cross-cultural similarities in ADHD-like behaviour amongst South African primary school children', *South African Journal of Psychology*, 34 (1): 122–38.

Moletsane, M. (2013) 'Cognitive and behavioural challenges', in C. Pienaar and E. Raymond (eds), *Making Inclusive Education Work in Classrooms*. Cape Town: Pearson, pp. 61–84.

Moodley, V. (2015) 'An investigation into the feasibility of the positive behaviour support model for Limpopo's primary schools (Grade R – 3): preliminary findings', in E. Walton and S. Moonsamy (eds), *Making Education Inclusive*. Newcastle upon Tyne: Cambridge Scholars, pp. 94–112.

Novartis (n.d.) *Attention Deficit Hyperactivity Disorder*. Kempton Park: Novartis.

Perold, M., Louw, C. and Kleynhans, S. (2010) 'Primary school teachers' knowledge and misperceptions of attention deficit hyperactivity disorder (ADHD)', *South African Journal of Education*, 30: 457–73.

Phillips, C. (2006) 'Medicine goes to school', *PLoS Medicine*, 3 (4): 433–5.

Picton, H. (1997) *Hyperactive Children: Caring and Coping*. Johannesburg: Witwatersrand University Press.

Prinsloo, E. and Gasa, V. (2011) 'Addressing challenging behaviour in the classroom', in E. Landsberg, D. Kruger and E. Swart (eds), *Addressing Barriers to Learning: A South African Perspective*, 2nd edn. Pretoria: Van Schaik, pp. 490–507.

Republic of South Africa (1996) 'South African Schools Act, 1996, Act No. 84 of 1996', *Government Gazette*, 377 (17579). Cape Town: Government Printer.

Roffey, S. (2010) 'Classroom support for including students with challenging behavior', in R. Rose (ed.), *Confronting Obstacles to Inclusion*. London: Routledge, pp. 279–92.

SAALED (2008) *From Inclusion to Belonging: Widening the Classroom Circle*, delegate conference book. Johannesburg: SAALED.

SAALED (2011) *From Inclusion to Belonging: The Language of Learning*, delegate conference book. Johannesburg: SAALED.

Savitz, J. and Jansen, P. (2005) 'Mainstream and remedial school Attention Deficit Hyperactivity Disorder boys : more alike than different', *South African Journal of Psychology*, 35 (1): 73–88.

Slee, R. (2010) 'Bad behaviour', in L. Graham (ed.), *(De)Constructing ADHD*. New York: Peter Lang, pp. 41–61.

Smit, A. and Liebenberg, L. (2003) 'Understanding the dynamics of parent involvement in schooling within the poverty context', *South African Journal of Education*, 23 (1): 1–5.

Snider, V., Busch, T. and Arrowood, L. (2003) 'Teacher knowledge of stimulant medication and ADHD', *Remedial and Special Education*, 24 (1): 46–56.

Staniforth, J. (2009) 'Improving school performance of the child with ADHD', in A. Decaires-Wagner and H. Picton (eds), *Teaching and ADHD in the Southern African Classroom*. Johannesburg: Macmillan, pp. 56–63.

Steinmann, W. and Botha, E. (2009) 'Playgrounds and play', in A. Decaires-Wagner and H. Picton (eds), *Teaching and ADHD in the Southern African Classroom*. Johannesburg: Macmillan, pp. 108–12.

Stobo, J. (2007) 'Do teachers push docs to overprescribe for ADHD?', *National Review of Medicine*, 4 (15). Accessed from: http://www.nationalreviewofmedicine.com/issue/2007/09_15/4_patients_practice09_15.html.

Swain, M. (2006) 'Languaging, agency and collaboration in advanced second language proficiency', in H. Byrnes (ed.), *Advanced Language Learning: The Contribution of Halliday and Vygotsky*. London: Continuum, pp. 95–108.

Tait, G. (2010) *Philosophy, Behaviour Disorders, and the School*. Rotterdam: Sense Publishers.

Taylor, N., van der Berg, S. and Mabofoane, T. (2013) 'Context, theory, design', in N. Taylor, S. van der Berg and T. Mabofoane (eds), *Creating Effective Schools*. Cape Town: Pearson, pp. 1–30.

Theron, L. (2009) 'Empowering children and adolescents with ADHD to be resilient', in A. Decaires-Wagner and H. Picton (eds), *Teaching and ADHD in the Southern African Classroom*. Johannesburg: Macmillan, pp. 178–84.

Van Vuuren, C. (2009) 'Coaching for teenagers with ADHD', in A. Decaires-Wagner and H. Picton (eds), *Teaching and ADHD in the Southern African Classroom*. Johannesburg: Macmillan, pp. 102–4.

Venter, A. (2006) 'The medical management of attention-deficit/hyperactivity disorder: spoilt for choice?', *South African Psychiatry Review*, 9: 143–51.

Walton, E. (2015) 'Working towards education for all in Gauteng', in F. Maringe and M. Prew (eds), *Twenty Years of Education Transformation in Gauteng 1994 to 2014: An Independent Review*. Somerset West: African Minds for the Gauteng Department of Education, pp. 210–17.

Walton, E. (under review) 'Developing PLCs for Inclusive Education: A University Community Engagement Opportunity'.

Wilke, J. (2009) 'The world of ADHD', in A. Decaires-Wagner and H. Picton (eds), *Teaching and ADHD in the Southern African Classroom*. Johannesburg: Macmillan, pp. xxiii–xxvi.

Website: https://www.facebook.com/ADHASA.ADHD (accessed 16 August 2015).

# 7
# READING AND WRITING IN/EXCLUSION

### Asperger's literature

Christopher Boone is the protagonist of the novel *The Curious Incident of the Dog in the Night-Time* (henceforth *Curious Incident*) (Haddon 2003). His behaviour and thought patterns have led readers to identify him as having characteristics of Asperger's syndrome or being on the autism spectrum. This award-winning novel was set as an English set-work text for Grade 10 learners in a Johannesburg school. A short time after reading the book, the learners were invited to reflect on the book and discuss issues of inclusion and exclusion in a university-led research project.[1] One question posed in the study was what advice the learners would give to Christopher's father, on hearing that he was thinking of enrolling Christopher in their school. Their responses were mostly cautious, with learners aware that their peer group may not be very accepting and that the school may not have appropriate facilities:

> I'd tell him to really think about the decision because I think I'd love to say that our school was very accepting. It is to a certain extent, but I think Christopher might find it hard to find friends who are willing to take the time to understand him and make friends with him. If this school did supply or have the facilities to accommodate Christopher in terms of his syndrome then yes I think it would be fine.

They imagined that the school would have to make some adjustments, like: 'separate bathrooms'; 'the school would have to explain to all the learners why he would act the way he acts and give ways to handle him'; 'children must not touch him'; and 'teachers would need to be more patient'. One learner saw that attitudinal changes would be needed, but was pessimistic about the possibility of Christopher's inclusion:

> The school's mindset would have to change as other accommodations would have to be brought in. Those in the school would have to be educated in the syndrome and understand specifically how he experiences it. He could never be truly included because he would have to be treated differently to be accommodated.

Another did not believe that anything should change: 'I don't think the school should change, yes he has Asperger's but in the real world, no one is going to change for him, he must get used to the real world.' Finally, one learner went so far as to say, 'I do not think that people with severe Asperger's should be allowed to enter normal schools'.

It has been argued that literature can become a means 'to engage children in social practices that function for social justice' (Botelho and Rudman 2009: 1) and can provide the opportunity to address social issues while meeting the academic demands of the school curriculum (Womack *et al.* 2011). With specific reference to autism, Hacking (2009) says that narratives 'tell neurotypical children how to accommodate and to respect autistic children' (502). The responses of this group of Johannesburg learners appear to belie the promise that fiction can play a role in the quest for more socially just and inclusive education. It seems that this fiction may also embed stereotypes and cement prejudice. This chapter, then, is the result of my reflection of the role of fiction in the popular imagination of a particular disability.[2] With reference to two novels: *Curious Incident* (Haddon 2003) and *House Rules* (Picoult 2010), I consider what it is that people come to know about Asperger's syndrome as a result of reading popular fiction.

Both of these novels were written while the fourth edition of the *Diagnostic and Statistical Manual of Mental Disorders* (DSM) (American Psychiatric Association (APA) 2000) had currency. Asperger's disorder is classified in the DSM-IV as a pervasive developmental disorder, discrete from autistic disorder. A lack of delay in language development distinguishes Asperger's disorder from autistic disorder in this classification system. The criteria for diagnosing Asperger's disorder are impaired social interaction which would present as at least two of the following: impaired use of non-verbal behaviours, failure to develop peer relationships, limited reciprocity in social interaction and a lack of interest in sharing experiences with others. In addition, stereotyped and repetitive behaviour and interests would be present, including at least one of the following: an abnormal preoccupation with particular interests, inflexible adherence to routines or rituals, repetitive motor mannerisms and/or preoccupation with the parts of objects (APA 2000). Readers of both *Curious Incident* (Haddon 2003) and *House Rules* (Picoult 2010) will identify many of these Asperger's disorder characteristics in the protagonists of the novels.

A subsequent edition of the DSM has been published, and this consolidates 'autistic disorder, Asperger's disorder, and pervasive developmental disorder into autism spectrum disorder' (APA 2013: xlii). The DSM-V presents a continuum of impairments from mild to severe in the domains of social communication and restrictive repetitive behaviours or interests. The revised classification addresses the considerable overlap between Asperger's syndrome and autism and makes the 'spectrum' important. This is not expected to alter prevalence rates, as 91 per cent of children who would have been diagnosed with a pervasive developmental disorder with the DSM-IV would meet the criteria for autism spectrum disorder (Kupfer et al. 2013). What this means, though, is that according to the DSM-V, there is no longer a disorder called Asperger's, as people who would previously have been diagnosed with Asperger's disorder would now be diagnosed with autism spectrum disorder. But the removal of this diagnosis from the DSM-V does not signal the immediate disappearance of the idea of Asperger's or the use of the term.

The *International Classification of Diseases*, 10th edition (ICD-10)[3] (World Health Organisation 1992), currently retains the distinction of Asperger's syndrome within the category of pervasive developmental disorders. This means that medical practitioners using the ICD-10 may continue to use the diagnostic label of Asperger's syndrome while it remains in this classification system. But beyond the diagnostic sphere, the *idea* of Asperger's disorder (or Asperger's syndrome as is commonly preferred) has entered the public imagination, leading McGeer (2009) to note that 'everyone versed in the comings and goings of everyday culture will have heard of autism (and/or Asperger syndrome) – and doubtless knows something about it' (517). It has become embedded in popular consciousness as a result of news, television and popular fiction (McDonagh 2008; Murray, S. 2006). Furthermore, having an Asperger's diagnosis, or being an 'Aspie', has become an identity marker appropriated by many people (Friedman 2012; Murray, D. 2006). It is thus doubtful that the term 'Asperger's' will recede from our lexicon in the immediate future.

An analysis of *Curious Incident* (Haddon 2003) and *House Rules* (Picoult 2010) is complicated by the changes in names and classifications. It can become quite difficult to distinguish whether or not references to autism imply Asperger's syndrome or vice versa, especially when (lay) writers use the terms interchangeably or imprecisely. For the purpose of clarity, I will make my reference point the decade between DSM-IV and DSM-V, when both novels were published and where Asperger's disorder/syndrome and autistic disorder were regarded as diagnostically discrete.

The literary portrayal of people who are deemed different, and different because of disability, is not new. Disability is found in literary works by Shakespeare (Richard in *Richard III*) and Dickens (Tiny Tim in *A Christmas Carol*), and contemporary film (Raymond Babbitt in *Rain Man* (Levinson 1988) and Sam Dawson in *I Am Sam* (Nelson 2001)) and fiction (Charlie Gordon in *Flowers for Algernon* (Keyes 1966)). The media also helps to construct popular notions of disability and is often the source of people's information about disability (Haller 2000). People with disabilities are variously portrayed in the media. Either they are presented as the pitiable victims of misfortune and the passive recipients of the goodwill of society, or they are shown as achieving great feats in spite of disabilities (Clogston, cited in Jones and Bentz 2005; Farnall and Smith 1999; Haller 2000). Autism and Asperger's syndrome, in particular, have featured prominently in the US news media (Haller *et al.* 2010) and have been a particular focus of narrative fiction in the past years (Murray, S. 2006). Hence my focus on *Curious Incident* and *House Rules*.

There are any number of interesting avenues to pursue in an examination of these two novels and they have much in common. Their main point of connection is that the protagonist of both is a young man who displays characteristics that have been described as typical of Asperger's syndrome. I am interested not only in how each book engages individually with Asperger's syndrome (and difference more generally), but what I see as the compounding *effect* of the themes and concerns presented. These effects may or may not be what the respective authors intended. I take the position that authorial choices are intentional and are worth examining in terms of the meanings they create rather than for the purpose of determining authorial intent. It is a fallacy, say Wimsatt and Beardsley (1946), that the intention of an author can be deduced either from within the text, or from the historical and contextual conditions in which the text was written, or indeed that identifying intention is necessary to judge the work. This is not an argument for a purely reader-centred approach to the texts, or to say that historical contingencies are not salient in understanding a text, or that biographical information of the authors may not have a bearing on the text. It is saying that a *focus* on deducing the intention of the novelists under discussion is to suggest that the meaning is fixed and that the texts can only mean what the authors intended them to mean. Rather, meaning is made in the interaction of readers, writers and contexts.

For those who have not read *Curious Incident* (Haddon 2003) and *House Rules* (Picoult 2010), it might help to know something about the plot and characters of each novel. Christopher Boone is the protagonist of *Curious Incident*. Readers meet him at seven minutes past midnight, looking at a dead dog lying on his neighbours' (Mr and Mrs Shears) front lawn. The reader learns that Christopher's mother was having an affair with Mr Shears and that she has left Swindon and now lives in London with Mr Shears. Christopher, however, was led to believe that his mother was dead. Christopher lives in Swindon with his father, Mr Boone. Mr Boone was looking for more than the platonic commiserations offered by Mrs Shears, and it emerges that, in frustration, he killed her dog. Christopher attends a special school run by Mrs Gascoyne, the principal. His teacher, who only seems to have a first name, is Siobhan. On discovering that his mother was alive in London and that his father killed Mrs Shears's dog, Christopher embarks on a journey to London to go and live with his mother.

Jacob Hunt is the protagonist of *House Rules*. He lives in the USA with his mother and brother. Emma Hunt, his mother, is a journalist with a local newspaper and her younger brother, Theo Hunt, has a predilection for entering other people's homes and imagining what it would be like to live their lives. Jacob's father, Henry Hunt, no longer stays with Emma, Theo and Jacob, and plays little role in their lives. The death of Jacob's social skills tutor, Jess Ogilvy, leads to Jacob being arrested and then tried for her murder. It emerges that Jacob had arrived for his social skills tutoring session and saw Jess dead and evidence of Theo's presence in the house. Using his forensic knowledge, Jacob staged the crime scene in order to implicate Jess's boyfriend rather than his brother. The trial forms a significant part of the novel, and Jacob is represented by his attorney, Oliver Bond. Jacob's Asperger's syndrome forms an important part of the trial and his psychiatrist, Dr Murano, plays a role in educating the court about this diagnosis.

Character names are intentional choices made by authors. The three young men who feature prominently in both these novels have names with Judeo-Christian associations. Christopher means 'Christ carrier', Jacob wrestled with God in the Old Testament and Theo is 'God-given'. These names suggest that these are no ordinary lives and that to touch Asperger's is a mark of exceptionality. There is a gift or benefit implied in the surname Boone, and the implication is that Christopher Boone either has some great advantages or is someone to be thankful for. Either way, the surname signals positive associations with Christopher. Jacob's surname is Hunt, which has various possible connotations in *House Rules*. It could refer to the hunt for Jess Ogilvy's murderer and the implied hunt for the truth. It may also represent the quest for understanding for people like Jacob who have an Asperger's syndrome diagnosis. H/hunt in *House Rules* can be linked with Christopher Boone's search to solve the mystery of the dead dog in *Curious Incident* and his subsequent expedition to London to find his mother. Character names are only one of the many intertextual connections between these novels, making them well suited for analysis as a dyad.

## A popular knowledge of Asperger's

Fiction plays a (mis)educative role in many spheres of life, irrespective of an author's intention. People build their ideas of different places through reading about them in books, while inhabitants of a place might well question the accuracy of their portrayal in fiction. This is also true of disability. Semino (2014: 145) confirms this, saying, 'Fictional representations of particular phenomena, including cognitive disorders, may well contribute to shape readers' knowledge and perceptions of real-life phenomena and people.' Asperger's syndrome is represented in these two works of fiction in various ways, with only a few aspects being explored in this chapter. First, I contrast the two novels in terms of acknowledging Asperger's syndrome. I then turn to the issue of the accuracy of the representation of Asperger's syndrome, drawing on scholarly and popular opinion. Because of my concern with inclusive education, the schooling experiences of the novels' protagonists are explored before considering how the families are shown as being impacted by Asperger's syndrome. Finally, I reflect on the voice of Asperger's by looking at the narration of the two novels.

### Acknowledging Asperger's

It is striking that at no time in *Curious Incident* does the author label or diagnose Christopher Boone as having autism or Asperger's syndrome. We, the readers, occupy the 'doctor's chair' (Wooden 2011: n.p.) and identify in Christopher deviance from our notions of 'normal', classify his 'symptoms' and diagnose him. As a result of this imposed diagnosis, the novel has been acclaimed as 'the best novel with an autistic character' (Osteen 2008: 40) and it has been stated that it '… constitutes a genuine, though highly stylized attempt to present the workings of an autistic mind' (Murray, S. 2006: 37). Mark Haddon, in response to an interview question that asked if he had to do research into the 'medical conditions' of Asperger's syndrome and autism, said 'I simply tried to make Christopher seem like a believable human being, rather than trying to make him medically "correct"' (Dasgupta n.d.). In his blog, Haddon (2009) explicitly distances the work from Asperger's syndrome, saying

> curious Incident is not a book about asperger's. it's a novel whose central character describes himself as 'a mathematician with some behavioural difficulties'. indeed he never uses the words 'asperger's' or 'autism' (i slightly regret that fact that the word 'asperger's' was used on the cover). if anything it's a novel about difference, about being an outsider, about seeing the world in a surprising and revealing way. it's as much a novel about us as it is about christopher.
>
> *(Punctuation in the original)*

That Christopher has no acknowledged diagnosis works to ensure that Christopher is read for who he is, as he is not defined by any particular label. This has merit in that it suggests a world where people are just who they are, without the determinism or stereotyping that accompanies diagnoses or labels. However, we cannot escape the Asperger's syndrome label that has been appended to Christopher by readers, critics and marketers.[4] Even Haddon only 'slightly regrets' the use of the term on the cover, and the book finds its place in the burgeoning market for stories about the misfortunes of others. In *Curious Incident*, Christopher never meets a psychiatrist but he does attend a special school. This suggests that irrespective of a formal Asperger's syndrome or autism diagnosis, Christopher's constellation of characteristics have been identified as somehow aberrant, warranting some kind of specialised intervention. The imposition of the Asperger's label by the novel's readership exemplifies one of the effects of the distillation of 'disorders' into the popular imagination, ironically through novels just like this. The recognition of Asperger's syndrome in others becomes a lay skill and this is evidenced in *House Rules* by Emma Hunt, Jacob's mother, who says of her ex-husband, 'I diagnosed him with a dash of Asperger's too' (7) 140.

In contrast to *Curious Incident*, Jacob Hunt's diagnosis of Asperger's syndrome is emphasised early in that novel. Much of the first chapter of *House Rules* is given to explanations of Asperger's syndrome in relation to Jacob, including the psychiatric diagnosis, various therapeutic interventions and characteristics like tactile defensiveness, intense focus and social awkwardness. The voice of this first chapter is Emma Hunt, Jacob's mother, who says that Asperger's is a term they use 'to get Jacob the accommodations he needs in school, *not a label to explain who he is*' (7) (emphasis mine). However, as the plot unfolds, she clearly finds in the Asperger's syndrome diagnosis an explanation for Jacob's characteristics and behaviour for herself and for others. The reader, too, is invited to share this understanding and see the label as an explanatory and exonerating device. Thus as Jacob flaps, growls and screams in the grocery store when the regular free sample lady is not at her post, and he backs into the shelf of pickle jars, breaking them, Emma angrily snaps at the staring crowd saying, 'He's autistic[5] ... Do you have any questions?' (11).

Picoult uses the authoritative voice of Jacob's psychiatrist, Dr Murano, and the court room setting to educate the judge and by extension the readers, of the nature, history and manifestations of Asperger's syndrome. As a narrative device, this serves to confirm the veracity and legitimacy of Asperger's syndrome and it validates the subjective accounts of the condition offered elsewhere in the book by Jacob, his mother and his brother. Dr Murano is invited to give a definition of Asperger's syndrome and she responds, confidently asserting that Asperger's is a 'neurobiological disorder' on the autism spectrum, and a 'developmental disability' distinct from that of a 'mentally challenged individual' (268). A range of characteristics and limitations associated with people diagnosed with Asperger's syndrome are described, with careful note that while many people might display some characteristics associated with Asperger's, it is the clustering and pervasiveness of certain behaviours that leads to diagnosis. It is striking that in the various descriptors of Asperger's syndrome, Picoult does not often let her psychiatric experts use hedges, those linguistic markers that signal tentativeness. Instead, these experts speak with the kind of confidence not always found in medical discourse, where hedges are often used 'as a resource to express scientific uncertainty, scepticism and doubt' (Salager-Meyer 1994: 151). This choice of linguistic strategy is noteworthy, particularly as Picoult's characters are referring to a relatively fluid diagnostic category (Frith 2004).

In these two novels, we have Asperger's syndrome as implicit (in *Curious Incident*) and explicit (in *House Rules*). With or without the label, though, the two main characters, Christopher Boone and Jacob Hunt, have similar characteristics, including their literalism, vocalisations when stressed, difficulties with social interaction and obsession with routine. They are both interested in crime and have similar aversions to touch, texture, food and colour. As a result, we have a popular imagination of Asperger's syndrome as a recognisable cluster of behaviours and characteristics. But, how accurate is this? One of the criteria that Landrum (2001: 254) suggests for evaluating books that portray people with disabilities is that 'all data pertaining to the disability is accurate'. In the section that follows, I consider various opinions on the accuracy of these portrayals of Asperger's syndrome and question the validity of this criterion.

## *Accurate Asperger's?*

Writers in medicine and psychiatry are measured in their appraisal of the accuracy of the representation of Asperger's syndrome in the two novels. The didactic possibilities of the works are suggested, together with an indication that the portrayals of the syndrome are sufficiently accurate to warrant their use in disseminating information. Freckelton (2009), the editor-in-chief of the journal *Psychiatry, Psychology and Law*, says that *Curious Incident* '... is not just a book about Aspergers's but it teaches a great deal about the disorder' (163). Wooden (2011) uses the text with medical students in the context of narrative medicine, suggesting that it can be profitably used for ethical enquiry. Disagreeing with these appraisals is *Huffington Post* blogger Greg Olear (2011), who is the father of a son with a diagnosis of Asperger's syndrome. Olear says that he has come to see 'what an inaccurate picture of Asperger's *Curious Incident* paints' on the basis that Christopher's behaviours would represent 'the most extreme forms of the disorder ever recorded' (n.p.). This observation echoes the views of another blogger, Richard Cooper (2010) who contends that the novel is not about a boy with Asperger's syndrome, but of 'a severely autistic boy'. Similar reservations about *House Rules* are expressed by Harrison and Damodharan (2012), who note that autism and Asperger's syndrome are conflated in *House Rules*, with Jacob's symptoms being excessive and exaggerated for the purpose of storytelling. They see in Jacob a compendium of stories or events which 'would individually be considered eccentric, but totalled together become quite pathological' (72). These authors do, however, see didactic value in this novel, noting that it 'may prove to be a useful tool for educating clinicians, patients, and their families on various aspects of the autism spectrum disorders' and that ultimately it may lead to 'greater insight into the syndrome' (72).

Accurate rendition of the diagnostic criteria for disorders or disabilities in fiction must necessarily be fraught. If we agree that illnesses and impairments are experienced differently by different people, then we cannot expect one person to exemplify the range of characteristics that might be associated with a particular diagnosis. In fact, we should be arguing that the rendition of people with disabilities in fiction ought to show the complexity of the experience of disability as it intersects with other aspects of identity, and is lived in different socio-cultural and economic contexts. We should probably question the demand that disabilities be portrayed 'accurately', as if there is an accurate way of being disabled.

The exaggerations in Christopher and Jacob's behaviours that their creators may have included for narrative effect and interest become associated with Asperger's syndrome in the popular imagination. As a result, we see the potential for this type of fiction to entrench the stereotyping of people with various disabilities. Instead of working to dispel these stereotypes by promoting an imagination of the Other, this fiction may confirm in the minds of readers just how very aberrant the behaviour of the Other is. Perceptions generated about the aberrant Other have important implications for inclusive education. For example, parents have been known to be resistant to the idea of the inclusion of diverse learners in their children's classes on the grounds that learning might be disrupted by challenging behaviour and that teacher attention will be compromised (Peck *et al.* 2004).

## *Educating Asperger's*

Christopher Boone in *Curious Incident* attends some kind of special school. He relates the fact that when he and others get off the bus, the children from 'the school down the road' shout 'Special needs! Special needs!' (56). Christopher claims that he takes no notice of this and he seems content within his educational environment. Christopher's school day resembles a kindergarten with little structure, no set curriculum and a teacher whom he calls by her first name, Siobhan – an infantilising environment. This is despite the fact that he clearly has exceptional mathematical abilities. There is nothing in *Curious Incident* that suggests critique of the separate special education placement, beyond Christopher's father having to get 'really cross' (57) with the principal in order to allow Christopher to take the A-level mathematics examination. In fact, the gratuitous gastronomic and scatological details of Joseph Fleming, Christopher's classmate, serve to reinforce perceptions of the deviant behaviours of children in special education (Walton 2012) and confirm the need for segregated settings for certain learners. Segregated special education in this novel is presented as the natural order of things and the processes by which Christopher was 'placed' in a special setting are not described or alluded to.

Jacob Hunt in *House Rules*, by contrast, goes to his neighbourhood school. His experience has been one of friendlessness and bullying, since an early age. There is, however, some evidence that the school has been responsive to Jacob's social and behavioural difficulties. Theo comments on the 'bazillion IEP meetings' (86) that his mother attends to make sure that the school is safe for Jacob. 'IEP' stands for Individual(ised) Education Plan and refers to a plan devised to ensure that a learner's unique learning and support needs are met in a school setting. In the context of the United States, where *House Rules* is set, the IEP 'serves the purpose of directing and monitoring all aspects of a student's special education program' (Christle and Yell 2010: 109). The extent to which IEPs (and similar iterations in other countries) serve the ends of inclusive education must be debated. On the one hand, an IEP can be the means by which support for learners is carefully considered, implemented, monitored and accounted for and is thus an essential feature of inclusive education (Aiello and Bullock 1999). Teachers see IEPs as beneficial in their planning and implementing the educational and social goals for learners with disabilities in their classes (Lee-Tarver 2006) and IEP meetings have the potential to promote collaboration with parents and other support professionals (Baglieri and Shapiro 2012). On the other hand, IEPs can function to ensure that learner difficulties remain an individual peculiarity, while the pedagogical status quo continues unquestioned. IEPs might also lead to stigmatising, something of which Jacob, in *House Rules*, is only too aware. Jacob has a 'cool-off pass' which allows him to leave his classroom if he is feeling overwhelmed by sensory stimuli and go to the 'sensory break room'. However, in Jacob's own words, 'The only kids who use the sensory break room are special needs, and walking through the door, I might as well just slap a big fat label on myself that says I'm not normal' (127). I shall return to Jacob's classification of others as 'special needs' and 'not normal', but here his avoidance of the 'concession' granted him can be seen as illustrative of the way in which this and other types of 'accommodation' serve as a public badge of difference and deviance.

Taken together, these novels present two recognisable responses to the 'problem' of educating learners who are deemed different or disordered. The one, exemplified in *Curious Incident*, is to remove the learner altogether from the neighbourhood school for 'placement' in a segregated special education setting. In this novel, the 'concession' that had to be fought for was the right to do what learners in the 'regular' school do – write an A-level examination. The other response is to see the learner with Asperger's syndrome in the 'regular' school, where the 'accommodations' are the right *not* to do what other learners do – stay in class irrespective of any 'commotion' (Picoult 2010: 269). Both responses are premised on the assumptions that learners with characteristics of Asperger's syndrome require educational responses different from or in addition to the regular educational provisioning. I do not wish to rehearse the wider concerns in the field regarding pedagogies and learner support, but rather point to the vocabulary that has accompanied the various responses to educational difference. In Chapter 4 I challenged the use of the word 'accommodation' with its associated hospitality metaphor. It seems that 'regular' learners belong in schools by right, but those who are deemed different have to have special arrangements to 'accommodate' them, as if they are perpetual guests in the system.

Then there are the various Individual(ised) Education/Support Plans to which I have referred. The foregrounding of the 'individual' in the phrase or acronym reflects a particular orientation to learner difference and ensures that it remains an individual problem. The individualisation of instruction or intervention according to specific diagnostic profiles reflects a particular cultural valorisation of the individual over the collective (Raveaud 2005). The individual focus also enables the containment of the 'problem' – ensuring that concerns about access and inclusion are reduced to 'compensatory measures' (Slee 2011: 108). Collective action against systemic exclusion is forestalled (McCall and Skrtic 2009), as parents, like Christopher's father and Jacob's mother, must advocate for the benefit of their own children. It is also worth noting where the noun 'individual' is verbed in this discourse,[6] as in the past participle 'individualised'. The verb form acknowledges some action taken to make the plan individually relevant, but obscures the subject, i.e. the one who *does* the individualising. By so doing, we are lulled into thinking that these plans just appear rather than being the outcomes of complex (and contestable) processes involving all sorts of people who claim expertise in the lives of the learners.

None of these concerns would necessarily be new to those steeped in the field of inclusive education, whatever their theoretical and ideological orientations are. However, popular fiction like the novels under consideration brings these concerns onto the bookshelves of the general public. We need to acknowledge the potential that novels like these have to shape and inform the popular imagination, and contribute to the conception that segregated placements or arrangements for learners deemed different or deviant are 'necessary and benevolent' (Ferri and Connor 2006: 11), both for their own good and to prevent them from disrupting or detracting from the education of 'regular' learners.

## *Asperger's families*

While it may be possible that readers of both *Curious Incident* and *House Rules* may develop some insight and understanding about Asperger's syndrome, I would argue that it is the parents with whom we are expected to empathise. Both novels present the parents of the child with Asperger's syndrome as overwhelmed by the demands that this presents. Both describe single-parent families, with the implication that the child with Asperger's syndrome is at least partly responsible for this state. Henry Hunt, Jacob's father, left home as he 'couldn't stand' (7) Jacob's tantrums, and was resentful of Jacob's mother's devotion to Jacob's therapeutic interventions. Christopher's father, Mr Boone, made advances towards their neighbour (Mrs Shears) after his wife left him for Mr Shears and moved to London. These advances were rebuffed, with Christopher's father acknowledging that 'we are a bloody handful' and 'not exactly low-maintenance' (151). Christopher's behaviour often exasperates his father, and his father's discovery of Christopher's detective novel leads to a physical fight. Nonetheless, Mr Boone carefully considers Christopher's dietary proclivities and tries to create a home environment that does not stress Christopher. Like Jacob's mother Emma, who has to advocate for her child's education by arguing for and monitoring 'all sorts of adaptations' (79), Christopher's father has to advocate for Christopher's right to write an A-level examination. Both parents find themselves having to explain their sons' behaviour to law-enforcement officials and other people who react negatively to various outbursts.

Readers of both novels find parents who are highly stressed by their children with Asperger's syndrome. There is some research to support this, with Lee *et al.* (2009) finding that having a child with high-functioning autism spectrum disorders negatively impacts parents' quality of life, and that the pervasiveness of the disorder and the demands of care and advocacy act as significant stressors on parents. This does not mean that the parents in these novels do not love their children, with Emma Hunt, Jacob's mother, saying that Jacob 'is not a cross to bear. He's my son' (311). Despite the protestations of parental affection and attachment that are interspersed through both novels, the reader is left with an overwhelming sense that these children represent a significant burden to their parents. Writing about Picoult's narrative preoccupation with 'the imperilled children of flawed middle-class parents', Montello (2010) finds Picoult presenting the view that 'taking care of these vulnerable victims seems to be more than ordinary parents can handle' (20). The state is notably absent in both novels and neither of the parents seem to (have) access to state services to support them. The novelists thus leave their readers with the impression of beleaguered parents made lonely by the demands of their children and with little support for the parenting challenges they face.

## *Asperger's voice*

The fiction writer can choose to narrate a story through the voice of one or more characters in the story. This device offers the possibility of revealing the inner thoughts of the storyteller in a way that eliminates the need for an omniscient third-person narrator. First-person narrative in fiction creates a sense of authenticity and immediacy by summoning associations with the genres of autobiography and diary. Both novels under consideration use first-person narratives. Christopher Boone is the only narrator in *Curious Incident*, but other voices are heard through the inclusion of letters from his mother and his prodigious memory and capacity for accurate rendition of conversations with others, like his father. As a first-person narrator, Christopher seems entirely reliable in that he does not conceal the facts as he knows them and does not hide his weaknesses (Kane and Byrne 2006). However, his perspective is limited and the reader is required to complete the narration with the intuition and understanding of the context that Christopher does not always exhibit. In *House Rules*, compensation for Jacob Hunt's limited perspective is provided by the voices of the other characters who are explicitly signalled by their names as chapter headings. This means that *Curious Incident* is mostly Christopher's story, but *House Rules* is narrated by a number of characters, and Jacob finds himself more told about than telling.

Both Christopher Boone and Jacob Hunt are extremely conscious of their idiosyncrasies and challenges, with Jacob engaging directly with his Asperger's diagnosis. Christopher is a self-conscious narrator, acknowledging that he is writing a book, albeit not a 'funny book' (10). As he tells his story though, the ('neurotypical') reader is invited by the author to find humour at Christopher's expense. This humour is derived, I suggest, from a number of sources. These include surprise at finding bodily excretion so nonchalantly mentioned in the formal space of a prize-winning book and a patronising indulgence that finds humour in the pedantry and insouciance with which events are narrated. Significantly, the reader enjoys a position as an outsider but is able to see layers of meaning that are not evident to those in a situation. Thus, as Greenwell (2004: 280) says, 'We are in on the joke, and Christopher isn't.' I have some reservations about how this humour works in contributing to the popular imagination of Asperger's syndrome. Christopher is a literalist. He acknowledges that he does not appreciate nuances in language, metaphor or facial expression. We thus read his accounts and laugh at him, not with him, as he is not, nor cannot be, aware of the humour that his narration creates. This is not a cruel laugh but it is a superior laugh.[7]

Christopher tells his story through a variety of genres and multiple modalities, and we read in the text the conventions of murder mystery, quest literature and diary, interspersed with diagrams, maths problems and maps. *House Rules* is more conventional in format. Jacob has a number of his own chapters where he offers his insights into who he is and why he is that way. Like Christopher, he is fond of lists. He itemises the food to which he is averse (very similar to Christopher's aversions), and indulges his mathematical abilities in a didactic chapter (260) reminiscent of Christopher's writing. Both young men reflect on their lack of what is known as 'Theory of Mind'. Christopher explains that when he was little, he 'didn't understand about other people having minds' (145), and that his parents were told that this would always be difficult for him. He claims that now this is no longer a problem because, like a puzzle, he can solve it. Similarly, Jacob claims that it is 'total bullshit' that 'Aspies like me cannot feel anything on behalf of others' (397) because they have no Theory of Mind. This rejection of the assumption of Theory of Mind deficit is borne out by research that suggests that while children with autism do struggle with the ability to infer others' ideas and intentions, adults who are deemed as high-functioning on the autism spectrum can pass tests that evaluate theory of mind deficit (Moran *et al.* 2011; Senju *et al.* 2009). In these and other sections, both Christopher and Jacob are given exceptional intrapersonal insight, and this insight is used to give the reader some understanding of what it might be like to experience the characteristics of Asperger's syndrome. For both protagonists, this insight extends to a view of themselves as superior to those deemed as having 'special needs'. Both young men are ardently concerned that they should not be categorised as having 'special needs'.

While many readers might be quick to assign both Christopher Boone and Jacob Hunt to that class of person deemed not normal, deviant or having 'special needs', these young men expressly resist this designation. Christopher is adamant that all the other children at his school are 'stupid', even though he knows he is not supposed to refer to them as such (56). He explains his distinction between having special needs, like spectacles or a special diet, and being 'Special Needs'. Across the Atlantic, Jacob also recognises a class of person called 'special needs' with whom he does not want to be identified. He is also concerned to refute an appellation of him as 'retarded', noting that his IQ score is 162, which is well outside the threshold for 'mental retardation' (66). Jacob does, however, often distinguish himself from people who are 'neurotypical', noting that he is 'just a tourist here' (184). Interestingly, the metaphor of the person with autism as a foreigner or visitor from another land is an image used by parents and professionals, and is not one used by people with autism themselves (Straus 2010).

## Reading Asperger syndrome: sympathetic imagination or *Schadenfreude*?

Sympathetic imagination, claims Nussbaum (1997), is the capacity to '… comprehend the motives and choices of people different from ourselves' (85). The ability to imagine the Other potentially mitigates judgment and scorn, promotes kindness and compassion and is, Nussbaum (1995) contends, 'a bridge to social justice' (xviii). Sympathetic imagination can be fostered through reading literature, as people are invited to learn about 'sameness and difference' (Nussbaum 1997: 95) in relation to Others. This imagining has powerful possibility in that it promotes

> … a respect for the voices and the rights of the other, reminding us that the other has both agency and complexity, is neither a mere object nor a passive recipient of benefits and satisfactions. At the same time, it promotes a vivid awareness of need and disadvantage, and in that sense gives substance to the abstract desire for justice.
>
> *(Nussbaum 1997: 97)*

In this regard, then, it could be expected that a reading of *Curious Incident* and/or *House Rules* would foster a sympathetic imagining of young people on the autism spectrum and their caregivers. The first-person narration could be seen as the means to access the 'inner faculties of thought and emotion' (Nussbaum 2010: 6) of the characters concerned and, as a result of this access, readers might become more understanding, considerate and respectful of the (difficult) lives of Others. Or not. It is also conceivable that literature like *Curious Incident* and *House Rules* feeds the public's fascination with the strange. The interest in these novels lies not in their potential to educate and inform, but in their contribution to the modern day 'freak-show' which, in the guise of infotainment, takes people on literary or televised tours of the medical and psychiatric hardships of others. Thus *Schadenfreude*, the emotion of experiencing joy or pleasure at the misfortune of others, contends with sympathetic imagination as the outcome of reading novels such as these. So the desire for justice that Nussbaum suggests might develop as a result of an awareness of need and disadvantage fades as readers are treated to gratuitous details and sensationalised accounts about the behaviour of Others.

I leave this topic with a sense that novels like *Curious Incident* and *House Rules* have the potential to educate *and* miseducate; to promote sympathetic imagination *and Schadenfreude*. I have shown that in many ways, these novels do accurately capture some of the difficulties people with the characteristics of Asperger's syndrome experience in a world not well disposed to difference. They also present difference in ways that ensure that it remains utterly aberrant. The grade 10 learners reading *Curious Incident* exemplify this in the study mentioned in the opening paragraph of this chapter. Over 90 per cent of them agreed that, as a result of reading the novel, they 'know and understand more' about Asperger's syndrome, and 80 per cent reported that they would now feel 'more understanding' towards a person with Asperger's syndrome. However, their vantage point is an assumed superiority as they gaze on Christopher Boone, wondering how they would 'deal with', 'manage' or 'handle' him if he came to their school. My conclusion must be that we are in urgent need of critical literacy, such that works like these can be enjoyed and appreciated, but also that the worlds they create are resisted.

## Notes

1 Forty learners completed self-administered questionnaires, and twenty of these learners participated in focus group interviews. The research is reported in full in Walton (2013).
2 I acknowledge that Asperger's syndrome and/or high functioning autism might not necessarily be regarded as a disability but rather a difference in cognitive style (Baron-Cohen 2000), hence the idea of people being either neurotypical or neurodiverse. The neurodiversity claim is that the wiring of the brains of people with autism is not defective, just different, and having the characteristics of autism is not deviance, just another way of being human (Jaarsma and Welin 2012). The terms 'neurotypical' and 'neurodiverse' are used in *House Rules*.
3 Current at the time of writing.
4 This represents an example of how texts come to have meanings beyond the author's stated intention.
5 The conflation of Asperger's syndrome and autism (despite their distinction in the then current DSM-IV) in this novel does point to the conceptual fluidity between these diagnoses.
6 The verbing of nouns is discussed with reference to 'being workshopped' in Chapter 5.

7 The issue of humour at the expense of people with characteristics of Asperger's syndrome has been explored in some detail with regard to the character of Sheldon Cooper in the television sitcom *Big Bang Theory* (Walters 2013). As in *Curious Incident*, humour is created in the incongruity between prodigious academic ability and restricted social skills.

## Literary texts mentioned

Dickens, C. (1990) *A Christmas Carol*. London: Penguin.
Keyes, D. (1966) *Flowers for Algernon*. Orlando, FL: Harcourt Brace.
Levinson, B. (dir.) (1988) *Rain Man* [film]. Century City, CA: United Artists.
Nelson, J. (dir.) (2001) *I Am Sam* [film]. Los Angeles: New Line Cinema.
Shakespeare, W. (1981) *The Arden Shakespeare: Richard III*. London: Methuen.

## References

Aiello, J. and Bullock, L. M. (1999) 'Building commitment to responsible inclusion. Preventing school failure: alternative education for children and youth, 43 (3): 99–102.
American Psychiatric Association (2000/2013) *Diagnostic and Statistical Manual of Mental Disorders*, 4/5th edn, text revised. Washington, DC: APA.
Baglieri, S. and Shapiro, A. (2012) *Disability Studies and the Inclusive Classroom*. New York: Routledge.
Baron-Cohen, S. (2000) 'Is Asperger syndrome/high-functioning autism necessarily a disability?', *Development and Psychopathology*, 12 (3): 489–500.
Botelho, M. and Rudman, M. (2009) *Critical Multicultural Analysis of Children's Literature*. New York: Routledge.
Christle, C. A. and Yell, M. L. (2010) 'Individualized education programs: legal requirements and research findings', *Exceptionality*, 18 (3): 109–23.
Cooper, R. (2010) 'Mark Haddon's Christopher Boone – Uncle Tom for the 21st Century?'. Accessed from: http://richardhcooper.blogspot.com/2010/05/uncle-tom-for-21st-century-as-someone.html.
Dasgupta, S. (n.d.) 'Interview with Mark Haddon, Author of *The Curious Incident of the Dog in the Night-time*. Accessed from: http://www.istituto-scalcerle.it/blog/testi/Mark_Haddon_Interview.pdf.
Farnall, O. and Smith, K. A. (1999) 'Reactions to people with disabilities: personal contact versus viewing of specific media portrayals', *Journalism and Mass Communication Quarterly*, 76 (4): 659–72.
Ferri, B. and Connor, D. (2006) *Reading Resistance*. New York: Peter Lang.
Freckelton, I. (2009) 'Book review. *The Curious Incident of the Dog in the Night-Time* by M. Haddon', *Psychiatry, Psychology and Law*, 16 (1): 163–4.
Friedman, M. (2012.) *Dude, I'm an Aspie! Thoughts and Illustrations on Living with Asperger's Syndrome*. Self-published through http://www.Lulu.com.
Frith, U. (2004) 'Emanuel Miller lecture: Confusions and controversies about Asperger syndrome', *Journal of Child Psychology and Psychiatry*, 45 (4): 672–86.
Greenwell, B. (2004) 'The curious incidence of novels about Asperger's Syndrome', *Children's Literature in Education*, 35 (3): 271–84.
Hacking, I. A. N. (2009) 'How we have been learning to talk about autism: a role for stories', *Metaphilosophy*, 40 (3–4): 499–516.
Haddon, M. (2003) *The Curious Incident of the Dog in the Night-time*. London: David Fickling Books.

Haddon, M. (2009) 'asperger's and autism', blog post 16 July 2009. From: http://www.markhaddon.com/aspergers-and-autism.
Haller, B. (2000) 'If they limp they lead. News representation and the hierarchy of disability images', in D. Braithwaite and T. Thompson (eds), *Handbook of Communication and People with Disabilities*. Mahwah, NJ: Lawrence Erlbaum Associates, pp. 273–88.
Haller, B., Ralph, S. and Zaks, Z. (2010) 'Confronting obstacles to inclusion. How the US media report disability', in R. Rose (ed.), *Confronting Obstacles to Inclusion. International Responses to Developing Inclusive Education*. London: Routledge.
Harrison, K. and Damodharan, S. (2012) 'House Rules', *Journal of the Canadian Academy of Child and Adolescent Psychiatry*, 21 (1): 72–3.
Jaarsma, P. and Welin, S. (2012) 'Autism as a natural human variation: reflections on the claims of the neurodiversity movement', *Health Care Analysis*, 20 (1): 20–30.
Jones, H. and Bentz, J. (2005) *Using Popular Media to Help Preservice Teachers Understand Disability*. Paper presented at the Inclusive and Supportive Education Congress, Glasgow, Scotland. Accessed from: http://www.isec2005.org/isec/abstracts/papers_j/jones_h.shtml.
Kane, G. and Byrne, D. (2006) *Selves and Others. Language, Identity and Literature*, 2nd edn. Cape Town: Oxford University Press.
Kupfer, D. J., Kuhl, E. A. and Regier, D. A. (2013) 'DSM-5 – the future arrived', *JAMA*, 309 (16): 1691–2.
Landrum, J. (2001) 'Selecting intermediate novels that feature characters with disabilities', *Reading Teacher*, 55 (3): 252–8.
Lee, G. K., Lopata, C., Volker, M. A., Thomeer, M. L., Nida, R. E., Toomey, J. A. et al. (2009) 'Health-related quality of life of parents of children with high-functioning autism spectrum disorders', *Focus on Autism and Other Developmental Disabilities*, 24 (4): 227–39.
Lee-Tarver, A. (2006) 'Are individualized education plans a good thing? A survey of teachers' perceptions of the utility of IEPs in regular education settings', *Journal of Instructional Psychology*, 33 (4): 263–72.
McCall, Z. and Skrtic, T. (2009) 'Intersectional needs politics: a policy frame for the wicked problem of disproportionality', *Multiple Voices for Ethnically Diverse Exceptional Learners*, 11 (2): 3–23.
McDonagh, P. (2008) 'Autism and modernism: a genealogical exploration', in M. Osteen (ed.), *Autism and Representation*. New York: Routledge, pp. 99–116.
McGeer, V. (2009) 'The thought and talk of individuals with autism: reflections on Ian Hacking', *Metaphilosophy*, 40 (3–4): 517–30.
Montello, M. (2010) 'Middlebrow medical ethics', *Hastings Center Report*, 40 (4): 20–1.
Moran, J. M., Young, L. L., Saxe, R., Lee, S. M., O'Young, D., Mavros, P. L. and Gabrieli, J. D. (2011) 'Impaired theory of mind for moral judgment in high-functioning autism', *Proceedings of the National Academy of Sciences*, 108 (7): 2688–92.
Murray, D. (2006) *Coming Out Asperger: Diagnosis, Disclosure and Self-Confidence*. Philadelphia, PA: Jessica Kingsley.
Murray, S. (2006) 'Autism and the contemporary sentimental: fiction and the narrative fascination of the present', *Literature and Medicine*, 25 (1): 24–45.
Nussbaum, M. (1995) *Poetic Justice: The Literary Imagination and Public Life*. Boston: Beacon Press.
Nussbaum, M. (1997) *Cultivating Humanity. A Classical Defense of Reform in Liberal Education*. Cambridge, MA: Harvard University Press.
Nussbaum, M. (2010) *Not for Profit. Why Democracy Needs the Humanities*. Princeton, NJ: Princeton University Press.
Olear, G. (2011) 'When popular novels perpetuate negative stereotypes: Mark Haddon, Asperger's and irresponsible fiction'. Accessed from: http://www.huffingtonpost.com/greg-olear/curious-incident-dog-night-time_b_1099692.html.

Osteen, M. (2008) 'Autism and representation: a comprehensive introduction', in M. Osteen (ed.), *Autism and Representation*. New York: Routledge, pp. 1–48.
Peck, C., Staub, D., Gallucci, C. and Schwartz, I. (2004) 'Parent perception of the impacts of inclusion on their nondisabled child', *Research and Practice for Persons with Severe Disabilities*, 29 (2): 135–43.
Picoult, J. (2010) *House Rules*. London: Hodder & Stoughton.
Raveaud, M. (2005) 'Hares, tortoises and the social construction of the pupil: differentiated learning in French and English primary schools', *British Educational Research Journal*, 31 (4): 459–79.
Salager-Meyer, F. (1994) 'Hedges and textual communicative function in medical English written discourse', *English for Specific Purposes*, 13 (2): 149–70.
Semino, E. (2014) 'Pragmatic failure, mind style and characterisation in fiction about autism', *Language and Literature*, 23 (2): 141–58.
Senju, A., Southgate, V., White, S. and Frith, U. (2009) 'Mindblind eyes: an absence of spontaneous theory of mind in Asperger syndrome', *Science*, 325 (5942): 883–5.
Slee, R. (2011) *The Irregular School*. London: Routledge.
Straus, J. (2010) 'Autism as culture', in L. Davis (ed.), *The Disability Studies Reader*, 3rd edn. New York: Routledge, pp. 535–59.
Walters, S. (2013) 'Cool aspie humor: cognitive difference and Kenneth Burke's comic corrective in the Big Bang Theory and community', *Journal of Literary and Cultural Disability Studies*, 7 (3): 271–88, 356.
Walton, E. (2012) 'Using literature as a strategy to promote inclusivity in high school classrooms', *Intervention in School and Clinic*, 47 (4): 224–33.
Walton, E. (2013) 'Inclusion in a South African high school? Reporting and reflecting on what learners say', *International Journal of Inclusive Education*, 17 (11): 1171–85.
Wimsatt, W. and Beardsley, M. (1946) 'The intentional fallacy', *Sewanee Review*, 54 (3): 468–88.
Womack, S. A., Marchant, M. and Borders, D. (2011) 'Literature-based social skills instruction: a strategy for students with learning disabilities', *Intervention in School and Clinic*, 46 (3): 157–64.
Wooden, S. R. (2011) 'Narrative medicine in the literature classroom: ethical pedagogy and Mark Haddon's *The Curious Incident of the Dog in the Night-time*', *Literature and Medicine*, 29 (2): 274–96.
World Health Organisation (WHO) (1992) *The ICD-10 Classification of Mental and Behavioural Disorders: Clinical Descriptions and Diagnostic Guidelines*. Geneva: WHO.

# 8

# SPEAKING AND HEARING IN/EXCLUSION

### No one understands what it's like to be me

A young teenager, whom I will call Naomi, was explaining to me why she hated school so much. She began with words which I will never forget – 'I spend the day being reminded of what I cannot do.' This young woman had a troubled past. She was in temporary foster care and had had a chequered schooling history. She explained how the day would start with mathematics, which she could not follow and found impossible to do. Then there would be an English class. She said that she enjoyed reading, but that she struggled to read the set works. The books she could read were too 'babyish' for her and she was self-conscious about her lack of fluency when reading aloud. Break times offered no respite. She was experiencing difficulties navigating the social complexities of the cliques of girls in her new school, and her inappropriate social behaviour was resulting in her being increasingly ostracised. The weekly physical education class was the worst, she said. She was carrying excess weight, was not fit and had no previous exposure to the rules of games like netball or hockey. No one wanted her on their team. This bleak account of a school day that endlessly reinforced a sense of inadequacy was summed up in her words 'No one understands what it's like to be me.'

Teachers often reflect on their own experience of school as enjoyable at best and at worst bearable. The system worked for them and they perpetuate its beliefs and practices, seldom considering how it might not work for others. In a quest for a more socially just and inclusive education system that is responsive to the needs of all learners, it becomes particularly important to listen to the voices of those who, like Naomi, find learning difficult and the way we do schooling insufferable. Their voices are usually silent and silenced. These are the learners who do not get prizes or awards. They do not get elected onto representative councils or prefect bodies. They occupy a precarious position as tenants on the margins of schooling (Slee 2011), mostly tolerated because 'being inclusive' is fashionable, but ultimately marginalised because their contribution and ways of being are not valued. So while the focus on the language of inclusive education in this book has been mostly on reading and writing, this chapter is concerned with talking about and hearing or listening to inclusion and exclusion in education.

## Listening to in/exclusion

The development of more inclusive education is partly made possible by finding out, as Naomi said, 'What it is like to be me.' This means striving to access the 'insider knowledge' of the educational world from the perspective of a child or young person. A powerful argument for listening to the voices of children and young people in the quest to develop effective inclusive environments is made by Messiou (2012a: 19). She says:

> … by engaging with students' voices we can reflect on what we offer to them and what they experience, and more importantly think of ways to make changes to improve these experiences.

Valuable insights can be gained by listening to children and young people who have been marginalised or excluded (Corbett and Slee 2000) and practices that need changing can be identified (Ainscow and Kaplan 2004). Those who are privileged in an environment are unlikely to recognise their own privilege and may well fail to recognise the obstacles to access and participation that others encounter (Wendell 1996). 'Insider perspectives' can work as a powerful pedagogic tool in teacher education (Jones 2014) by alerting teachers to ways in which their practices are experienced by learners.

To access the opinions of children and young people we need them to communicate their experiences. This might be through talking, but some young people do not use spoken language and some are proficient in languages different from those who listen to them. Some are better able to communicate through other mediums, such as signs, play, art or drama. The term 'voice', although technically related to sound and speech, has come to represent various forms of communication, including visual representation. Thompson (2008) suggests that children and young people's capacity and right to speak come together in the notion of voice. All children and young people have a voice, even if it is expressed as silence (Lewis 2010). As novelist Arundhati Roy (2004) reminds us, '… there's really no such thing as the "voiceless". There are only the deliberately silenced, or the preferably unheard.'

Whereas hearing and listening might appear synonymous, an argument can be made for differentiating between the two processes. Bodie and Crick (2014: 105), for example, maintain: 'Hearing denotes a capacity to discriminate characteristics of one's environment through aural sense perception, but listening is a relationally oriented phenomenon.' Listening, for these authors, is 'an acquired art', 'difficult and contingent' and 'qualitatively different' from hearing (105). Significant for my purpose is the idea that listening creates the possibility for considering 'that things could be other than what we had assumed them to be' (Bodie and Crick 2014: 105). Listening to the voices of children and young people presupposes intentionality, relationship and an openness to new perspectives. But before abandoning 'hearing' in this discussion in favour of 'listening', it is worth noting that 'hearing' can be used to emphasise understanding and empathy, as in Roberts' (2008) chapter title: 'Listening to children: and hearing them'. The implication of this title is that listening is possible without 'hearing' which, says Roberts, is 'taking full account of what they tell us' (Roberts 2008: 260). Whether the word listening or hearing is used as the stronger word, the issue remains that children and young people need to know that their contributions are valued, that participation is meaningful and that consultation is genuine.

## Listening through research

Research offers a formalised space in which to listen to children and young people about their experiences of inclusion, exclusion and marginalisation. In what has become known as 'voice research', children and young people are engaged as participants with, rather than subjects of, research. South Africa lags behind other countries when it comes to listening to the voices of children and young people in the context of inclusive education. The focus of research in this country has been overwhelmingly biased towards hearing about teachers' attitudes and opinions on inclusive education (Walton 2011). Relatively little is known about how young people experience education under the providence of inclusive education. In the sections that follow, I will recount some findings from research done by five postgraduate students and present the voices of some of the young people with whom they worked. These students each identified a group of young people whom they knew from their own experiences to be vulnerable to marginalisation or exclusion within the 'inclusive' education system. The students spent time with these young people, listening to 'what it is like to be them' and then reporting what they heard. Each student's sample was small but, taken together, the young people who participated provide compelling insights about what it is like to negotiate marginalisation and exclusion where learners are assumed to be 'included'. In Table 8.1, I have summarised these projects for ease of reference in the discussion that follows.

### *Voices of young South Africans*

Many affluent independent schools in South Africa offer financial assistance to disadvantaged learners who would otherwise be unable to afford the fees. Geyer (2014) was interested in the experiences of this group of young people, and the extent to which the sponsorship programme is as inclusionary as its benefactors intended. Geyer reports that the young people who received financial assistance expressed gratitude for the opportunity. However, once admitted to the school, these learners found that the limitations of the sponsorship cast a shadow over their experiences. Although their tuition fees were paid, they lacked technological devices that their

TABLE 8.1 Five voice research projects

| Project designation | Investigator name | Participant identity | Participant* details | Data collection methods |
|---|---|---|---|---|
| Project A | A. Combrink | Grade 8 and 9 learners in mainstream high schools who attended remedial primary schools | Seven young people across six schools in Johannesburg | Two individual interviews with each learner, spaced across one academic year |
| Project B | L. Dolowitz | Young people with a diagnosis of Tourette's syndrome | Eight young people | One in-depth individual interview with each young person |
| Project C | K. Geyer | Economically disadvantaged learners who received scholarships to attend affluent independent schools | Sixteen young people across four schools in Johannesburg | Two individual interviews with each learner, spaced across one academic year |
| Project D | W. Kimani | Young mothers who returned to school after the delivery of their babies | Eleven young women across two Johannesburg schools | Prompted 'Mxit' diaries; 'sister-sister' videos; one focus group interview with all participants in each school; each individual participated in another small group (three mothers) interview |
| Project E | T. Taylor | High-school learners in special schools | Seventeen young people across five special schools in Johannesburg | Three focus group interviews with the learners in each school, and one individual interview with each participant in one academic year |

*Most participants in these studies are not specifically identified by gender, race or age in the research reports.

peers used for learning and they were constrained in their sport participation because of a lack of equipment. Their peer relationships and sense of belonging varied. Some felt that their relatively poor background resulted in (self-imposed) ostracism, like one young man who would refuse weekend invitations home with classmates because he knew that reciprocation would be expected. Others felt 'inferior' and 'excluded' (55) because they could not join in the conversations about lavish overseas holidays that their classmates enjoyed. Despite this, most learners reported that, over time, they developed 'trusting friendships' (54). While these learners were candid with the researcher, their voices were silent or silenced in the school. Often the silence was self-imposed in the sense that they withdrew from conversations because they felt they could not participate or feared exposure as scholarship recipients. One learner reported being silenced on account of her family not being able to afford school fees. Geyer (2014) says, '… learners were complaining about not having a class for a particular subject'. The scholarship recipient was prevented by her peers from participating in the conversation because '"you don't pay, you don't get to complain"' (56).

Although the independent schooling sector is relatively small in South Africa, it has been shown to be proactive in terms of inclusive education (Walton *et al.* 2009). As a result, many independent high schools are willing to enrol learners who, because of various learning difficulties, attended 'remedial' primary schools. In Project A, Combrink (2014) was concerned to find out what it was like to be a learner from a remedial primary school now in a mainstream high school. She reports that the experience of these learners was characterised by significant academic difficulty and epistemological marginalisation. Combrink (2014) records one learner saying, '"Teachers always say that I didn't listen when I say to them I don't understand"' (47). In a form of epistemic injustice (Fricker 2007), this learner's expression of difficulties with understanding was contradicted by teachers. Another learner silenced him/herself for fear of being thought of as 'stupid', telling the researcher, '"Most of the times I don't understand the work, but I don't want to say so because teachers will think I'm stupid or I don't listen"' (48). The social experience of these learners was mixed. Some had good friends for whom primary school background did not matter. Others felt as though they were 'judged' by their peers because they 'are' 'remedial' and are deemed 'stupid' (52). The young people who shared their experiences with Combrink had mixed views of their primary school education in remedial schools. On the one hand, they appreciated the assistance they received with learning from supportive teachers there. On the other hand, they found it left them with a label that led to 'marginalisation, exclusion and teasing' (59) in their mainstream high schools.

Learners in special schools are also ambivalent as they reflect on their 'placement'. In Project E, Taylor (2014) was motivated to engage with young people in special schools after watching them remove all garments displaying the school insignia on leaving the school property. The reason, she reports, was that learners were embarrassed to be identified with the school as it 'had a negative impact on the ways others viewed [them]' (1). Taylor reports that learners in the special schools were generally positive about the educational support they received from teachers and enjoyed positive peer relationships within the school. It was, however, when they interacted with people outside of the school that they felt '"embarrassed"' or '"ashamed"' (66) to name their school. A significant finding relevant to the concern of voice is that Taylor found relatively few learners aware of why they were in a special school. Some noted their disability and assumed this as the reason, while others remarked on learning difficulties they had experienced in previous schools. For ten of the participants, there had been no consultation about a move to a special school, with Taylor quoting one as saying, '"My parents dumped me at the special school"' (71). Taylor noted the learners' frequent use of the noun 'placement' or passive form of the verb 'was placed'. She says:

> Placement is often seen as a decision made by parents and teachers with little consideration of what learners, the individuals who are ultimately affected by the placement, think. (71)

Taylor confirms what Slee (2011) notes in the context of Queensland, Australia. 'Placement' is for learners with disabilities, whereas 'enrolment' is for 'ordinary' learners.

The school experience of young people with a diagnosis of Tourette's syndrome was generally less positive than the experiences of those interviewed by Taylor. The accounts heard by Dolowitz (2014) in Project B were of anxious young people trying with varying success to control tics at school and mostly misunderstood by teachers and peers. Their overall experience was of impatient teachers who do not understand Tourette's syndrome. One young person asked '"Why can't my teacher realise that I can't help moving or making noises?"' Another said that the teacher '"… is always shouting at me to stop making noise and sounds"' (69). They said that their teachers were generally unsupportive, critical, irritable and unhelpful. Peer relationships were similarly fraught. The young people Dolowitz interviewed acknowledged their aggression, poor impulse control and socially inappropriate behaviour, but linked this to a cycle of teasing and bullying. One said, '"They make fun of me because I twitch … they imitate me and laugh"' (74). Another wished for peer support and understanding, saying:

> 'I wish they [peers] would support me and understand what I am going through … I wish I had more friends and that people would like me.' (72)

Dolowitz concludes by capturing the complex and dynamic interplay of physical, psychological, social and scholastic factors that make for a generally negative school experience for these young people.

Stigmatisation, bullying and unsupportive teachers have also been the experience of young women who return to school after the delivery of their babies (Kimani (2014), in Project D). While South African policy has had some success in encouraging young women to stay in school during pregnancy and return to school after delivery, many of these young women do not complete their secondary education. Kimani (2014) focused her research on listening to young schooling mothers better to understand the inclusionary and exclusionary practices that confronted them. She found them to be determined to persevere and committed to their studies. They were encouraged to continue by a few teachers and a friendship bond with others in similar situations. However, the obstacles they faced were significant. They were very aware that they were constructed as a 'problem' and they were stigmatised by 'Teachers and classmates who make disparaging comments in class about pregnancy and motherhood' (Kimani 2014: 87). Various pregnancy prevention discussions and programmes in the school reinforced this attitude, and the young women felt demeaned by the content and moralising tone of these events. The young schooling mothers faced academic difficulties as a result of inflexible assignment submission dates or after-school classes scheduled when they had to collect their children from child care. Kimani listened to these young women through a number of innovative methods and concluded that schools '… need to recognise their motherhood in ways that are helpful and in ways that preserve their dignity' (Kimani 2014: 93).

## *Concurrent experiences of inclusion, exclusion and marginalisation*

These accounts present a complex picture of concurrent experiences of inclusion, exclusion and marginalisation. Access, participation and belonging are not absolute experiences, they are relative and constantly in flux. Young people's accounts show that they are aware of contradictions and dilemmas. For example, young schooling mothers (Project D) sometimes want their identities as mothers acknowledged so they can be supported, while at other times they don't want to be identified as different. Furthermore, young people's accounts of their experiences do not always match the researcher's expectations, giving credence to the idea that listening can disrupt preconceptions. For example, learners in special schools (Project E) did not view their schooling provision as inherently demeaning or discriminatory. Together with learners from remedial primary schools (Project A), they were almost unanimous in praising the teachers and teaching in these schools. On the surface of things, these findings may frustrate the advocate of inclusive education, who is keen to find fault with segregated special education. In this regard, Gabel (2010: 10) asks:

> Are separate contexts (i.e., self-contained classrooms) always oppressive or can they sometimes be liberatory, and who decides whether an educational context is oppressive or liberatory? This question assumes that there can be liberation and oppression in any educational context but interrogates the power relations in making claims about such matters.

The voices of young people confront adults with questions about who gets to decide who is seen as included or excluded, and disrupt adult views of what is or what should be. The research reported in these five projects '… endorse[s] complexity, partial truths and multiple subjectivities' (Lather 2007: 136) in the schooling experience of a variety of South African young people. Having noted ambiguities and contradictions, however, it is clear that the young people across these studies seem to know that they are not the 'smiled upon' (Slee 2011: 42) ones. The educational and social structures of schools and schooling do not always favour who they are and theirs is an ongoing struggle for a recognition of their worth and value. They are silenced, but they find ways to assert their voice.

## Silence and voice

While the young people in these studies gave their voice to the postgraduate researchers, they revealed how they were tacitly or explicitly silenced in their schools. In the face of an environment and culture that valorises certain ways of being and learning, all these learners had learned to silence, if not make something of who they are invisible. Scholarship recipients in Project C were loath to reveal their status as such, given the affluence of their peers. They withdrew from conversations and social interactions where overprivileged pastimes were discussed. Young people in mainstream high schools were silent about their remedial primary school backgrounds, fearing judgment and teasing (Project A). They had learned to be quiet in lessons when they did not understand something, lest they were thought to be inattentive or stupid. If they spoke about not understanding, they were contradicted. While many young people in Project E were not unhappy in their special schools, they avoided identifying with their schools because they knew of the associated stigma. They hid their school clothes and preferred not to name their school. In many cases, they were not consulted about schooling decisions. Silence was demanded of young people with Tourette's syndrome (Project B), and they expended much of their energy and attention on suppressing tics and vocalisations. Young schooling mothers in Project D were shamed into silence during class discussions on sexuality and were actively discouraged from attending pregnancy prevention programmes.

But just as the young people's experiences defy caricaturing as either inclusionary or exclusionary, their silence was not absolute. All found ways to navigate a schooling system that is not necessarily premised on their inclusion. They expressed their agency in various ways, and showed resilience and even resistance. With the possible exception of the young people with Tourette's syndrome, all the young people formed supportive friendships which mitigated some of the academic and other challenges they faced. They found creative ways to circumnavigate some of the constraints on their inclusion. One scholarship recipient in Project C, for example, judiciously avoided sports that demanded extra equipment (like cricket) but chose rugby and soccer where he could use the same boots all year (Geyer 2014). Even the aggression of the young people with Tourette's syndrome in Project B could be seen as a way of communicating frustration to a community that is intolerant of difference.

## Imagining schooling as different

There is much that could be deduced about the workings of exclusion in schools from the accounts of the young people in these five projects. But this is not always necessary as many of them explicitly gave voice to how schooling could or should change. Teachers were the focus of attention, with young people able to articulate the kind of teacher behaviour and attitude that supports and includes rather than that which demeans and excludes. In most cases, this involved recognition of difference and an appropriate response to this difference. Learners who attended remedial primary schools noted that teachers should realise that they have different learning needs and that they '"sometimes struggle to learn in the same way as other learners"' (Combrink 2014: 59). They also thought that that teachers should be aware of the bullying that took place and intervene in some way. Young people with Tourette's syndrome had a number of injunctions for teachers, including that they should '"stop criticising me ... as I am trying my best"' (Dolowitz 2014: 71). Learners in special schools emphasised the need for teacher patience, saying that in an ideal school, '"teachers should actually just be patient with all the students"' (Taylor 2014: 83). Young schooling mothers expected teachers to be understanding and encouraging, especially since many are mothers themselves.

While many of the young people who participated in these studies found support in friendships, their biggest challenge was the negative attitudes and behaviours of peers either within their schools or in their wider circles. Scholarship recipients wished they '"could be around friendlier people"' and wanted to see changes in '"... the perceptions of learners and how humans treat each other"' at school (Geyer 2014: 57). Learners in special schools or who attended remedial primary schools or who have Tourette's syndrome are unanimous in identifying the need for understanding and acceptance from peers. Prejudice and stereotyping abound and mitigate against friendship. A learner in a special school said:

> 'They [learners in mainstream schools] hear we [are] from this school and they [are] like 'Don't come near me. I don't wanna have you as a friend.' And it hurts a lot, 'cause I want friends too. It's hard to get friends.'
> 
> *(Taylor 2014: 76)*

Learners with Tourette's syndrome wished that their peers knew more about the syndrome and how it affected them. One said: '"I'm never the in-crowd ... I wish they [peers] would be more comfortable with the TS [Tourette's syndrome] issue"' and another wanted '"... my friends to know that I am who I am because of my condition"' (Dolowitz 2014: 73).

There is abundant international and South African research that documents the negative attitudes that children and young people have about peers whom they deem different (Walton 2013). The problem is that this research is mostly for academic interest. The voices of the young people who bear the brunt of these negative attitudes and cruel behaviours serve as a reminder of real lives affected by prejudice and discrimination. Nor is the solution merely to advocate change in attitude. As Slee (2011) reminds, attitudes do not operate in a vacuum. They are engendered and sustained by structures that give them legitimacy. Young people are given tacit permission to ostracise or demean Others by watching how their teachers treat them (Messiou 2008). The South African education system familiar to young people is one of

> ... flourishing separate special schools for learners deemed to have disabilities or additional support needs; an elite independent school sector granted the

right to exclude by setting admission criteria; and an ordinary school sector where 'clauses of conditionality' (Slee 1996: 107) govern ongoing enrolment.
*(Walton 2013: 1181)*

It shouldn't surprise us that young people have negative attitudes to Others, when the processes and structures around them give credence to the idea that some learners do not really belong in 'their' classrooms or schools.

The young people who participated in the five research projects had limited perspectives on issues of exclusion at school level and rarely imagined changes beyond their classroom experience. Nor did they look to the wider context in accounting for some of the exclusionary pressures they faced. Recipients of financial assistance did not interrogate the wider impact of scholarship programmes. They did not consider how these initiatives represent an individual solution to a systemic problem, in that while individual learners may benefit from enhanced educational opportunities, systemic inequities remain (Geyer and Walton 2015). Learners were able to identify how their association with special and remedial primary schools leads to labelling, but also recognised the educational benefits of schooling in these contexts. But they never questioned the premise on which schools are segregated on the grounds of learner ability. Learners with Tourette's syndrome and young schooling mothers acutely feel prejudice and discrimination in the school context but do not relate these to wider societal constructions of deviance.

The limited horizons of the young people's experiences must be acknowledged when hearing their voices as an impetus for change. Gable (2013: 93) reminds us:

> While student narratives of their experiences are undeniably important, a hermeneutic account will not access the social relations that exist beyond this student's consciousness.

The researcher's role in mediating the narratives of the young people is crucial in situating these experiences within the wider social context. For if we take the voices of the young people I have reported here at face value, we might conclude that nothing needs to change in the system of separate special education because the learners in that system are mostly happy and appreciative of the education they are receiving. Likewise, we might forestall all critique of scholarship programmes on account of the positive experiences of those who are selected to participate in them. The wider field of disability research warns about an 'obsession with experience' (Mercer 2002: 235) or 'methodological individualism' (Oliver 2009: 112). Inclusion and exclusion in schools should not be understood as an aggregation of individual experiences. Instead, experience needs to be seen as embedded in wider social, cultural, political and economic processes (Skeggs 1995, in Mercer 2002: 235). It is thus important to remember that children and young people who participate in 'voice' research give us 'experience-near concepts' (Geertz 1983: 57). These are the familiar, spontaneous and readily understandable concepts that they use to account for their experiences. It is the responsibility of the specialist theorist to provide the 'experience-distant' concepts, that is to 'capture the general features of social life' (Geertz 1983: 58). The voice researcher enables an understanding, not just of 'what it is like to be me', but what it is like to be *us*, where 'us' are groups of people constituted in a wider social world. This builds our understanding of who education privileges and disprivileges, and the mechanisms by which this occurs.

## Dilemmas, concerns and caveats in voice research

In the introductory paragraphs of this chapter, I described the potential for change that listening to children and young people offers. There are, however, some difficulties and dilemmas that need to be acknowledged. Researchers entering the field to listen to children and young people need to be conscious of a number of difficulties at every stage of the process, from the conception of the problem, to selecting participants and finally to (re)producing their voice. They also have to answer to those who question the epistemological value of voice research.

### What (or who) is the research problem?

There is a dilemma that must be acknowledged in conceptualising research with children and young people to understand their experiences of marginalisation (Walton 2011). There is a choice between working with an entire learner population, like a whole class or grade, and singling out certain subgroups of learners based on some predetermined characteristics. The former approach has advantages. It acknowledges that all children might experience marginalisation (Messiou 2006) and means that analysis cannot use specific (arbitrary) categories of learner difference to account for behaviour or experience (Walton 2013). But the whole group approach might not necessarily give us the nuances of understanding that teachers need to bring about change.

The alternative is to identify a particular subgroup of learners based on a particular identity marker (like disability) and listen to them. This approach was taken in the five student projects reported on in this chapter. The advantage of doing this is that specific children and young people have the potential to offer insight into the extent to which inclusive policies and practices actually include. In this regard, Slee (2011: 169) asks: 'Who is better able to talk about the needs and aspirations of disabled children than the children themselves …?' These are the children and young people who are most likely to be 'information-rich' (McMillan and Schumacher 2001: 401) about experiences of inclusion, exclusion and marginalisation in relation to their identities. In addition, their collective stories remind us that we are not dealing with isolated individuals whose experiences, on their own, might be regarded as idiosyncratic. Instead, we can recognise the systematic oppression of a particular group of children and young people.

There are also disadvantages to listening to the voices of a particular subgroup of children and young people. The first is that it is inextricably bound up with labelling. From an entire group of children and young people, some have to be selected and invited to participate in research on the basis of a marker of their difference. There are many examples of published research in this tradition (see Cocks 2008; Mitchell 2010; Whitehurst 2006). It is problematic, however, when categories of difference are uncritically presented as self-evident. Research legitimates and perpetuates these categories when they are used as selection criteria for participants, and it creates the impression that these categories are discrete, fixed and objective. Then, the act of selecting research participants out of a general group on the basis of a particular identity marker is signalling the expectation that their experience is different. Research situates them as the 'exotic other' (Allan 2007: 44). I have argued that:

> Unlike the experiences and views of 'regular' learners, their experiences and views are presumed unusual, unfamiliar or strange, therefore warranting investigation. The act of research thus produces these children and young people as strangers.
>
> *(Walton 2011: 87)*

The idea that some learners are strangers is reinforced by the hospitality metaphor[1] that pervades discourses of inclusive education. Research compounds this by asserting that not only are some learners different, but they are different in ways that are potentially problematic.

The assumption that certain children or young people are necessarily vulnerable, marginalised or excluded because of some or other identity marker exemplifies deficit thinking. It also might skew the research lens such that research does not reveal the ways children and young people are resourceful and resilient. For example, in their study of refugee children in a Durban school, Sookrajh *et al.* (2005) found that the refugee learners did not validate their teachers' construction of them as vulnerable. In addition, special need, disability or barrier to learning does not necessarily account for the marginalisation or exclusion of children and young people. There are potentially a number of contextual and other influences on their school experiences. The life-world and identities of children and young people reflect the complex interplay of any number of factors, including race, language, ethnicity, culture, rurality, gender, class, age and sexual orientation. Any of these individually or in combination might contribute to an experience of marginalisation and exclusion. If this is not acknowledged, we risk essentialising children and young people by constructing their identity and experience as monolithic (hooks 1994: 90).

Research to promote inclusive education through listening is thus faced with a dilemma that is familiar to the field. This dilemma is the dual (contradictory) imperative of responding simultaneously to the universal and the individual (Allen 2007; Ferguson and Ferguson 1998; Lunt and Norwich 1999). In 'voice' research, the dilemma is:

> To promote inclusive education, we need to understand the experience of inclusion and exclusion in schools from the inside and so we have to listen and respond to the voices of children and young people who have been

included and or excluded. But in doing this, our research selects, labels and positions them as 'the included' or 'the excluded', marks 'them' as different from 'us' and so undermines the very essence of inclusive education.

*(Walton 2011: 87)*

Dilemmas must be acknowledged, but they cannot have satisfactory solutions. But this should not detract from the possibility that the findings of such research could jolt the education community into realising that not everyone benefits from our current structures and arrangements (Slee 2011). Slee (2011: 157) warns, however, that in countenancing 'the voices of marginalized people' their voices should be represented rather than inscribed.

## *Power, voice and writing the Other*

The process in which one person (in this case a researcher) presumes to listen to and then recount the voice of an Other (in this case children and young people) is inevitably problematic. The researcher's relationship with participants is ethically complex, especially as a result of the unequal power relations implicit in an adult researcher engaging with children and young people. Despite measures to ensure voluntary participation and informed consent, adult authority may tacitly compel children or young people into giving their voice. Once in the research setting, the adult researcher may constrain what young people feel they can say (Thompson 2008). The researcher can easily become the inquisitor, with the power to select research questions and direct conversations (Walton 2013). Then, in a process mostly invisible to the children and young people, their voice becomes data to be cleaned, coded and categorised. It is then overlaid with the researcher's more authoritative voice, and only allowed to whisper through the subsequent report in small snippets that support the researcher's 'findings'. No wonder that concern has been raised that children and young people have been exploited by researchers who 'mine' them for data (Fleming 2010).

What it means to 'write the Other' is a concern wherever a researcher presumes to (re)produce an Other's voice, in a different context and via a different medium. This concern must be magnified in research with children and young people, given that the power relations are so very unequal. I often wonder if children and young people really are giving 'informed consent', not just to an interview or other means of participation, but to the wider dissemination and critical consumption of what they say. I am not convinced that they always can imagine the journal article or the book chapter, and how their utterances are rewritten in contexts and for purposes they cannot apprehend. Nor might they think that they will grow up and their opinions might change, but their current voice is frozen in print. The reflexivity of the politically committed researcher goes little way to disrupting the 'privileged fixed position from which the researcher interrogates and writes the researched' (Lather 2001: 484). But at least there must be some recognition of the intractable dilemmas inherent in being both confidant and researcher, in leaning towards participants in order better to hear them, then leaning away to share what they've told us with the academic community. We can never be smug because there really is '... no ethically unassailable position' (Josselson 2007: 560) and researchers doing this work must tread carefully. In going forward, perhaps we should jettison talk of 'giving voice' to children and young people, as if it is a gift in the power of adults to bestow rather than a right to be asserted. Instead, we could talk about children and young people trustingly giving their voice as a gift to be respectfully stewarded by those who listen. We may concede that voice is a gift, but have to confront the question of whether it constitutes knowledge.

## *The epistemological value of voice*

The findings of voice research have been criticised for their 'epistemological weakness' (Arnot and Reay 2007: 317) and for 'privileging the mundane' as 'experience replaces theory as the author of knowledge' (Moore and Muller 1999: 202). The knowledge(s) generated by voice research are limited by both their dependence on context and their segmented, rather than hierarchical, organisation (Arnot and Reay 2007; Bernstein 2000; Moore and Muller 1999). The findings of voice research are unlikely to be abstractable (Moore and Young 2010) and, as such, cannot count as knowledge with general explanatory power. These concerns need to be acknowledged, but not necessarily so that voice research is abandoned. Young (2000: 530) reminds us of 'the role of experience in the production of new knowledge' and Maton (2010) affirms the legitimation of claims to knowledge based on knowers' attributes and experiences. The focus in what Maton calls a 'knower code'[2] is a 'privileged subject of study, the "knower"' (Maton 2010: 46). Truth, in a knower code, is defined by the privileged and unique voice of the knower or the client knower group. These client groups are often those 'said to be silenced within official educational knowledge' (Maton 2010: 42) and include endlessly proliferating knowers, fragmented by gender, class, race, ability and other identity markers. Thus research that aims to 'give voice' to a particular (marginalised) group has to acknowledge the epistemological limitations of its endeavours and recognise that the knowledge structures developed by this research have a stronger social rather than epistemic relations (Maton 2010) with the object of study.

## *Other ways to listen*

Research is not the only way to listen to children and young people – there are other opportunities and avenues for listening to their voices. What remains important is an acknowledgment of 'children's capacity to reflect on issues affecting their lives' and that they are given 'responsibilities and opportunities to share in decision making' (Rudduck and Flutter 2000: 86). Clark (2005: 491) urges those who work with children to engage in 'everyday listening', in addition to the one-off consultation that might occur when their views are sought over a specific issue or event. Messiou (2012b: 1318) believes that, '[L]earners' voices provide practitioners with wonderful opportunities for thinking about the way that children themselves perceive practices within the school.' She advocates that teachers engage in dialogue with their learners to build trust and potentially to change the culture of the classroom. Linington *et al.* (2011: 40) promote a community of enquiry approach among very young children, noting this is 'a relational pedagogy in its emphasis of listening to children in contexts that are meaningful to them'. Participation of high-school learners in school governance structures through representatives is legislated in South Africa (Carrim 2011) and could provide opportunities for the voices of young people to be heard.

Article 12 of the 1989 United Nations Convention on the Rights of the Child states that children have the right to express their views and be heard in matters pertaining to them (UN 1989). Furthermore, there is a particular injunction in the Convention on the Rights of People with Disabilities (UN 2006: Article 7.3) that children with disabilities

> ... should have the right to express their views freely on all matters affecting them, their views being given due weight in accordance with their age and maturity, on an equal basis with other children, and to be provided with disability and age-appropriate assistance to realize that right.

Whether through research or other mechanism, realising this right acknowledges that the experiences and opinions of children and young people are valuable and useful, and can help to bring about change.

## The potential for more dialogue in voice research?

I have, in this chapter, offered some perspectives on voice research and have presented some findings from research done with young people in South Africa. I conclude by suggesting that within this type of research, there is potential for more dialogic interaction, or a mutual speaking and hearing. The research reported here is quite traditional, with participants giving voice (in some way or another) and researchers listening and then analysing and disseminating what they have heard. The researchers' function tends to be seen as channelling the voices of the young people. There are more interactive possibilities, such that participants also learn and grow in their understandings of themselves and others. Some scholars have engaged children and young people as co-researchers (see, for example, Carrington *et al.* (2009), Messiou (2013), and Messiou and Jones (2015)). These approaches disrupt the researcher/researched binary and address some of the challenges of voice research described in this chapter.

Engaging with the voices of learners enables adults to think about how to improve learners' experiences. There is also the possibility that learners themselves might '... think about their own behaviour and, in so doing, have an active role in confronting marginalisation' (Messiou 2012a: 19). If the research space becomes more of a dialogue, there is the potential for a mutual consideration that things might be different. And as much as adults enter the space open to hearing and understanding, children and young people may also be challenged to look beyond their limited horizons and reflect critically on their own views and behaviours. In so doing, researchers may become, as Fleming (2010) says, builders rather than borrowers.

## Acknowledgment

I acknowledge the kind permission of Perspectives in Education to use work which was first published as E. Walton (2011) '"They discluded me": the possibilities and limitations of children's participation in inclusion research in South Africa', *Perspectives in Education*, 29 (1): 83–92.

## Notes

1 See Chapter 4.
2 Knowledge-knower structures are explored in more detail in Chapter 2.

## References

Ainscow, M. and Kaplan, I. (2004) *Using Evidence to Encourage Inclusive School Development: Possibilities and Challenges*. Paper presented at the Australian Association of Research in Education Annual Conference, Melbourne, December.
Allan, J. (2007) *Rethinking Inclusive Education*. Dordrecht: Springer.
Arnot, M. and Reay, D. (2007) 'A sociology of pedagogic voice: power, inequality and pupil consultation', *Discourse: Studies in the Cultural Politics of Education*, 28 (3): 311–25.
Benjamin, S., Nind, M., Hall, K., Collins, J. and Sheehy, K. (2003) 'Moments of inclusion and exclusion: pupils negotiating classroom contexts', *British Journal of Sociology of Education*, 24: 547–58.
Bernstein, B. (2000) *Pedagogy, Symbolic Control and Identity*. Lanham, MD: Rowman & Littlefield.
Bodie, G. D. and Crick, N. (2014) 'Listening, hearing, sensing: three modes of being and the phenomenology of Charles Sanders Peirce', *Communication Theory*, 24 (2): 105–23.
Carrim, N. (2011) 'Modes of participation and conceptions of children in South African education', *Perspectives in Education*, 29 (1): 74–82.
Carrington, S., Bland, D. and Brady, K. (2009) 'Training young people as researchers to investigate engagement and disengagement in the middle years', *International Journal of Inclusive Education*, 14 (5): 449–62.
Clark, A. (2005) 'Listening to and involving young children: a review of research and practice', *Early Child Development and Care*, 175 (6): 489–505.
Cocks, A. (2008) 'Researching the lives of disabled children', *Qualitative Social Work*, 7 (2): 163–80.
Combrink, A. (2014) 'The Experience of Grade 8 and 9 Learners in a Mainstream High School after Attending a Remedial Primary School'. Unpublished MEd research report, University of the Witwatersrand, Johannesburg. Accessed from: http://wiredspace.wits.ac.za/handle/10539/18238.
Corbett, N. and Slee, R. (2000) 'An international conversation on inclusive education', in F. Armstrong, D. Armstrong and L. Barton (eds), *Inclusive Education: Policy Contexts and Comparative Perspectives*. London: David Fulton, pp. 133–46.

Dolowitz, L. (2014) 'Listening to the Voices of Learners with Tourette's Syndrome'. Unpublished MEd research report, University of the Witwatersrand, Johannesburg. Accessed from: http://wiredspace.wits.ac.za/handle/10539/15813.

Ferguson, P. and Ferguson, D. (1998) 'Constructive tension and the potential for reflective reform', *Childhood Education*, 74 (5): 302–8.

Fleming, J. (2010) 'Young people's involvement in research – still a long way to go?', *Qualitative Social Work*, 10 (2): 207–23.

Fricker, M. (2007) *Epistemic Injustice. Power and the Ethics of Knowing*. Oxford: Oxford University Press.

Gabel, S. (2010) Introduction: disability studies in education', in S. Gabel (ed.), *Disability Studies in Education*. New York: Peter Lang, pp. 1–20.

Gable, A. S. (2013) 'Disability theorising and real-world educational practice: a framework for understanding', *Disability and Society*, 29 (1): 86–100.

Geertz, C. (1983) *Local Knowledge*. New York: Basic Books.

Geyer, K. (2014) 'The Voices of Disadvantaged Scholarship Recipient Learners in Affluent Independent High Schools'. Unpublished MEd research report, University of the Witwatersrand, Johannesburg. Accessed from: http://mobile.wiredspace.wits.ac.za/handle/10539/15874.

Geyer, K. and Walton, E. (2015) 'Schooling in the shadow of benevolence: the experience of scholarship recipients in affluent schools', *South African Journal of Higher Education*, 29 (1): 335–53.

hooks, b. (1994) *Teaching to Transgress*. New York: Routledge.

Jones, P. (2014) 'Whose insider perspectives count and why should we consider them?', in P. Jones (ed.) *Bringing Insider Perspectives into Inclusive Teacher Learning*. Abingdon: Routledge, pp. 1–8.

Josselson, R. (2007) 'The ethical attitude in narrative research', in D. J. Clandinin (ed.), *Handbook of Narrative Inquiry: Mapping a Methodology*. Thousand Oaks, CA: Sage, pp. 537–66.

Kimani, W. (2014) 'Lenses from the Margins: Young Schooling Mothers' Experiences in Two High Schools in Gauteng'. Unpublished MEd research report, University of the Witwatersrand, Johannesburg. Accessed from: http://wiredspace.wits.ac.za/handle/10539/18237.

Lather, P. (2001) 'Postmodernism, post-structuralism and post (critical) ethnography: of ruins, aporias and angels', in P. Atkinson, A. Coffey, S. Delamont, J. Lofland and L. Lofland (eds), *Handbook of Ethnography*. London: Sage, pp. 477–92.

Lather, P. (2007) *Getting Lost: Feminist Efforts Toward a Double(d) Science*. Albany, NY: State University of New York Press.

Lewis, A. (2010) 'Silence in the context of "child voice"', *Children and Society*, 24 (1): 14–23.

Lewis, I. (2008) *Young Voices*. Oslo: Atlas Alliance.

Linnington, V., Excell, L. and Murris, K. (2011) 'Education for participatory democracy: a Grade R perspective', *Perspectives in Education*, 29 (1): 36–45.

Lunt, I. and Norwich, B. (1999) *Can Effective Schools Be Inclusive Schools?* London: Institute of Education, University of London.

McMillan, J. and Schumacher, S. (2001) *Research in Education: A Conceptual Introduction*, 5th edn. New York: HarperCollins.

Maton, K. (2010) 'Analysing knowledge claims and practices: languages of legitimation', in K. Maton and R. Moore (eds), *Social Realism, Knowledge and the Sociology of Education*. London: Continuum, pp. 35–56.

Mercer, G. (2002) 'Emancipatory disability research', in C. Barnes, M. Oliver and L. Barton (eds), *Disability Studies Today*. Cambridge: Polity Press, pp. 228–49.

Messiou, K. (2006) 'Understanding marginalisation in education: the voice of children', *European Journal of Psychology of Education*, 21 (3): 305–18.
Messiou, K. (2008) 'Understanding children's constructions of meanings about other children: implications for inclusive education', *Journal of Research in Special Educational Needs*, 8 (1): 27–36.
Messiou, K. (2012a) *Confronting Marginalisation in Education*. Abingdon: Routledge.
Messiou, K. (2012b) 'Collaborating with children in exploring marginalisation: an approach to inclusive education', *International Journal of Inclusive Education*, 16 (12): 1311–22.
Messiou, K. (2013) 'Working with students as co-researchers in schools: a matter of inclusion', *International Journal of Inclusive Education*, 18 (6): 601–13.
Messiou, K. and Jones, L. (2015) 'Pupil mobility: using students' voices to explore their experiences of changing schools', *Children and Society*, 29 (4): 255–65.
Mitchell, W. (2010) '"I know how I feel": listening to young people with life-limiting conditions who have learning and communication impairments', *Qualitative Social Work*, 9 (2): 185–203.
Moore, R. and Muller, J. (1999) The discourse of "voice" and the problem of knowledge and identity in the sociology of education', *British Journal of Sociology of Education*, 20 (2): 189–206.
Moore, R. and Young, M. (2010) 'Reconceptualising knowledge and the curriculum in the sociology of education', in K. Maton and R. Moore (eds), *Social Realism, Knowledge and the Sociology of Education*. London: Continuum, pp. 14–31.
Oliver, M. (2009) *Understanding Disability. From Theory to Practice*, 2nd edn. Basingstoke: Palgrave Macmillan.
Roberts, H. (2008) 'Listening to children: and hearing them', in P. Christensen and A. James (eds), *Research With Children: Perspectives and Practices*, 2nd edn. Abingdon: Routledge, pp. 260–75.
Rose, R. and Shevlin, M. (2004) 'Encouraging voices: listening to young people who have been marginalised', *Support for Learning*, 19 (4): 155–61.
Roy, A. (2004) *Peace and the New Corporate Liberation Theology*. The 2004 Sydney Peace Prize lecture, at the Seymour Theatre Centre, University of Sydney. Accessed from: http://www.smh.com.au/news/Opinion/Roys-full-speech/2004/11/04/1099362264349.html.
Rudduck, J. and Flutter, J. (2000) 'Pupil participation and pupil perspective: "carving a new order of experience"', *Cambridge Journal of Education*, 30 (1): 75–89.
Slee, R. (2011) *The Irregular School*. London: Routledge
Sookrajh, R., Gopal, N. and Maharaj, B. (2005) 'Interrogating inclusionary and exclusionary practices: learners of war and flight', *Perspectives in Education*, 23 (1): 2–13.
Taylor, T. (2014) 'Inclusive Education: Learners' Perspectives on their Special School Placement'. Unpublished MEd research report, University of the Witwatersrand, Johannesburg. Accessed from: http://wiredspace.wits.ac.za/handle/10539/15824.
Thompson, P. (2008) 'Children and young people: voices in visual research', in P. Thompson (ed.), *Doing Visual Research with Children and Young People*. London: Routledge, pp. 1–20.
United Nations (1989) *United Nations Convention on the Rights of the Child*. New York: UN.
United Nations (2006) *Convention on the Rights of Persons with Disabilities and Optional Protocol*. Retrieved from: http://www.un.org/disabilities/countries.asp?navid=12andpid=166#S.
Walton, E. (2011) '"They discluded me": possibilities and limitations of children's participation in inclusion research in South Africa', *Perspectives in Education*, 29 (1): 83–92.
Walton, E. (2013) 'Inclusion in a South African high school? Reporting and reflecting on what learners say', *International Journal of Inclusive Education*, 17 (11): 1171–85.

Walton, E., Nel, N., Hugo, A. and Muller, H. (2009) 'The extent and practice of inclusion in independent schools (ISASA members) in Southern Africa', *South African Journal of Education*, 29 (1): 105–26.

Wendell, S. (1996) *The Rejected Body*. New York: Routledge.

Whitehurst, T. (2006) 'Liberating silent voices – perspectives of children with profound and complex learning needs on inclusion', *British Journal of Learning Disabilities*, 35: 55–61.

Young, M. F. D. (2000) 'Rescuing the sociology of educational knowledge from the extremes of voice discourse: towards a new theoretical basis for the sociology of the curriculum', *British Journal of Sociology of Education*, 21 (4): 523–36.

# BOOK ENDS

### Condemned and privileged to a life of alertness

On completing a master's level course in inclusive education, a student wrote as part of an informal course evaluation:

> We are now part of the inclusive activists' movement and so condemned and privileged to a life of alertness. We will share the difficulty, tension and struggle this creates, but also share in the new relationships it builds.
>
> *(Coetzee 2012)*

This student saw inclusive education as an activist movement of which she and her classmates were now a part. Clough (2000: 6) does not agree that inclusion represents a single movement, but that it 'is made up of many strong currents of belief, many different local struggles and a myriad forms of practice'. Whether inclusion represents one or more movements, it is significant that the student did not see inclusive education primarily as a field of study, despite a semester of engaging with theories, research and debates in the inclusive education literature. Instead, she was left with a personal response to inclusion as something we do to ourselves (Allan 2005). By talking of a life of alertness, she echoed the need for vigilance that is often mentioned in connection with inclusive education (see, for example, Artiles and Kozleski (2007) and Slee (2009, 2011)). Rice (2006) frames vigilance as 'critical consciousness' and quotes Kincheloe in defining this as

> ... an ability to step back from the world as we are accustomed to perceiving it and to see the ways our perception is constructed through linguistic codes, cultural signs and embedded power. (26)

A life of alertness, vigilance and critical consciousness is both a privilege and a sentence, because once one is aware of the workings of power to exclude, indifference should no longer be possible.

The inclusive activist might be alert to many things – exclusionary pedagogical practices, inaccessible buildings and facilities, inequitable distribution of resources and policies that privilege the few are just some that come to mind. But the alertness imagined by this book is towards language and the linguistic codes to which Rice (2006) refers. Language 'builds things' (Gee 2011: 16) in the world. The reading, writing, speaking and listening described here have contributed to the building of what we now know as inclusive education. In turn, inclusive education has spawned thousands of books and journal articles, fed the policy mill, contributed to the proliferation of courses in higher education institutions and bolstered options on the international conference circuit. But to assume that the language of inclusive education is necessarily neutral, if not benign, in its effects is to underestimate the power of language.

South Africa's Truth and Reconciliation Commission (TRC) to which I referred in the introduction of this book has much to say about the role of language. In particular, the Commission exposed ways in which language was harnessed by the apartheid regime *and* those struggling for liberation to further their ends. Notwithstanding the explicit references to the role of language in promoting and sustaining violent acts in defence of and in resistance to apartheid, it is worth noting what it is that the TRC found language doing because the language of inclusive education does similar things. For example, the TRC report noted that 'apartheid discourse constructed socialised categories, enshrined in the language of laws, which forged differences and distance between groups' (TRC 1998: 295). This book has shown that the language of inclusive education constructs socialised categories, particularly of children and young people. This occurs in and through policies, textbooks for teachers and research, as some children and young people are categorised as needing inclusion and others as the presumed included. Forging difference and distance occurs as 'they' are distinguished from 'us' in hospitality metaphors and in a phalanx of educational interventions deemed necessary for effecting 'inclusion'. Popular fiction buttresses the language of difference by presenting young people with whom we might sympathise, but whose aberrant behaviour is offered as a source of entertainment that ensures their distance and reinforces their alterity.

Language builds identities and relationships (Gee 2011) as socialised categories are ascribed, described and inscribed. So while textbook writers construct categories of learners who are deficient and a problem for teachers and the education system, the textbook writers also use language to enact their identities as experts in inclusive education and cast teachers as non-experts and un(der)skilled. These experts assume, through various linguistic devices, the authority to instruct readers and so signal a fundamentally unequal relationship. Other texts make their readers into gazers who stare and scrutinise the characteristics of others, particularly the different Other. These Others are the gazed upon, unable to return the stare. Being alert to the workings of the language of inclusive education means being aware of how socialised categories and various identities are built in speaking, writing, reading and listening, and what the effects are in terms of forging difference and distance. Alertness requires critical questioning, resisting and even rejecting these categories and identities.

Language, says the TRC report, 'calls people up' and motivates them to action (TRC 1998: 295). The TRC was adamant that language works explicitly or implicitly to compel or justify action, and the language used by the apartheid regime and the liberation struggle gave the impression that certain (violent) actions were condoned, if not encouraged. The link between words and deeds is emphasised by the TRC report, and being alert to the workings of language in inclusive education requires acknowledgment that language and action are inextricably linked. While not suggesting that anyone languaging inclusive education is motivating for violent acts, there must be some recognition that material consequences for real children and young people result from how inclusive education is languaged. This may be because of policy discourses which create conditions for the possibility of removing some children from schools that cannot 'cater' for them, or of professional discourses that produce some children and young people as needing behavioural or pedagogic interventions to 'manage' their disorders, or of metaphorical constructions of inclusive education that exonerate teachers from their responsibilities to particular learners. It is worth noting, too, that violence can also be symbolic, 'a gentle violence, imperceptible and invisible even to its victims, exerted for the most part through the purely symbolic channels of communication and cognition' (Bourdieu 2001: 1–2). This gentle violence is perpetuated through the responsible sounding language of support and meeting needs and through the benevolent sounding language of welcome and accommodation. Being alert means perceiving and then making visible the symbolic violence that the language of inclusive education may motivate.

Language and ideology are intertwined, and the TRC report states that 'Language, in its many and varied forms, is the central element in ideology as power' (TRC 1998: 296). The language of apartheid was the language of a repressive ideology which, through various discourses, enabled and sanctioned one of the gross human rights violations of the second half of the twentieth century. Significant for my purpose is the TRC's observation of the effect of multiple discourses which intersect, intertwine and combine in an 'arrangement of sequences and spirals that enmesh' in a process which resulted in 'ideological acceleration' (TRC 1998: 296, 297) and an inevitable commitment to violent acts. The effect of any one inclusive education text may not be significant in and of itself but it is necessary to acknowledge the cumulative and compounding effect of the speaking/listening/writing/reading of (the accelerating ideology of) inclusive education. Pre-service and practising teachers, for example, find inclusive education languaged as *technē*, or practical (rather than professional) knowledge across a range of policies, textbooks and other publications, and conferences. The script of the otherness of people with disabilities, the 'burden' they represent to teachers and parents, and the 'challenges' of including 'them' is rehearsed across fiction, newspaper reports, policies, research and various publications in the professional domain. Without alertness, this script is endlessly re-enacted and never disrupted.

Language, says the TRC report (1998: 296), 'instructs and advises people'. Not only does it motivate people to action, it determines what and how people think. The knowledge project of inclusive education has been a concern raised in this book, with particular reference to what the legitimate knowledge of inclusive education is, who can claim to produce this knowledge, and what the limits or boundaries of this knowledge might be. Where language informs people that the meaning of inclusive education is necessarily context-bound, determined by local historical-cultural contingencies and constituted by insider perspectives, the result is a field characterised by extreme semantic gravity (Maton 2011) and the potential for inclusive education to mean anything to anyone. The knowledge of inclusive education recontextualised in textbooks and curricula has a significant bearing on what and how pre-service and practising teachers think about inclusive education. Depending on what knowledge is selected and foregrounded, they may find inclusive education informed by theoretical perspectives on in/exclusionary schooling in an *epistēmē* discourse, or by the exigencies of current policy, or by the experiential knowledge of various participants in the education system.

By giving something attention, or ignoring it, language instructs and advises people about what is significant (Gee 2011) in inclusive education. This might be by making inclusion an individual, classroom, school, education system or societal issue; or by making the target/s of inclusion significant – all children, or children with disabilities, or marginalised children with any identity marker; or by foregrounding particular concepts like school improvement, social justice or learner support. Textbooks make differences among children and young people significant (or not) through chapter allocations – some differences get chapters, some share chapters and some are ignored entirely. The same applies to research, as distinctions are drawn and some identity markers are made significant and research-worthy while others are not. Popular fiction makes story-worthy difference significant but less entertaining difference is ignored. In efforts to be relevant and meet the 'needs' of ill-equipped teachers in inclusive classrooms, practical knowledge is made significant while theoretical knowledge that might lead to enhanced professional judgment is given less significance. Being alert to what it is that the language of inclusive education instructs and advises means considering the nature and extent of inclusive education as a field in epistemological terms, and confronting the limitations of current conceptualisations of inclusive education. It also means recognising the role of language in building and lessening what and who is deemed significant. Questions must be asked about whose interests are served when significance is built or diminished, and who is included, marginalised or excluded by the significance made.

The TRC did not shy away from naming key people as it reported on the role of language in the struggle both to preserve and resist apartheid. Many submissions by these key people contained (reluctant) acknowledgment of the effect of language. For example, a former minister of Law and Order in the Apartheid government said, 'I realise with shock now, with shock and dismay that this language usage obviously and apparently gave rise to illegal actions' (TRC 1998: 295). What should not be forgotten in an analysis of the language of inclusive education is the languagers. Slee (2011: 2) contends that inclusion and exclusion are about 'real people who should not be abstracted' and I maintain that the real people who language inclusive education should also not be abstracted. As Allan and Slee (2008: 19) remind us, '… we are in the discourse and we *are* the discourse' (emphasis in the original). Althusser (1970/2012) lauded the efforts of teachers who teach against the system and practices. But he said that these teachers were rare, and that the majority do not suspect their own complicity in the 'maintenance and nourishment' (119) of the ideological representation of the school as natural, indispensable and beneficial. Being in a discourse (or ideology or field) makes the kind of distanciation required for alertness, vigilance and critical consciousness particularly difficult. Despite this difficulty, I (we) need to take responsibility for how I (we) language inclusive education and the cumulative effects of what we have constructed together.

## Con-clusion

This book began with in-clusion and ex-clusion, the closing in and out, and also dis-clusion, some kind of temporary ejection and put down. I now con-clude, which is to close together, and put the second 'bookend' in place. Engaging with the language of inclusive education is more than 'playful post-modern deconstruction' (Slee 2011: 2) or academic indulgence. At the time of writing this conclusion, two issues in South Africa that have bearing on the language of inclusive education have made headline news. The first is the issue of transformation in South African higher education institutions. This has been foregrounded in the wake of student protests demanding the removal of a statue of the British imperialist Cecil John Rhodes at the University of Cape Town. These protests have led to wider discussions about the continued presence of colonial and apartheid era symbols in the country as a whole and about deeper issues of persistent inequality. These forms, whether material or semiotic, serve as a constant reminder that places and spaces were not designed for all South Africans. Many people who now occupy previously 'white' areas or institutions cannot go about their business without an evocation of their past (and even present) exclusion. It is the view of some that changing place names or removing statues is an unnecessary waste of money and resources, but this view mostly comes from those whose privilege is reflected in these symbolic forms. And privilege is usually invisible to those who have it (Kimmel 2010). In education, language is used by those with the power to name or to address, and to speak and write in/exclusion into being. And often they are unaware of the power they exercise through language or of the symbolic violence that it produces. The effects are experienced by countless young people who must navigate the schooling system with constant reminders that the system was not designed for them.

The second issue is a wave of violent xenophobia that has swept across South Africa. Xenophobia is a euphemism, because we have seen more than a fear of foreigners, but a kind of hatred that has resulted in the looting and destruction of shops and loss of life. The xenophobic refrain is that foreigners take local jobs and put pressure on the health and education systems to the detriment of locals. Language has played a role here too, as observed by journalist Mina Demian in a piece aptly titled 'When ill-considered street semantics turn into acts of destruction and murder':

> Out of this crisis emerges the foreigner/local binary. Far from being an accident, this binary pervades media reports about the violence. The country is accustomed to talking about the 'other'. If you're black or white or coloured, there's always that 'other'. The foreigner/local duality is an expression of its awareness, the idea of something called 'us' and something called 'them', something called 'good' and something called 'dangerous'.
>
> *(Demian 2015)*

The anti-xenophobia campaigns that have been mounted in the wake of the violence go some way to show a South African majority who do not condone the attacks, but they do not disrupt the assumed naturalness of the local/foreigner binary. To South Africa's shame, it seems that despite the TRC report clearly showing the role of language in the instigation and perpetuation of violence, the effect of semantics remain ill-considered on our streets.

Inclusive education has not found a way of avoiding the language of 'us' and 'them', even in its best efforts towards welcoming 'them', the previously or potentially excluded. While inclusive education might cast itself as educational xenophilia, it still languages some learners as 'that other' who must be accommodated. Like the anti-xenophobia campaigns, the anti-exclusion language of inclusive education has not succeeded in disrupting the binary of locals (those for whom the schooling system is designed) and foreigners (those for whom a place in the schooling system must (reluctantly?) be made). 'They', or those who must be included, are languaged as representing additional effort and expenditure that must be made on their behalf. Including 'them' is a 'challenge' for policy-makers who must generate guidelines to direct (and bureaucratise) inclusion, for teachers who must be equipped through courses, conferences and textbooks, and for researchers who must discover how inclusion best occurs.

In response to the #Rhodesmustfall campaign, the Rhodes statue has been removed. And the violent xenophobic attacks have abated (for now) with a groundswell of support for #NoToXenophobia. These issues, while ostensibly unrelated to inclusive education, serve as a point of reflection on the role of language in endeavours to exclude and include, impose and resist. The South African context in which these events took place is a particularly poignant point of reference, given its history of exclusion and repression and the struggles for transformation rather than mere change.[1] Unlike statues which are visible and relatively easy to target (and deface), the workings of language are less easy to identify and even more challenging to resist. As we language our world, it is difficult to see that what seems to be the natural order of things is, in fact, built by language. And, as I have argued, this difficulty is exacerbated for people actually using the language. This book is a call for an ongoing and critical engagement with the language that enables, buttresses and conceals exclusion, even disguised as the language of inclusive education. It is also a call for those, including myself, who presume to speak and write the language of inclusive education to live a life of critical alertness to what it is that our language builds.

## Note

1 The reader is reminded here of the point made in Chapter 3, with reference to the words of a South African poet: 'Replacing white people with black people is therefore not transformation in itself ... If black people replace white people but the same structures, systems, visions and attitudes are retained, you merely have change' (Krog 2003: 126).

## References

Allan, J. (2005) 'Inclusion as an ethical project', in S. Tremain (ed.), *Foucault and the Government of Disability*. Ann Arbor, MI: University of Michigan Press, pp. 281–97.
Allan, J. and Slee, R. (2008) *Doing Inclusive Education Research*. Rotterdam: Sense Publishers.
Althusser, L. (1970/2012) 'Ideology and ideological state apparatuses', in S. Žižek (ed.), *Mapping Ideology*. London: Verso, pp. 100–40.
Artiles, A. J. and Kozleski, E. (2007) 'Beyond convictions: interrogating culture, history, and power in inclusive education', *Language Arts*, 84: 357–64.
Bourdieu, P. (2001) *Masculine Domination*. Cambridge: Polity Press.
Clough, P. (2000) 'Routes to inclusion', in P. Clough and J. Corbett (eds), *Theories of Inclusive Education: A Student's Guide*. London: Sage, pp. 1–34.
Coetzee, C. (2012) Informal Course Evaluation, EDUC7068, Wits School of Education, May. Used with permission
Demian, M. (2015) 'When ill-considered street semantics turn into acts of destruction and murder', *Mail & Guardian*, 24 April. Accessed from: http://mg.co.za/article/2015-04-23-when-ill-considered-street-semantics-turn-into-acts-of-destruction-and-murder.
Gee, J. P. (2011) *An Introduction to Discourse Analysis: Theory and Method*, 3rd edn. New York: Routledge.
Kimmel, M. (2010) 'Introduction: toward a pedagogy of the oppressor', in M. Kimmel and A. Ferber (eds), *Privilege*. Boulder, CO: Westview Press, pp. 1–10.
Krog, A. (2003) *A Change of Tongue*. Johannesburg: Random House.
Maton, K. (2011) 'Theories and things: the semantics of disciplinarity', in F. Christie and K. Maton (eds), *Disciplinarity: Systemic Functional and Sociological Perspectives*. London: Continuum, pp. 62–84.
Rice, N. (2006) 'Teacher education as a site of resistance', in S. Danforth and S. Gabel (eds), *Vital Questions Facing Disability Studies in Education*. New York: Peter Lang, pp. 17–31.
Slee, R. (2009) 'The inclusion paradox: the cultural politics of difference', in M. Apple, W. Au and L. Gandin (eds), *The Routledge International Handbook of Critical Education*. New York: Routledge, pp. 177–89.
Slee, R. (2011) *The Irregular School*. London: Routledge.
Truth and Reconciliation Commission (TRC) (1998) Truth and Reconciliation Commission Report, Volume Five. Accessed from: http://www.justice.gov.za/trc/report/finalreport/Volume%205.pdf.

# INDEX

Ainscow, M. 30, 53, 56, 70, 91, 137
alertness, life of *see* language of inclusive education: critical consciousness of
Allan, Julie viii, 4, 12, 24, 24, 31, 36–7, 39, 42–3, 48–9, 54, 71, 91, 93, 108, 147, 155, 159
Althusser, L. 159; Marxist theory of state 29–31, 42n1&2
American Psychiatric Association (APA) 114n5, 120–1
apartheid 2; language/discourse of 7n2, 34, 77, 156–9; symbols 159
Apple, S. 87–8, 100
Aristotelian terms in inclusive education 24; epistēmē 11–14, 40, 158; technē 11–14, 17, 41, 55, 157
Armstrong, D. 32, 40, 69
Artiles, A.J. 4, 24n3, 32, 40, 48, 53, 155
Asperger's syndrome 119–23, 125, 128, 133n7; critical literacy approach to 6, 129–32; impact on parents 129; languaging of 6, 125, 131; popular knowledge of 123–6
aspirational discourse of inclusive education 15–17, 20
Attention Deficit and Hyperactivity Support Group of Southern Africa (ADHASA) 110, 112–13
Attention Deficit Hyperactivity Disorder (ADHD) viii, 103–5; accommodation/management of 98, 105, 110–11, 113–14; languaging/metaphors of 6, 68, 77, 105–7, 109–15; three categories of 104, 107–14

authoritarianism 36, 114
autism 3, 68, 96–7, 110, 119–21, 123–6, 129–31, 132n2&5
autism spectrum disorders 97, 114n5, 119, 121, 125–6, 129; sympathetic imagination or Schadenfreude regarding 131–2

barriers to learning and development 34, 37, 51, 57, 59, 74–6, 81, 93, 94–5*tab*, 96–8, 105–6, 111–12, 114, 147; identifying and addressing 17, 23, 34, 52, 59, 92, 97–9; located within learner 112; poverty as 53, 55, 71
Bernstein, Basil 5, 38–41, 86, 91, 149
Black-Hawkins, K. 87, 97–8, 100
Blommaert, J. 31; definition of discourse 10
Booth, T. 40, 56, 69
Bornman, J. 17, 34, 41, 88–93, 94–5*tab*, 97–9, 105, 107, 112–13
Brantlinger, Ellen vii, 12–13, 29, 31–2, 37, 68, 87, 97, 99, 108

Cameron, L. 3, 67–8
Chen, H. 37, 39
children with special needs 2, 4, 6, 9–10, 14, 18–20, 34, 51, 66–7; accommodation of 6, 16, 21–3, 57, 75–6, 98; disembodiment of needs 57–8; *see also* metaphorical terms in inclusive education: hospitality; *see also* special needs education
Christian-Smith, L. 87–8, 100

cognitive metaphor analysis 3, 67–9; *see also* metaphorical terms in inclusive education
colonialism 49, 96, 159
Combrink, A. 139*tab*–40, 144
Connor, D. 18, 21–2, 128
Constitution of South Africa 15, 51, 64, 94
*The Curious Incident of the Dog in the Night-time* 6–7, 120–2; Asperger's voice in 129–31; Christopher Boone in 119–20, 123, 125–6, 129–32; learner responses to issues 119–20, 132; role of parents in 129

Danforth, S. 68, 77, 114
Dednam, A. 98, 108–12
definition of inclusive education *see under* inclusive education as concept
Deignan, A. 3, 67–8
Department of Basic Education (DBE) 25n10, 71, 104
Department of Education (DoE) 6, 21–2, 51–2, 72, 77, 79, 92, 95*tab*, 105; provincial 58
Department of Higher Education 88
Derewianka, B. 37, 39
desegregation 18, 22
*Diagnostic and Statistical Manual of Mental Disorders* (DSM) 107, 109, 114, 120–1
difference and disability 1, 4, 6, 15, 38; categories of difference 41, 97–8, 146–7, 156–7; disability discourse/theories 12, 19, 24, 38–9, 99–100; as identity markers 18–19, 35, 53, 60, 110, 121, 126, 146–7, 149, 158; labelling and stereotyping 32, 104–5, 109, 14, 120–1 , 124, 126, 144–6; languaging of child as burden/problem viii, 3, 6, 19, 24, 35, 69–70, 76, 86, 96–100, 109, 111–14, 129, 141–2, 157; medical/psychological orientation 39, 96; negative peer/community attitudes towards 20, 119–20, 140–1, 143–5; portrayal in media 18–23, 121–2; *see also* ADHD; Asperger's syndrome; autism; diversity
disabled children not in school 25n10, 71
discipline of noticing 4; value of critical incidents in 3–4
disclusion, notion of vii–viii, 1, 159
discourse, three domains of 5, 10–11, 24, 29, 106–7, 112; *see also* policy domain; professional domain; public domain
diversity 27, 32, 34, 51, 69, 76, 82, 91; management of/response to 3, 42, 58, 78–80*tab*, 98–100, 104–5, 112, 157; as problem 99–100

Dolowitz, L. 139*tab*, 141, 144
Dyson, Alan 12, 14, 33, 42, 91

Eagleton, Terry vii, 29–31
educational exclusion vii–viii, 1, 5–6, 9, 12–13, 53, 59, 70, 73, 77, 137–8, 146–8; media reports of 18–21; naming/positioning children as Other/different 18, 32, 34, 75–6, 132, 156; out of school youth 19, 25n10, 71; systemic/endemic 20, 32, 55, 95–6, 145; *see also* exclusionary pedagogical practices; marginalisation in schools
educational support 17, 22, 47, 51–2, 54–5, 57–9, 73–6, 94*tab;* classroom strategies 16, 23, 78*tab*, 97–9, 105–6, 108, 113; district-based support teams 16; sponsorship/financial assistance, 138–40, 143–5
epistemologies of inclusive education 12, 29, 37, 53, 73, 99, 140, 158; value of voice 146, 149; *see also* marginalisation in schools: epistemological
exclusionary pedagogical practices 59, 76, 96, 99, 136, 141, 150, 156; identifying and addressing 54–5, 57, 74, 77, 86, 137, 146, 159

Fairclough, N. 10, 67
Ferri, B. 18, 21–2, 128
Forlin, C. 13, 31, 40, 105
Foucault, M. 24, 105, 108, 111
full-service schools 16, 78, 81, 103; Professional Learning Communities (PLCs) 103–4
functional linguistics 3, 50

Gee, J. 3, 7, 11–12, 48, 60, 68, 156, 158; definition of discourse 10–11
Geyer, K. 138–40, 143–5
globalisation 12, 34, 49, 96
Graham, Linda 2, 32, 34, 36, 49, 106
Gramsci, A. 29–32
Grobbelaar, R. 19, 22, 25n10

Haddon, Mark 119–22, 124; *see also The Curious Incident of the Dog in the Night-time*
higher education 16, 37, 50, 52, 87, 156, 159
*House Rules* 6, 120, 132; Asperger's voice 129–31; Jacob Hunt in 122–31; role of parents in 129

identities of inclusive education 5, 10, 29, 42–3n12, 60; collective 15, 34; teacher 81 implementation discourse 15, 19–20, 41, 51, 56, 59, 79, 91, 94; barriers to implementation 20; *National Strategy on Screening, Identification, Assessment and Support (SIAS)* 16–17, 82

inclusion vii, 1, 4, 73; critique of full inclusion 31, 34; discourses of 2, 10–12, 14, 18; as ideological task vii, 3, 5, 13; as metaphor of segregated schooling viii, 3

inclusive education as concept 2–5, 11–12, 42; contextual issues 48; definitions of 5–6, 9–10, 42, 47–50, 52–61; responsiveness 35, 51, 54, 57–9, 91, 127, 136; shift from access to quality 52–3

inclusive education as discourse 10–11, 29, 42, 61, 69; fragmentation around identity groups 35–6, 38; saying-doing-believing of 10–11, 24

inclusive education as ideology 5, 10, 29–33, 42, 86, 91; counter-hegemonic tenets of 30, 32–3, 56; Thompson's modes of operation 5, 33–7, 72

inclusive education as knowledge field 5, 11, 29, 34, 37–42, 61–2, 86, 89, 91–2, 96, 158; practical knowledge 13, 40–2, 90, 93, 157–8; *see also* knowledge-knower structures; pedagogic discourse

inclusive education textbooks 3, 34, 41, 85–8, 100, 158; *Addressing Barriers to Learning* 88, 91, 96–7; *Believe That All Can Achieve* 88, 97; *Making Inclusive Education Work in Classrooms* 88, 92, 97; writers 3, 41, 87–9, 91–3, 96, 99–100, 156

inclusive education textbooks, analysis of: audience design 88–90; construction of learner difference/barriers to learning 88, 93, 96–100; explanation of inclusive education 90–3; gateway analogy 93, 94–5&*tab*, 96, 100

inequality 53, 100, 159

inspirational discourse of inclusive education 15–17, 20

Johnson, M. 67–8

Kim, T. 68, 77
Kimani, W. 139*tab*, 141–2
knowledge-knower structures 24n2, 35, 37, 149; client knowers 38, 149; horizontal or hierarchical 38–40; knower code 24, 37–8, 149; specialised/ideal knowers 37–40, 49; *see also* Legitimation Code Theory
knowledge production; *see* inclusive education as knowledge field

Kozleski, E.B. 4, 24n3, 32, 40, 48, 53, 155
Krog, Antjie 55, 161n1

Landsberg, E. 88, 91, 94–5*tab*, 96, 98, 102, 106, 111

language of inclusive education viii, 2–3, 5, 12, 18–19, 21–2, 33, 39, 58, 60, 159; accents 3, 61; critical consciousness of vii, 7, 155–6, 159–61; language of effectiveness 54–7, 61; listening and hearing 3, 6–7, 137–8, 146–7, 149–50, 156; reading 3, 6–7, 137, 156; relationship between words and meaning 1, 5, 17, 47–8, 57, 60; speaking 3, 7, 10, 156; writing 3, 6–7, 10, 137, 156; *see also* metaphorical terms in inclusive education

languaging 6, 11, 24, 61, 71, 157, 160; *see also under* ADHD; Asperger's syndrome; difference and disability

Legitimation Code Theory (LCT) 37, 40–1; and potential for knowledge progression 41; semantic gravity/semantic density 37, 40–2, 43n9, 92–3, 158

Lewin, K. 53, 99
Liasidou, A. 12, 14, 31, 92

mainstream 32, 51, 56, 95; inclusive education 56–7, 61, 78–9, 81; schools 12, 18–20, 22–3, 58, 139*tab*–40, 143–4; *see also* ordinary schools

marginalisation in schools 3, 6, 13, 32, 36, 95, 136, 146–7; epistemological 32, 36, 53, 99, 140; and lack of access 21, 25n10, 38, 52–3, 71; value of listening and hearing 137–8, 145, 148

Marxism vii, 29–30, 39
Mason, J. 4, 58
Maton, Karl 5, 11, 24n4, 35, 37–8, 40, 42–3, 149, 158
McCall, Z. 35, 128
McNiff, Jean 4, 50
metaphorical terms in inclusive education 3, 6, 67–70, 77; buildings 6, 71–3, 80*tab*; goal 6, 29, 67, 69–73, 77, 78–9*tab*, 95, 110, 127; hospitality 6, 22, 69, 74–6, 81*tab*; machine 68; process (journeys and steps) 6, 69, 72–4, 79*tab*; *see also* cognitive metaphor analysis

negation of inclusion 1, 54, 59–60; link to classroom practice 13–14
nominalisation of inclusion 12–13, 36, 49, 62, 72

Novartis 107–9, 114
Ntombela, S. 90–2
Nussbaum, M. 131–2

ordinary schools 2, 16, 58, 75, 79, 81, 106, 113, 145
organic ideologies 30, 32

paternalism 36, 49, 76
pedagogic recontextualisation 11; 24n4, 40–2, 86–7, 91, 96, 100, 158; *see also* inclusive education as knowledge field; inclusive education textbooks
pedagogical discourses 6, 24n4, 86–9, 96, 100; construction of difference 97, 99
pedagogical status quo 32, 55–6, 96, 114, 127
Pettipher, R. 90–1
Picoult, Jodi 6, 120–2, 125, 128–9; *see also House Rules*
Pienaar, C. 88–90, 94–5*tab*, 97–8
policy and legislation 15–16, 51–2, 58, 75, 78–80*tabs*, 92–3; guideline documents 51–2; *Guidelines for Inclusive Teaching and Learning* 75; South African Schools Act 51, 106; *see also* White Paper Six
policy domain viii, 5, 10–11, 14; contested 14–15, 92; *see also* aspirational discourse; implementation discourse; inspirational discourse
power relations 3, 14, 30–1, 36, 86, 108, 110–11, 142, 148, 156; and dissimulation 34; legitimation of 33–4; *see also* Legitimation Code Theory
professional development of teachers 93–4, 103–5; *see also* teacher education
professional domain 5, 10–14, 17, 20, 24, 106–7, 110–12, 158
psychology 39, 61, 86, 96–7
public domain 5, 10–11, 14, 19–20; role of newspapers/media in 18–25n8&9, 56

Raymond, E. 88–92, 94–5*tab*, 97–9
relations of domination and oppression *see* power relations
research in inclusive education 4, 6, 40, 91; link to classroom practice 13–14, 59; South African context 4–5; teacher education 86; *see also* voice research
Rose, R. 10, 14, 34, 41, 88–95, 97–9

*Salamanca Statement see under* UNESCO
Sapon-Shevin, M 57, 60, 69
Schmitt, R. 3, 67, 69

school improvement 39, 51–2, 54–7, 59, 61, 81, 91, 114
school restructuring and effectiveness 52, 54–7, 60–1
schooling mothers 142–5
segregated education/schooling viii, 5, 34, 51, 106, 127–8, 142, 145
Sfard, A. 67, 69–70
Skrtic, T. 35, 128
Slee, Roger 3–4, 11–12, 14, 20, 24, 31–2, 34, 36–7, 39–40, 42, 48–9, 52, 54, 60–1, 69, 76, 91, 95–6, 105, 128, 136–7, 141–2, 144–6, 155, 159; re-righting language 2
Spandagou, I. 32, 40, 69
special needs education 4, 9–10, 12, 24, 31–4, 36, 39, 43n12, 50, 57, 59, 61, 68, 71, 97, 99, 145; special schools 2, 16, 37, 47, 51, 58–9, 66–7, 74, 106, 140–4; *see also* children with special needs
Swart, E. 88, 91, 94–5*tab*, 96, 102, 106, 111

Tait, G. 104, 107
Taylor, T. 139*tab*–41, 144
teacher education 2, 6, 9, 13, 20, 39, 41, 49, 82, 89–90, 99, 103–4; and challenge of learner diversity/difference 85–6; in-service programmes 6, 13, 87, 100n2, 104; pre-service 6, 13, 66, 85, 87, 100n2
teacher practice, improved viii, 3, 13–14, 97–8; reflection towards 4
teacher qualifications: requirements 87, 114, 104; underqualification 103
teacher resistance to inclusive education 22, 33, 36, 54–5, 66–7, 76–7, 86, 97
Thompson, J. 3, 5, 31, 36, 72, 137, 148
Tourette's syndrome 139*tab*, 141, 143–5
transformation of education 5, 56, 59, 72, 159–60; Consortium for Research into Equity, Access and Transformation in Education 53; distinction between change and 55, 161n1; Truth and Reconciliation Commission (TRC) 2, 156–60

UNESCO: *Guidelines for Inclusion: Ensuring Access to Education for All* 56; Salamanca Statement and Framework for Action 2, 14, 33, 35, 95*tab*
United Nations 93; Convention on the Rights of People with Disabilities 33, 150; Convention on the Rights of the Child 150

Venter, A. 109–10
violence, role of language in 2, 157, 159–60

voice research 138–45; dilemma of 146–8; epistemological value of 149; potential for more dialogue in 150–1; writing the Other 148–9

Waitoller, F.R. 4, 24n3, 32, 40, 48
*White Paper Six: Special Needs Education* 15–17, 49, 51, 58, 69–72, 75, 78–81, 92, 94–5*tab*, 106, 111; *see also* policy and legislation

xenophobic violence 76, 159–60

Žižek, S. vii, 32

CPSIA information can be obtained
at www.ICGtesting.com
Printed in the USA
LVHW030336210120
644186LV00006B/89